The Weather Witch

(Building a Log Home in the Great North Woods of Minnesota)

Michael N. Felix

Copyright © 2004 by Michael N. Felix

All rights reserved. This book may not be reproduced in any fashion or by any means, without the express written permission of Michael N. Felix.

Also see www.theweatherwitch.net

Library of Congress Control Number: 2004090341

ISBN: 1-57579-279-6

Cover Design – Natalia Blanks
Illustrations – Natalia Blanks, Florence Luzar, Lindsay Nohl

First printing, 2004

Printed in the United States of America
PINE HILL PRESS
4000 West 57th Street
Sioux Falls, SD 57106

Table of Contents

Some Explanations vi

Grand Rapids, Minnesota, Moose Lake 1
August 12
September 19
October..32
November...41
Building Your Log Home, Part One.....................................51
December 66
January 78
February 90
March 97
April 104
Building Your Log Home, Part Two 119
May 139
June 153
The Bars of Grand Rapids (and Other Topics) 168
July...191
August 215
September 225
Building Your Log Home, Part Three 242
October..255

Epilogue 267

About the Author 281

To my Literary Irish mother, to papa who loved telling stories and to my sister Mary who supported me while these events were occurring

Some Explanations

In the summer of 1993 I set about building a log home on the shores of Moose Lake, north of Grand Rapids, Minnesota. This is the story of that year.

All of the principal events of this story, with a couple of unimportant exceptions, are true so far as I saw them, though due to the vagaries of memory some may be out of sequence. So for what it's worth, I have put these events down on paper. I hope you enjoy my story.

mnf

Grand Rapids, Minnesota, Moose Lake

I suppose I gave her that name because the wind and the weather in that place seemed so very wild and personal. Whatever the reason, I called her the Weather Witch and that winter night I lay in my bedroom listening while the rising wind became a long keening wail pitching up, up to a shriek, then pausing for a moment as if gathering its strength, only to build again to another furious gust. Late in the day I had seen the storm coming, a low roiling cloud absorbing the dark line of the woods a mile or so away and advancing quickly across my frozen white lake. In front of the storm the ferocious wind whipped the snow into ghastly white whorls, snow tornadoes twenty and thirty feet tall, dancing and whirling like debutantes at some demented cotillion.

I lived then in a large but poorly insulated mobile home, which; aside from being drafty, had the unnerving habit of shaking and creaking alarmingly at each buffeting of that wild wind. The wind quieted for a moment and I tried to settle down to sleep, but it had only gathered itself again over the lake and soon made another fierce, wailing rush at the shore. Suddenly something torn loose in the wind slammed kabang! into the side of my trailer and I sat bolt upright. That did it. I wasn't going to get much sleep for a while anyway. I rather groggily got up, made myself some tea and sat reading a little, listening to the storm, half-fearful that wind would send my trailer rolling end over end toward the county road. Through the night the temperature fell and the driving wind raked the scrag ends of the alder and willow. Finally, later in the night, I crawled back into bed and fell into a ragged sleep. When I woke in the early morning light the wind had quieted to sighs.

Morning. White snow, frightening cold. A pale sun finally made its appearance and weakly illuminated some pale white frost tracery on the windows. When I went out to start my old truck, it was so cold that the dry snow squeaked loudly underfoot and the seat of the truck was rock hard. The truck had an engine heater, which was supposed to warm the engine oil, but the engine screeched as if in pain when it finally roared to life. A large cloud of exhaust surrounded the truck, slowly rising straight up in the still, cold air. Deciding to head for town to find somewhere warm and, not incidentally, some other actual live human beings, I jammed the shift lever into gear and stepped on the gas. The truck lurched stiffly. I rocked the truck back and forth to try to loosen the stiffened grease in its joints. When it would actually roll, I began backing up to get on the county road. Suddenly to my horror the temperature needle, which previously had been shivering down at the lowest extremity of the temperature gauge, shot up to that part of the gauge marked only by an ominous red band. At that same moment steam began billowing from under the hood. This could not be good.

I turned off the engine and stood helplessly in a snowdrift, half frozen, my nose dripping, staring at the truck, the only sound being my breathing and a soft hissing from the radiator. The air smelled faintly of steamy antifreeze. The truck was my only means of transportation and I was fifteen miles from town. If I had damaged the engine I would be in serious trouble. I then did the first sensible thing I'd done for a while and clumped my half-frozen feet back to my kitchen to brew a cup of coffee and think the matter over. The propane burner on my kitchen stove worked fine, and I soon had a hot cup of coffee that I was sipping gratefully, enjoying the silence. Silence? I went to check the thermostat for the furnace. The furnace in the trailer had stopped working. I frantically twiddled with the dial but nothing seemed to turn it back on. I had no phone to call anyone. I was going to have to solve this on my own.

Fortunately I had a wood-burning stove, sort of a round, missile-shaped contraption, which I now stuffed with wood until I had a roaring blaze whereupon the living room and kitchen reached sauna-like temperatures while the bedrooms hovered somewhere around freezing. I had removed my coat, was gulping hot coffee and had begun to massage my frozen feet when, to my astonishment, I heard boots on my deck and someone yelling cheerfully, "Anyone home?" It was my neighbor Dale from the resort a quarter mile to the east who came plowing through the dry snow in his mukluks, a grin appearing from the dark hole of his heavy parka. Dale was intense and very religious, a slant of mind I thought at the time related to the situation we were in. He came over a few times that winter and made a few perfunctory but earnest attempts to save my soul, which he felt was in danger of being lost. I inquired that, considering the conditions outside, how it was that he knew the world hadn't ended and that this wasn't hell. He responded that, aside from the fact that it was too cold to be hell, he was there and that meant the world hadn't come to an end. This did seem logical.

I brewed a cup of coffee for him and explained my predicament. He chuckled. "Oh you probably need more antifreeze in your truck" was all he said, and then he glanced at my little propane tank and said I needed a bigger one, none of this being apparently unusual. For some reason these comments, and perhaps the fact of there being one other actual live person in this frozen wilderness, reassured me. We sat and talked a little. In a while he headed off down the county road, which had promptly been plowed by the county.

I had moved to my property on Moose Lake, which I had purchased years before as a summer cabin, allegedly to work on a writing project. Actually it was the only property I had left after a prolonged financial drought. The property included more than eleven hundred feet of wooded lakeshore but it was mostly swampy and narrow. It had an old whitish mobile home on the west end of it. This trailer-park artifact was fairly large with two bedrooms, a kitchen and living room, but it had seen better days. My brother came up in the fall to fish. His joking comment prior to leaving was, "Well, if you run out of food, you could always ice-fish for your dinner." He left on a gray, cold Sunday, and when he left I was there to face what future I could make for myself. I had no job, very little money, an old brown Chevy truck as transportation and I was living in an equally old mobile home on the only property I owned. And on that property I still owed ten thousand dollars. My future did not look promising.

I got along. After Dale left that cold day, I found some antifreeze, and when I had poured some in the truck, it started and ran just fine. In fact the truck seemed to adjust itself to the cold, and so long as you plugged in its oil heater and kept it full of its necessary fluids it ran very well. At very cold temperatures I resorted to the local expedient of sticking a piece of cardboard in front of the radiator. I had built a temporary garage constructed out of two-by-fours and plastic. The garage did keep some of the snow off my old truck, but it did little to ameliorate the cold conditions. The propane furnace in my trailer never did work very well and normally stopped working when the temperature descended below minus twenty.

The mobile home itself afforded only the most meager protection from the cold. In about midwinter, when there were two feet of snow on the ground, I got the idea to shovel snow along the sides of the trailer to shield it from the wind. Strangely, my first thought about this idea was wondering what the neighbors would think. I got over this trepidation fast and started shoveling snow assiduously, my survival being at risk. In a few days the trailer practically disappeared into a large man-made snowbank.

Early that winter I busied myself working on a story I was writing. I ran out of wood in January, but here providence in the form of the woodlot and my trusty chain saw came to my rescue. There was a lot of downed dry wood on my land, mostly poplar, but also some ash. So I had a virtually unlimited supply of wood in my woodlot if I had the initiative to go out and cut it. That winter the snow was thigh deep, but with freezing as a motivator, I did manage to get out fairly frequently to cut wood. My friends also took pity on me, and sometime in late winter one of them dumped a load of oak next to my house. Some of this wood was dry and burned a little. The rest seemed impervious to heat. Still, it was the thought that counted.

I had saved strips of fat from a deer and deep in that winter put some of it out on the porch. On very cold days, a large pileated woodpecker came to the porch frequently to peck huge chunks out of the strips. Later in the winter a skunk came most nights to eat scraps of food that I put out. He or she, one doesn't inquire, ate delicately and was so quiet that I could hear him chewing unconcernedly, as only a skunk can. When he finished he waddled back to the woods leaving only a trail in the snow and a faint odorous reminder of his visit.

I did not totally lack for entertainment. The county road had a deceptively sharp, dropping turn by my house. In full winter when it is cold, the paved road is fine and usually dry and not slippery. But the road would regularly be slippery in late winter or spring with the freezing fog and mists. When the bars closed for the night there would be traffic by the house at one-thirty or thereabouts in the morning. More than one car did not make the corner. One March night the weather was misty and close to freezing. I heard a car go by and then a crash, so I got up, took a flashlight and went to investigate. The surface of the county road was as slippery as a skating rink. Down the road a bit I saw a flashlight waving around.

A car was hanging precipitously over the shoulder of the road, its nose poking into the ditch, which was about ten feet deep. Flashlight man was staggering around, looking at his car as if it would get itself out of the ditch, and bleeding profusely from some sort of head injury. I invited him to my place, and when we got in, I gave him a towel to sop up the blood on his head. He sat in my living room, a lanky man with swept back longish hair, but bald as a newborn baby on top. He smelled like a barroom and waved back and forth on the chair, sporadically bleeding. An alarming thought suddenly occurred to me that he might expire right there if I didn't do something. So I told him that I had no phone, but that I would go next door if he wanted and call the police. This seemed to animate him. "No cops! No cops!" he said with rather more energy than I expected from him.

Finally, after bleeding a bit more, but none on my carpet, he talked me into giving him a ride to his home, which he said was only a couple of miles up the road. Ten miles later we found his house. After drunkenly pledging his eternal friendship and vigorously shaking my hand with one hand while holding my towel to his head with the other, he got out and staggered into his house never to be seen again. While gingerly negotiating that road-cum-skating rink on my way home, it occurred to me that I was in some danger of exiting the road myself, and I wondered if anyone would give me a lift home if I did. One hopes. In any event, my eternal friend must have gotten help and returned immediately to the site of his accident, because by daylight his car was gone from my road.

One frigid night with a brilliantly full moon out, I heard a dog barking loudly in my yard. I staggered out to look at what was causing this accursed noise. A smallish brown and white dog was sitting in the bright moonlight in my driveway, barking at my house. As soon as I walked outside and called to him, he turned and trotted away into the dark. A week later, the same thing, a little dog sitting in my driveway barking at my trailer. I go out. The dog takes a look, wags his stubby little tail a few times and trots off. This happened several times after that, always with the same result. This was my introduction to Casey the Dog. He must have been lonely or more likely was looking for a new source of snacks. Maybe he just wanted to see what I looked like. Whatever his doggy motivation, he must not have liked the prospects just then, so he retreated for the time being, and I didn't see him again at my place until the next fall.

By the next summer, having had time to thaw out and consider my fate, I resolved to build myself something more substantial in the way of a dwelling. So moving as quickly as I could, I sold the mobile home and a portion of the land and bought a little camper to be used as a construction trailer. The camper was designed for summer and fall camping. I had no idea what I would do when winter came, but having passed more or less successfully through one winter without expiring, I didn't worry about it. Winter is, of course, always less of a challenge the more comfortably distant you are from it. The people who bought my old trailer showed up all too soon and there I was then, out of the only home I had, up north with no house. But I had paid off what I owed on the land and had some money to go toward starting a house. Not a really good position but there was no going back.

In Grand Rapids there was a log home supply company, a unique business. The proprietor, a friendly and earnest little man with a humorous mischievousness about him, had worked in the woods early in his career until he got the idea to sell log home products. It turned out that there were lots of people all over the country willing to part with very considerable amounts of money to buy products related to log homes, and so he gradually built a substantial business. I didn't have any money to speak of, but I had started to think about what I would do about a house. So I began to occasionally stop in to nose around and exchange pleasantries with the always-genial proprietor. I did this apparently on the theory that contact with professionals would rub off on my job, assuming I ever started. It didn't, but I still wish it had. One day as I was perusing the merchandise, he, having pegged me by the outré nature of my wardrobe and the desperate look in my eye, and rightly thinking I was starved for company of my own, mentioned that some people got together in a sort of coffee house. He said it was called the Common Ground.

The Common Ground coffee house was held Friday and Saturday nights in a downtown art gallery. Doorbells jingled against the glass street door as I entered. The gallery was simply a very long and spacious room in an off-street brownstone. At the rear of the gallery I could see a small knot of people, from where emanated the pleasant smell of brewed coffee accompanied by the sound of guitar chords. I made my way toward them perusing the art as I went, which ranged in quality from adequate to bad, with bad winning hands down, most of it resembling the offerings of bored retirees. Of course I'm the person who went to a Picasso exhibit and thought his sculptures looked like broken attic furniture and that his paintings would have looked a lot better with less paint. I'm still not sure those sculptures weren't attic refuse.

I finished looking at the assembled offerings and made my way to the rear of the gallery and the knot of humanity gathered there. At the far end of the gallery there was a small kitchen and an area with some working tables of the sort one sees in school lunchrooms. Eight or ten people were sitting at the tables under glaring fluorescent lights. Two of them looked as if they had been in a beard-growing competition and were presently attempting to determine who had lost. Two comparatively normal-looking guys, one wearing a porkpie hat, had finished tuning their guitars and were playing gospel tunes. One of the listeners included a guy with dark, bushy, long hair, like a reject from a bad California hippie flick.

At an adjacent table was a woman who looked as if she would run out the door if you spoke to her and next to her a woodsy-looking fellow with long wild hair and a slightly crazed look in his eye. A woodtick if ever I saw one. And standing at the coffeepot next to a jam jar, which held about a buck fifty in change, was a very tall person with a ponytail who had apparently stepped out of some alternative lifestyle magazine. He was fiddling with the coffee maker, muttering something about how he wished someone else would bring coffee just once, but paused in these important machinations to greet me with a practiced, instantly familiar and comfortable manner. Tom was an artist and had thought up the simple, but wonderful, idea that there needed to be a place in town where various artists and others could get together to talk, play music and generally socialize. He had talked the art gallery, of which then he was a board member, into letting him use it on Friday and Saturday evenings to have his coffee house. He named it the Common Ground.

The only other guy whose name I noted then was Lon. He was a pretty good guitar player, and he had several people gathered around him. He was one of the first to greet me in a friendly way, but he seemed to evaluate me according to some personal meter of his own.

I settled into the evening and eventually did talk to the woodtick. He had long hair, a loopy smile and seemed to be a nice fellow with a quirky sense of humor who eked out a living working at various jobs as a carpenter and a laborer. He lived in the woods up north twenty miles or so. Lately he'd been making willow furniture that he'd sold to some rich tourist who was building a half-million-dollar log home on some lake, of which there are hundreds in the local area. He was in town this time to train to be a firefighter. There were a lot of fires then in the west and they were hiring men for that duty. Apparently the pay was relatively good since they didn't lack for people to go fight fires. Fighting fire is hard work mostly done at higher elevations, breathing thin air full of smoke. He said he was going to fill a small container with water to carry to Montana. He was going to pour it on the ground there for luck.

"Got to prime the pump," said he.

I mostly sat and listened or talked with Tom. He and I had been to the same college at the same time but had never met. A young lady got up and read her poetry. There was music. Nothing really dramatic, but it was a good time and when the evening came to a close, I helped clean up. The Common Ground coffee house was perfect for me since it didn't cost much and there was music. I began to show up virtually every weekend.

August

By August I had sold my creaky mobile home and part of my property to a family whose apparent goal in life was to catch and eat every fish in the lake, and who showed up with every beer-swilling relative and friend they had to get started on the project. My new home was a red, white and blue sixteen-foot-long camping trailer, which I parked next to the new power pole on my construction site. The power company people, in typical, efficient, northern Minnesota style, had very promptly gotten power to my site. I suppose one could derive some symbolism from the fact that I, just as promptly, parked my habitation about ten feet from the source of all my power, but I had no time for symbols just then, thank you. I hunted around in vain for a place to plug in my home to this power. It became apparent, in approximately ten seconds, that there was no plug-in. I called the power company to report this obvious oversight.

"Oh no, we don't install the plug-in," he said. "You get your electrician to do it."

I didn't know any electricians and didn't want to spend money on one. Upon hearing this, the power company representative cheerfully indicated that I could do the job myself. He gave me a list of the items I needed to purchase to do the job. Really there wasn't that much, a plug-in, some conduit and some other doodads, which were of no real importance and needn't be mentioned, except that, combined with me inserting my fingers into close proximity to several hundred amps of power, they had a fair prospect of killing me.

I admit I have always been a little trepidatious about electricity. Once when I was a kid I laid on a live extension cord, and although I didn't lay there very long, I have never forgotten it. And I've never understood wiring concepts well. In high school, I caused an experiment in electricity during physics class to emanate bright sparks and explode. I'm not sure if there were any gledes accompanying the sparks. Probably. It was very pretty, but the physics instructor took a dim view of my having anything to do with his electrical experiments after that. One could, of course, ask why a school was allowing high schoolers to mess around with 110 volts. But in those days, both in physics and chemistry, it wasn't unusual for students to be allowed to experiment with the real thing. With predictable results, I might add.

On another occasion, some not-all-that-bright acquaintances of mine had prepared a concoction of sulfur, charcoal and other interesting ingredients. Whereupon one fool bet another fool ten dollars that he wouldn't hit it with a hammer. The resulting explosion put one of them in the hospital. By the way, there was certainly concern about the students, but no litigation. Imagine that today. At any rate, there was no way I was going to actually pay for a couple of outlets. So with a care occasioned by the prospect of electrical death, I installed the necessary doodads and plugged myself in to the grid. It worked! Oh power grid, thy mercy to gain!

One day while driving down the road, I saw an old Buick with a for-sale sign on it, parked in front of a horse stable. I needed a backup vehicle and I didn't want to spend a lot of my limited resources, so I stopped. In a while, a youngish-looking middle-aged man came over from in back of the barn, followed by a collie and a black dog of indeterminate origin, the latter of whom made a few perfunctory barks for appearances' sake, and then settled down to watch these interesting activities. My erstwhile representative of the horsy set smelled faintly of horses and hay. Either that or I had stepped in something.

The Buick was the color of a pumpkin in fall, as long as a boat and in good condition. Very old though. It had been owned by his parents, who now also old, had recently become somewhat confused of mind. His father had been in the habit of going for a drive on weekends with his wife. Forgetfulness hadn't stopped him though. Periodically he and his wife would get dressed up, jump in the Buick and hurdle around the highways and byways of Itasca County. The trouble was they had only the vaguest idea of where they were going or where they were when they arrived. Several months before, they had decided to go for a ride on Sunday and had ended up in Bigfork some miles north. Not really knowing where they were, they had cheerfully asked for directions home from a local. Whereupon they backed into a mailbox and roared off down the highway— in the wrong direction. The local guy, concerned that they would collide with a logging truck or more likely, run over some tourist, called the county sheriff. The sheriff stopped them. After talking with the oldsters and not getting anything coherent—except for their names—the sheriff then called the son. The couple eventually got home, the son took the keys and that was the end of their traveling life. Shortly after that they both took up driving beds at the nursing home. Too bad.

I bought the pumpkin-colored Buick for three hundred dollars. The horse person seemed to be relieved that his parents would no longer have a chance to get at their car. Incidentally, it had a huge eight-cylinder engine but it still got twenty miles to a gallon of gas. I presently drive an eight-cylinder truck, which is thirty years newer than the old Buick, and my truck gets fewer miles to the gallon.

Early in August a short, smiling block of a local earthwork contractor named Ernie came over and built a pad, upon which I was to build my house. He had stubby arms and callused thick hands so that shaking hands with him was like grabbing the end of a thick tree branch. I was always happy to see him, since he gave the impression of being able to get things done. Ernie had an oversized backhoe on tracks, a track hoe he called it. I filled the footing trenches about three quarters full of large crushed rock. The ground upon which I was building my house was very wet and the crushed rock would resist frost heaving and provide a good base for the concrete block footings that I was going to build.

Cold is both good and bad. Cold will kill you, but then keep you intact practically forever. They've found woolly mammoths in Alaska that have been frozen in the ground for ten thousand years. Then there was the guy over toward Bena who got drunk one night and, eschewing indoor plumbing, decided to use the outhouse in the backyard of the bar. He passed out sitting there, and it being twenty below or so, he froze to death. It then snowed, covering up any tracks, and after a while the people stopped looking for him. They just figured that he'd show up eventually in one form or another. He wasn't located until the next spring when he was found by someone who was looking for a tool and thought it might be in that unused outhouse. He was still sitting there, essentially unchanged, except for being very desiccated. Probably the longest period he'd been dry in his life. Even now loggers haul logs out of the backcountry through wetlands and marshes by making "winter roads," which are built by waiting until the real cold starts in December or January and then packing down the snow with a tracked machine. In a couple weeks, the cold will then freeze down deep enough to drive a truck on the winter road.

Back at my place I had filled the trenches with the crushed rock, and to quote a long-forgotten politician, here's the beauty part: any water would go to the unfrozen bottom of the trench and wouldn't be able to freeze below the blocks and heave the walls. Furthermore, the noncompressibility of the rock would make a good base for the footings and heavy log walls. That is the theory anyway. As they say in the media, only time will tell.

At the Common Ground coffee house a kid named Russell has been coming to the coffee house, not more than ten or twelve years old. He has an engaging look and a fun mischievous manner. He is also smarter than everyone else. He is smarter than you. He can sit at your table and discuss anything like an adult. Then he goes off and plays a game like a kid. Someone decides to play him at chess. That was a mistake, the game is over in about ten moves. But Russell doesn't gloat, helpfully offers tips on the fellow's game, quotes a few moves by some obscure Russian grandmaster and inquires as to whether the person wants to play another. The person declines.

I had gotten to know most of the main individuals at the coffee house and had begun to recognize most of the people who drifted in occasionally. I usually helped Tom clean up at the end of the evenings. The coffee house had been going on for a year or more and the burden of always having to be available to open it was beginning to wear on him. Tom wanted the coffee house to change, to grow into something other than a group getting together on weekends. Money was an issue. Tom had been supporting the coffee house from his own pocket, plus he was on the board of the gallery and between his own artwork, time for the board and the coffee house, he was feeling the pressure. This situation couldn't go on forever. And then there was the matter of meeting under those glaring fluorescent lights. The place, aside from the art, just didn't look like a coffee house.

Lon didn't want the coffee house to change. He, his family and several others had been the first to support the idea of the coffee house and showed up virtually every night. Besides playing music, Lon's wife helped out and was generally a positive force in this little group. But while they were friendly to everyone, it seemed to me that the attention always returned to Lon. It was quickly apparent that he liked the coffee house to be just what it was, a small informal group meeting a couple of times a week. He seemed most comfortable when there was no structure except when the structure revolved around him. In that environment his personality was being fed, but the coffee house was stagnant. I didn't mind since I was having fun. I met lots of people. Various musicians came in from around the area to play. People drifted into the gallery from off of the street and then sat down to listen to the music. But mostly it was just a group of six or eight people, like some sort of encounter group.

But new people were beginning to come in and help. Sally, a straw-haired, energetic Finnish woman with a nasally officious competence began to come in regularly and to help with the closing of the coffee house. Several others pitched in so that Tom didn't have to be there for each opening and closing.

One evening we were doing the usual when a woman of about fifty came in. It was summer and there were a lot of tourists around, drawn into the coffee house through the art gallery. The lady came in, sat for a while listening, and then asked if she could play some of her tunes. Thinking she was going to get her instruments, we as a chorus assented enthusiastically. She and her husband then dragged in one of those recording and music-playing machines. Then with the assistance of various mixed percussion and background vocal tracks, she began to treat us, in a quavering but determined voice, to religious music. She sang tune after tune while we waited for her to quit. Time passed. She sang on. Those who had watches glanced nervously at them. We listened while devil and angel struggled in our name. Several people left. Tom shifted uneasily, a virtually unheard of thing. Finally someone grabbed his guitar and made as if he wanted to play. Protocol suggested that she would stop and let someone else have a chance. She played on, her electronically augmented voice ecstatic. Finally, and amazingly, Tom stepped up at the end of another musical attempt to save our souls and quietly motioned to her to stop, which she reluctantly did.

September

In the first week of September Casey the Dog tried to bite a porcupine. This is virtually always a bad idea; so if you by some chance get the notion to bite one, restrain yourself. I happen to like porcupines; they make cute urrring noises when they're in heat and then they mate ... carefully. And they walk around unconcernedly like the skunk for the same reason that nations act the way they do. They have weapons. But poor Casey didn't know this. He had started showing up again about the time I started working on my log house, usually coming in the morning after his owners left for the day. They mostly ignored him, and since he had a little door by which to come and go, he used it to tour the neighborhood, hustling up some action.

Casey was a Brittany, born and bred for bird hunting, and since his owners wouldn't hunt him, he took to amusing himself by driving red squirrels crazy. Having spotted a likely red squirrel, he would plant himself at a sporting distance from the base of the tree and stare at the squirrel. After some minutes of this staring, the squirrel would get more and more excited, chattering and twitching. Then, as if pulled by a string, the squirrel would start slowly coming down the tree. I was horrified the first time I saw this, thinking, of course, that the poor mesmerized squirrel was about to be easily killed by Casey the Svengali dog. Usually, however, the squirrel would get near the bottom of the tree and make a run for it with Casey in hot pursuit.

He loved any gathering of people. If you had a party going, Casey would be there. One group of tourists were celebrating something, the catching of fishes perhaps, when Casey showed up. They thought he was cute. They drank beers and carried on until a late hour. No one seemed to notice when Casey left, but the next morning at first light the man heard a scratching and whining at the door. With a beer hangover, at six in the morning, little Casey didn't seem so cute.

Besides human company, food, sex and chasing squirrels were the three main things on Casey's mind. Substitute work or hobbies for the squirrel part and that is of course the recipe followed by most humans also, so this is understandable. Casey assumed that whatever I was going to eat, he would eat also. And truth be told I looked forward to Casey coming almost every morning. Mostly we would eat together, but sometimes he had cadged food from someone else in the neighborhood that day and wasn't particularly hungry. So he would take whatever I gave him and, sneaking away to avoid my prying eyes, bury it. If it were winter, he would bury it in the snow, carefully tamping the snow with his front paws. I don't know if he ever found the cached food again, and I never got quite hungry enough to raid his stashes. I have some pride.

On the evening of the porcupine Casey had started home when I heard him yelp. A few minutes later he was whining at the door to my camper. When I went to let him in, there he was with numerous quills embedded in his nose and all over the roof of his mouth. Now getting a mouth full of quills is serious enough, but it's the getting them out that is the problem. The quill goes in easy, but each quill has a little hook on the end, which makes it hard and painful to remove. Many animals in the wild have died from starvation from having quills in their mouths. Normally what one does is to take the dog to the veterinarian who sedates the excited animal. Then he puts the dog to sleep and pulls the quills… I took Casey to his house to find his owners. No one was home, but I knew the man's girlfriend and went to her house. She called several veterinarians, but no one was one available.

Finally, I decided we would have to pull the quills ourselves. We got a belt to wrap around his jaw and a stick to prop Casey's mouth open. One of the boys, a strong young football player, held Casey. We began pulling the quills from the dog with a pliers. Grab one. Jerk. With each quill being pulled, the dog yelped and struggled frantically. First from the nose. Those were the worst. Casey struggled wildly. Two or three and then rest the squirming, crying dog. More and more quills came out from his lips and then the roof of his mouth. Casey got so that, at the sight of the pliers, he would begin struggling and crying. I felt a little like crying myself. Finally, after an hour of this dog torture, we had gotten all of the quills and were done. We gave Casey some water, he drank for a long time and I went home exhausted. The next day Casey showed up as if nothing was wrong, though he seemed to avoid that patch of the woods where he had run into the porcupine.

As if to make up for Casey's bad luck, the weather suddenly turned good for a change, with cool fall-like mornings and bright summer afternoons. By then I had a very nice-looking pad and footing trenches that I filled with crushed rock, and upon which I could theoretically build my log home. On the crushed rock I would build the concrete block footings.

I had bought an old bulldozer, allegedly a 1939 Allis-Chalmers. That's what its owner told me it was, but he probably just took a stab at its age. It was heavy and Allis-Chalmers yellow, which, I'm told, any old farmer could remember. It had a gasoline-powered motor and was perfect for knocking things down or grading. The bad part was that it was all sharp edges. Almost everything on the Allis could hurt you, or worse. The little bulldozer was unloaded at my place and its owner showed me how to run it. It had various levers designed to turn the thing to the left or right.

Unfortunately a previous owner had taken the bulldozer apart and had forgotten a part when he put it back together. It was, or so the story went, too much work to take it apart again and bedamned if he was going to do it. So only some of the turning levers worked. It turned left when going forward just fine but the right-turn levers didn't work. To go right, one had to put it into reverse and swing it around so the front end turned right, then put it in forward. But the bulldozer started and ran well, and once you did get it going, roaring and smoking, it would push or pull anything. Brute force was its thing. By working with the bulldozer and then with a shovel, I managed to smear the crushed rocks into the trenches, and then with a few hours of hand-work, I leveled the crushed rock. On top of the crushed rock I was to lay three courses of concrete blocks.

The concrete blocks for the footings showed up one afternoon in late September. The deliverer of said blocks took one look at my driveway and wouldn't come down to unload the blocks. After arguing with him for a while, I gave up and told him to unload the blocks in the ditch alongside the county road. This was a very bad mistake since I now had to somehow get several hundred very heavy blocks down a steep bank to my construction site. Also I somehow got the damned fool notion into my head that someone might steal my footing blocks from where they were deposited in a steep roadside ditch. I actually camped by the construction site for one night to guard against those notorious concrete block thieves, much to the amusement of one neighbor to whom I made the mistake of relating this.

Eventually I rigged a cable from a tree by the pile of blocks down to the other side of the site. I then hooked a pulley onto the cable and a hook, which I had shaped by a welder, underneath the pulley. Then I called up a friend to come over and help. Once he was done laughing at the sight of my contraption, we got to work, me hooking the heavy blocks onto the pulley and then letting them down the hill. The friend would then unhook the block and I'd pull the pulley back up the hill. Worked great as long as you had two people. Of course it would have worked better to have gotten the block truck down the damned driveway.

One of the nice things about the Common Ground coffee house was the way it blended into our lives. It was held on Friday and Saturday nights and the art gallery was open also on weekends. Opening the coffee house was easy and fit my life perfectly. I would usually clean up at my place and drive in to town about seven o'clock in the evening. Someone was covering the art gallery until then, and when one of us would arrive that person would leave. At that time of the evening, not many people would be around, there usually would be no one in the gallery and there was a nice quiet feel to the place. There was a sort of kitchen area where we could store our coffee and supplies, so I would first set up the coffeepot. When the coffee is done percolating I pour a cup for myself and wander around the gallery to see the new art.

Let me admit right here that I am a little hard on the art in the gallery. This is because most of it was very bad. There are, of course, many good artists in northern Minnesota. And also one must remember that this gallery is a public gallery that presents a great range of talent. With those thoughts rattling around in my head, I continue sauntering slowly around the gallery and come upon an exhibition of very original and lively art done by the middle school students in town. Had some of these submissions been framed, they would have easily exceeded the general run of the art in the gallery. I applaud but no one hears.

After my five-minute tour of the gallery to see the new art, I get ready for the evening. By this time we had made a few tables for the coffee house. The tables consisted of two pieces for the base and a top. One of the bottom pieces was slotted and to assemble them one simply slid one piece into the other and you had a base for the table. The hexagonal top fit onto the lower sections and was secured with small bolts and wing nuts. A tablecloth and lighted candle completed the table. By this time we also had a small stage that could be assembled and disassembled for storage. With the lights lowered we had a suitable atmosphere for a coffee house.

Speaking of wing nuts, Glen comes floating in. He is a pleasant, waif-like little man with long, white-gray hair. He has a well-traveled face and a placid but interested look in his eyes. Put a white robe on him and he would be the picture of some California cult leader. He lives in a little camper trailer that he drives to California every winter and back here every summer. At least several winters he parked his trailer in various parking lots there or so he told me. Recently he had become better off since he qualified for Social Security. This made a huge difference to him, and it is the only way I could tell you how old he is. In a bit he picks up his flute and begins tootling.

The little bells on the street doors jangle and clash against the glass and Sharon and her husband Tom (a different Tom from the one who started the Common Ground) come in and, perusing the art as they go, make their way slowly back to where I'm working. Without being asked Sharon helps put out the cups and cookies. They seem to me to epitomize the best of the coffee house: positive, cheerful and helpful people, a couple whom I saw together so often I came to refer to them as Tom-and-Sharon, one unit. They relish the chance to sit and talk with anyone about any subject and yet weren't one of those couples who are constantly finishing each other's sentences or who come out because they stopped having anything interesting to say to each other about ten years previous. They were a single unit with independent voices. Very classy.

Tom's lanky form appears at the back door, he waves a greeting and heads to the little kitchen where we make our coffee. As I have mentioned, Tom started the Common Ground. These days people expect to be entertained when they go out for an evening. But a coffee house is subtly different. It implies that you will be a contributor to the process through music or your ideas presented in conversation. Actually, at a coffee house, in some odd way, just sitting quietly and listening seems to be a contribution. Still the thought that people would want to get together to merely talk and play music, and could actually do it week after week without killing each other, is amazing to me. It's like having a party a week at your house. Please note I said your house; I wouldn't do it. I suppose it is a variation of the back porch where people get together to play music and talk.

Tom ambles over to talk with some people sitting at a table. He seems to have a particular talent for sitting down at a table of people and making them feel comfortable. This is an important skill when you have strangers regularly coming in to the coffee house. Some people just want to sit quietly for a while and it is the function of a good coffee house to let them do that. It is a skill to judge their needs and Tom is very good at this. Without intruding, he would plop himself down with anyone who came in and usually in a few minutes they would be laughing and talking as if they'd been coming to the coffee house for years. As the evening went on he would work his way around to all of the tables, and for a few minutes that table or group would be the center of attention.

Tom is visiting with a middling-aged person whom he knows from somewhere. The guy is a wood-carver of some sort. Only instead of a knife or carving tools, apparently he uses a chain saw. He lives in a large camper and alternates between living on some land next to a highway near the Twin Cities and Arizona, where he spends the winter. He mentions the place where his land is and indicates that it is marked with a large bear carving that he made from a tree stump. I think I remember it. It looked vaguely like a gigantic prairie dog standing on its hind legs. I also seem to remember a menagerie of rather curious-looking carved creatures. As supporting characters to the prairie dog, one supposes. Upon closer inspection these turned out to be animals. I think.

The wood-carver is with a blonde. She is quite nice, not bad looking, but with dried-out platinum hair, too many miles on the chassis and a smoker's cough. A hairdresser back in Arizona.

I head into the little kitchen, from where I hear only snatches of talking.

"...don't **really** know why I go along with him."

A burst of laughing from another table. "... ya ... once in a while...in the sauna." (Pronounced "sow oo na")

"...of the kids got...ya know... Sounds of more laughter, the shuffling of feet and chairs scraping.

The door jangles again, indistinctly now, since there is a lot of chatter and someone has produced a guitar that he is playing idly, more like tuning really, midst the smell of fresh coffee and a few scented candles. It is two regulars, the first a fellow who, according to others, has taken recently to hanging around all-night gas stations. We don't know why this night owl hangs around the gas station. Someone speculates he is afraid to go home. Maybe he likes the smell of gas. There is much speculation about it, but of course no one would ask. If the gas station doesn't mind him hanging around, it's his business why he does it. All that I know is that he is genial and funny, and he and I always have a good time talking and joking. The guy with my erstwhile night owl is a bushy-haired person who lives with his mother and is writing a book. A case of arrested development if I've ever seen one, but he plays the guitar pretty well.

Have you ever put on a great party and everyone had a good time so you decided to do it again in a week? Naturally it fizzled the second time. In some regards it's a matter of expectations, which of course is the case with anything. If you don't expect too much, life is usually great most of the time. On good nights at the coffee house the evening would take whatever form it wanted, but always, talking and music were the central activities. New people seemed to blend in very easily. Not infrequently the evening includes poetry, particularly from the high school crowd. One night we were doing our usual thing, nothing special, when a group of bubbly and outgoing young ladies from the high school came in. The whole group laughed and sang and generally had such a great time that the atmosphere was wonderful.

But sometimes there would be a good crowd, and for no reason that I could think of, all of the air would go out of the occasion and the coffee house would acquire the atmosphere of stale bread or worse—in our case a sort of strained tension. I mention this because Lon and his wife come in, go directly to a table where Lon takes out a guitar and begins strumming, ignoring the fact that someone else is playing. Lon's wife, who is smart and pretty, goes to get a cup of tea, smiling at someone she knows. She generally tries to be positive, but something strained, contrived and negative seems to suddenly permeate the atmosphere. Lon is deadpan and nonchalantly keeps on playing. There is a sense of isolation about him. The other player stops playing and looks at Lon who, having made some point, stops also and wanders to the far end of the gallery to sulk.

The street door jangles again, faintly now over the chatter, and some juveniles come in, cast a few perfunctory glances at the art and come on back sitting quietly and a little warily. There seems to be a great need among juveniles to be able to hang out at this type of an adult setting. I cannot tell you what it is, but the coffee house is … alternative. It had people who didn't always think the way everyone else did. The juveniles seemed to respond well to this, a setting within which they were acting normal, without being in some teen center. And since there is no drinking or drugs, it is an entirely safe setting for them to come in for a while.

Once, however, a cute girl came in with her mother who, no doubt thinking of her own misspent youth, was rather chary about her own daughter's tendencies. This mother was determined to guide her daughter's actions and so accompanied her to the coffee house. The mother then left, apparently thinking her daughter, who was about fifteen years old, luscious of body and whose eyes were an invitation to lust, was safe amidst this aggregation of unrequited hippies. Shortly thereafter, however, a rather hyperactive young man showed up out of the blue, and with practically no introduction began kissing and generally assaulting the young girl's budding virtue. After letting this go on for a little while, one of us, I don't remember who, sat down with them and explained that this was a coffee house and not a kissing and fondling room. As for me, I was just jealous. Shortly thereafter, before the mother returned, the teenage boy left, talking not being in his sweaty retinue of action.

Later midst the chatter, the music and the smell of candles I am talking to a rather well-endowed woman named Marilyn. She is explaining that she was a "financial advisor" to various retired people in the area.

"Oh, you mean you sell insurance," says I.

This is the wrong thing to say and apparently one of the numerous mistakes I make around her, and she went on at some length about how she helped these people with their financial plans and that the selling of insurance was not the most important part of this, no doubt, sanguine and sagacious advice. Anger seemed to emanate from her very skin.

Her husband comes in a little later and sits with her, not saying a thing. A mystery. His skin is the color of paste or something that hasn't seen the sun for about six months. Interesting, considering the fact that summer had passed and gone, and it would have been virtually impossible not to soak up some sun. Once when I first bought my land and came up to see it in early April I found two beefy guys, an equally beefy woman and a scrawny, scraggly guy with a wispy beard reveling in the delightful forty-five-degree air of early April, soaking up the sun. Oh well, maybe her husband had been sick. A little later he sits quietly to one side talking intermittently and absently with someone and watching his wife, who was talking with someone I don't know with an odd intensity.

The wood-carver yells goodbye to everyone, and he and his girlfriend leave. She is fumbling for her cigarettes halfway to the door. A sudden flare and glow at the door and an exhaled cloud of smoke about two feet onto the sidewalk. I find myself staring at that fading white puff in the air and can suddenly taste and feel that first drag. Coffee and a cigarette. I shake it out of my head. I'm busy in the kitchen again.

From the kitchen I hear a small burst of good-natured laughing midst the chatter "...Well it ain't her hairspray he's....in," someone says. I don't catch the rest. I bend down to get something and suddenly catch a very faint whiff of cool outside air and cigarette smoke that has traveled the length of the gallery, not stopping at all to goggle the art, and I can taste that cigarette and dame nicotine whispers right into my brain how much she needs me, and more importantly, how much I need her.

The evening has gone pretty well. There is a lot of laughing, talk, music and singing. One of the juvenile ladies got up and read some poetry that was full of angst and mystery. Almost everyone paid for their coffee and cookies. Lon found someone to visit with and his wife got into an animated conversation with Tom. Everyone had a pretty good time. There was no set closing time, but most evenings wound up about eleven o'clock unless the music was good and the people were reluctant to leave. Wound up is a good description since after a few cups of coffee the patrons would be more than a little hopped up on caffeine. The good part of this was that everyone had a lot of energy to help put away the tables and the stage and wash the coffeepot and whatever utensils we had used.

October

In October the Weather Witch makes some days warm and fat, like smiling babies, and fills them full each night on milk from the breast of the enormous birch-white moon rising just there behind the trees. Just a few nice days, gurgling and cooing, full of sunbeams and dragonflies that dart and hover in the late afternoon haze like dancing little fairies. Of course she's also a bitch and time a mere nothing, and her babies soon turn sullen and cold and when they're grown she stalks the empty woods and frozen wastes shrieking her approval.

At my construction site I was finally underway, actually working on my house. My goal was to build a log house, completing it enough in one year so that I could live in it. I wasn't at all sure whether I could do it, but I had chosen my course. And really, even considering the mistakes I made related to planning, there is some redeeming value in not thinking and instead just blundering ahead. I have an acquaintance who gets a great idea and is very enthusiastic about it. Then he starts thinking about it and all of the work, and the time it would take, and the other things he needs to do, and the fishing trip he might have to miss. Pretty soon he decides to just think about it for a while and eventually he forgets about it. There is some value in not thinking too much.

Have you ever started doing something and about sixty seconds into the task realized that you just absolutely hated doing it? I only say this because after laying, oh, say one concrete block, I was reminded of the fact that I detest cement work. A long time before this I had worked myself through college as a cement laborer in the summers. I had apparently suppressed this fact, but with that first incredibly heavy concrete block, memories of sweating, shoveling, toting blocks and wheeling cement came flooding back and reminded me that one of the reasons I continued in my pursuit of an education was my dislike of anything cement.

In a day or so my arms ached as if something had been trying to yank them out of their sockets, this condition resulting from my attempts to carry two blocks at a time, something I'd done when I was twenty years old. Just in case you haven't figured it out, I haven't been twenty for a while. In addition I'd tripped over one of them and had skinned a knuckle trying to keep myself from sliding down a wet bank and got slapped hard in the face with a branch for my flailing. At the end of each day I staggered to the camper and collapsed. A quivering mass.

I finished the footings in a week and a half, but I didn't like it at all. Poor me. This dislike of large, heavy concrete objects led to one of the mistakes I made on my house. I should have laid at least one more course of blocks. Believe me, you need a good size crawl space under your house if you don't have a basement. Enough for now. Later I will elaborate upon the no-doubt fascinating topic of basements and crawl spaces. I still don't like concrete so instead of talking about it now, I'll tell you a bear story.

A Bear Story

When I started building the house there was an old bear den about twenty yards to the west of the house. Sometime in the past, an enterprising black bear had dug a hole into the bank of the county road, which was the southern boundary of my property and which in that place was wooded and quite high, probably going up some twenty-five vertical feet. I had walked by the den numerous times, and it didn't look like it had been used recently. Finding a bear den is, of course, unusual but in recent years there have been a lot of bears in our area. Rather like humans, they reproduce prolifically so long as there's a good food supply. Like humans they are omnivorous and will eat meat, bugs, vegetables, grass and roots, not to mention the odd dog. In fact I'm told if you examine a bear carcass next to a skinned human you'd have difficulty telling the difference, except that perhaps the human might be uglier. Which reminds me of the old deer-hunting joke up there about the guy who was accidentally shot. The punch line went, "I think we could have saved him, Ole, if you hadn't of gutted him out." Hey, it's still a good one. Anyway, the difference between a bear and a human isn't as great as you think, being largely in the teeth.

I knew there was a big bear in the neighborhood because I occasionally saw his rather large paw prints in the mud on my driveway. I assumed he was a male since I never saw any cubs, but anyway, he was a very large bear with very long legs and a huge head. A very huge head. No kidding, hold your hands about eighteen inches apart.

That was the length of his head from the tip of his nose to the back of his skull.

The reason the bear hung around the neighborhood was, as usual, food. There are only three reasons anything hangs around anything else, namely, food, sex and money. And since it wasn't money, and sex seemed to be out unless there was something about my neighbors that I didn't know, it had to be food. Most people and animals aren't inclined to move so long as they're making a living. Oh certainly people move for political or religious reasons, but most of them came because they didn't have squat going where they came from. In Norway the land inheritance got smaller and smaller. In Germany there got to be too many Germans. Just kidding. Most of the immigrants to the United States came when agriculture was the main occupation of people. All of those Norwegians, Germans and Swedes who came here were mostly just looking for more and better farmland.

Anyway, the bear had figured out that by hanging around the lake, he could scrape up a pretty good living, dining alfresco, on fish heads and associated fish parts. My neighbor Dale ran a resort in the summer. Virtually every day some of the tourists would clean fish, and of course there would be fish head and entrails. Dale would try to dispose of this fish offal. Therein lay the problem. Fish offal gets pretty rank, pretty fast and is hard to get rid of to boot. If you bury it, pretty soon it starts to stink and voilà! some animal digs it up for food. You put it in plastic bags and the slightest leak and very shortly the local animal population shows up to dine. Why, you ask, can't you throw the fish heads, scales and guts back into the lake? Once in a while that's fine, but not if people catch more fish every day.

Some resort owners transport their fish stuff out into the woods and there remand it to nature, just as you and I will be remanded whence we have cast off the mortal coil. The trouble with this approach was that it gets tedious, not to mention smelly, to have to load and dump this stuff every day. And remember you have to dump it somewhere far enough so it doesn't come back with the neighborhood mutt. So in the face of these offal logistical difficulties, Dale had taken to storing up garbage in the back of an old pickup truck for a week or so until he could haul it to the dump. And this is where the bear came in. He took to showing up pretty near every night in the summer to sample the fish head cuisine. So you see, from Dale's perspective, he and the bear had worked out a good system, the bear being sort of a living garbage disposal.

Dale kept a couple of vicious animals chained at his resort. He claimed they were dogs. Now I like dogs, but these things scared me a lot worse than the bear ever did. His dogs had the unnerving habit of synchronizing their barking, which was loud anyway, so that when one was finishing a bark the other was just starting. This was not a pleasant thing to hear. They were on chains most of the time, but periodically they would escape and go streaking down the county road, grinning maniacally, frothing at the prospect of freedom, with Dale in hot pursuit in his truck. The subject of Dale's dogs is certainly interesting but it doesn't play out in this particular story.

Except that the bear figured out in nothing flat that the dogs were on chains and so he would ignore their insane barking. After a while even the dogs got used to the bear and stopped barking when the bear appeared, since they concluded that he had come to dinner and they wouldn't be part of the main course. So virtually every night the bear would emerge from the woods, jump up on the tailgate of Dale's pickup truck, and walk around the railing of the pickup bed sniffing the pickings prior to diving in for dinner.

This predilection for garbage is what gets bears in trouble with humans. And that's what happened to this bear. During one week in the summer the fishing hadn't been too good and Dale's garbage pickings weren't so great, or maybe the bear just got sick of fish heads. Whatever was going on in the big bear's head, he decided to dine at another neighbor's garbage can restaurant. This particular neighbor had cutout bear silhouettes on his front yard, apparently liking the fake kind of bears, but not the real ones. At any rate, one night the bear mangled the guy's garbage cans so he called the Department of Natural Resources. The government, being here to help, brought out a culvert trap, which, if you don't know, is a section of a large-diameter steel culvert with one end welded shut and a trap door on the other end. They baited it with more garbage and naturally the bear took the bait. Bears aren't all that smart. Some northern Minnesota hunters think bears are quite clever, but then they aren't exactly the smartest bunch themselves.

That was in August. I had heard about it and didn't like it, the poor bear hadn't hurt a soul, but he was gone. I heard that they'd taken him to the other side of Lake Winnibigosh and let him loose, more than fifty miles from our lake. I didn't think much more about the bear. He wasn't coming back. And I was too busy getting things arranged, the footings dug and getting those miserable blocks laid on top of the crushed rock and living in the little camper trailer next to the work site. I had completely forgotten the Big Long-Legged Bear.

Then one night in early October when that first giant, yellow, glowing moon had risen again behind the poplar trees, a soft warm breeze was blowing and there weren't any mosquitoes to speak of, I was lying on the bed in the little trailer, semi-exhausted and a little depressed, since it seemed that progress on the house was slow, with the light from that big moon pouring in, the last of the tree frogs cheeping, and some late running bats out looping around this way and that across the face of that moon, laying there wondering about everything that was going to happen to me.

And then I heard the sound of feet padding steadily along, past the camper. I sat up. And there in the moonlight was the bear. The Big Long-Legged Bear had walked home fifty miles, and there he was, plodding past my little trailer, down the driveway, heading straight for Dale's fish head restaurant. I lay back and my heart somehow lifted a little. The moon poured in and it seemed to smile on me. I thought of the night after night of the bear steadily walking and walking, walking home and I started laughing for some reason, and when I stopped, I suddenly felt very sleepy and safe.

At the Common Ground coffee house my friend the woodtick showed up again one night. Remember him? He had been out west fighting fires for part of the summer. He was a nice enough, expansive-talking sort of fellow with a quirky, slightly loopy and humorous outlook. He had said that he was going to bring a vial of water out west and pour it on the ground out there—to encourage the rain, he said. I asked him whether the water had worked.

He stared at me for a moment, one of those slightly crooked smiles on his face, apparently searching among the sizzled synaptic wiring in his head for something about water. "What water?" he finally asked.

"Why, the water you poured on the ground out there to prime the pump," said I.

Then he remembered, lit up a little at the memory, but quickly there was that fractured grin again. "I did pour it on the ground. But I got thirsty and decided it wouldn't hurt if I drank it before it went on the ground," he said.

I asked him how hard the fire fighting was. He waved his hand as if fighting various conflagrations were nothing and said he had put most of them out by stamping on them with his foot. That was as much as I got out of him since he was then leering at a woman who had come in and had been interested in all of this talk. After all, he had actually held a job for several months and thus had acquired tinges of respectability, a trait that might prove useful around the ladies.

A guy who played bagpipes came in, another of the summer visitors. He had once heard a Scottish bagpiping band play "Amazing Grace" and very much wanted to do the same. Being in Minnesota, he hadn't had a lot of opportunities to exercise his bagpiping skills. Or perhaps he wasn't up to the standards of the other bagpipers in the area. So he ventured into the Common Ground. The patrons of the Common Ground, mostly considering themselves liberal in their thinking and tolerant of every musical inclination, quickly assented to his plan, which was to tune up in an adjacent room and then to come marching in, in full regalia, skirling mightily to the lugubrious strains of "Amazing Grace." This he did and, to his credit, even hit several notes reminding me of that tune. It also occurred to me at that moment that if the place were ever overrun with rodents, he could have been hired to drive them out, such was the piercing quality of his bagpiping.

As it was, his musical efforts merely moved me several feet toward the door. His outfit and skirt, however, were a hit—a light-blue cotton long-sleeved blouse and a somehow understated red plaid skirt over dark long stockings, just in case you go for that sort of thing. He did eventually stop playing and became a regular at the coffee house, apparently rightfully concluding that any group whose collective constitutions could stand listening to his bagpiping indoors were his kind of people. He was a nice guy, and only brought out the bagpipes on special occasions or when he was in a bad mood, neither of which occurred frequently. So that was okay.

November

The Big Long-Legged Bear had come back and it would have been great and highly inspirational if I had taken some sort of lesson from his methodical, plodding, fifty-mile homeward trip. If I did it wasn't apparent to me then, since I was too busy trying to get some actual work accomplished in the weeks before too much snow rendered the place unworkable. In early November my brother showed up again to go deer hunting for a couple of days. You might picture the scene he saw at my place when he cautiously descended my driveway. An unfrozen, dark, cold lake. Bleak trees against white snow. My little trailer parked next to the power pole, rather like some sort of large red, white and blue striped bug chained to a post, not to mention piles of logs and wood shavings, the old pumpkin-colored Buick, a wreck of a bulldozer, various tools scattered around and the black footprint of my house footing in the snow. And this was a good day. Later my brother told me that he was shocked at my living situation. If he was, he didn't show it then, and we went off for a couple of days of hunting. Strangely I don't remember if we got any deer; the meat would have come in handy.

When I got back from hunting, I worked every day. The weather in October had been good, but November is gray, hard and cold under the best of circumstances in the north, and the circumstances in '93 weren't the best. After a few preliminary rounds of jabbing cold and snow, it proceeded to snow steadily almost every day. Actually, from my perspective things weren't all that bad. Both of my vehicles worked pretty well. I wasn't broke. So long as I was frugal, I wouldn't starve for a while, and my place was comfortable enough. I didn't expect perfection. Probably the biggest problem was that it snowed frequently so I had to sweep off the work every day and clear the snow off of the driveway.

Shortly thereafter a logger from Effie, showed up with a semi-trailer load of logs that were to become my house. My driveway is very steep where it drops off the county road, and in those days it was not in good shape. Actually, even considering the improvements I've made, bringing a loaded semitrailer down it would be no picnic. To try it with slippery snow on the ground would seem insanity. In contrast to the concrete-block guy, however, who took one look at my driveway when it was fairly dry and refused to bring his load down, this logger took a careful look and then hopped back into his semi truck and brought the whole load of logs right down onto the site. I hope I can impart to you just how difficult this was. He had to get fifty thousand pounds (or more, the load itself of green logs probably weighed thirty thousand pounds) of semi and trailer, forty feet long or so, down a steep snow-covered driveway.

One could argue, I suppose, that he had to get the logs down onto the site and driving that load down there was the only way to do it. But driving that huge load down and unloading it wasn't the most serious problem. Getting his rig turned around and back up that hill and out of there was the real problem. I had prevailed upon my neighbor Dale to come over and plow my driveway, but you can't get all of the snow. And this logger did it twice. He brought his semi into my place with two loads, got it out safely and I had the logs for my house. All that I can say is that he was one hell of a truck jockey.

Dave was an old gentleman from Effie who came to help me get started building my log home. He had been a soldier in World War II, and when he got home from the war he had gone to work building log homes. He had built hundreds of log homes in his day, and this is what he said more or less in his words.

"When I got home from the war I needed a job and there wasn't many jobs around. Someone told me there was an Irishman might hire somebody, so I went on over to where this man name of Flynn was building a house. Flynn had a hard eye and didn't talk much. He looked me up and down, heard my story without saying a thing, pointed at a pile of logs and said, 'Peel those and we'll see.' Well, I was used to working and taking orders, so I did as I was told and after a day or so I guess it was sort of assumed I'd keep working. We made log houses the old-fashioned way, with hand tools, adze, axe and saw. We cut the logs, scribed and chipped out the tops of the logs and made the window frames, all by hand.

"I worked for Flynn for seven years. There was a big demand for log cabins about then. And then the demand for log homes died down a little in the '50s, but it came back in the '60s and ain't settled down yet. Anyway, we had work every year, so that was okay. After that I guess he was getting old and wanted to retire. It wasn't easy, that work you know, and he'd been at it a long time. So one day he came up to me when we finished a job. 'I'm quitin' the business, here's five letters from people who want houses built. You can do what you want with them.' That's all he said and that was his way. We was never close you know, Flynn wasn't like that, though I know he respected me for the way I worked. And that's how I come to build houses."

Dave was unusual in a couple of respects. He had never used alcohol in his life. His father had drunk up the farm that Dave's grandparents had hacked out of the north woods, built up and that he had inherited. His father regularly got drunk and abused him. Once he found Dave who was driving tractor for a neighbor and demanded money, presumedly to use for drinking. When Dave refused, his father hit him in the face with a heavy leather belt, knocked him down and took all of his money. After that Dave procured a pistol, and the next time his father appeared to ask for money, he produced the pistol instead of cash, pointed it at his own father and told him he'd kill him if he came closer. His father left. Such was life then.

Dave had never married. He spent his money on trucks, guns and hunting dogs. Once I asked him why he had never married. He paused while sharpening a chain saw blade, ran a stubby thumb on an edge and stared a little at me. "Woman…Soft shoulders and cold hearts," he said, snapping the saw around and jerking hard on the starter cord.

Incidentally I was amazed to find out that he had never lived in a log house himself. He had built a little frame shack where he lived with his hunting dogs and his guns. He drove his truck down from Effie every day to work with me, the cab jammed to the ceiling with hunting paraphernalia, a chocolate lab puppy riding alongside on top of the pile. The puppy romped around our building site biting this and that and annoying Casey. Eventually the rambunctious pup found a place in the sun where he promptly fell asleep while we worked.

We started by cutting half logs for the ends of the house. Suffice it to say, splitting a large log in half isn't easy so we took turns cutting the log with a chain saw and smoothing the flat side by brushing it with the chain saw. The rest of the first-course logs are perpendicular to the half logs and are scribed over the half logs so that they are also flat on the concrete footings. (This process is in any good instruction book.) By the way I put strips of insulation under the logs to seal any airflow between the logs and the house. This was a mistake since water gets under there and this space stayed moist. Moisture is bad where wood is concerned. Having air under there is better. Eventually I pulled out the insulation, got that area dried out and chinked the space between the concrete footing sill and the first log. There are several products you can use for this space, including foam insulation, which is water-resistant.

I noticed several things about the work during the first week. First, my job didn't look as clean as the one in the book. I wasn't that clean either, come to think of it, and Dave didn't seem to be worried about it, so I didn't let that bother me. He was anxious to get off of the first course and didn't seem to be as careful as I expected. I didn't think much about that at first since I was in a hurry myself. Also Dave couldn't really do any heavy work, not that I expected any very heavy work out of him. He was enthusiastic but he didn't seem in good condition and his chain saw work was very rough.

But the problem that became obvious immediately was that I was going to have trouble due to the excessive length of one of my walls and the resulting tapers on my logs. In log home building you're putting the fat end of a log on top of a thin end of the log under it. If they're too long and the difference in size is too great it looks ugly, but more importantly, large differences in the overlapping logs create trouble cutting and fitting the corners. This was apparent to me the minute I started. I would have had a better-constructed house if I had stopped right there to rethink the whole process. I didn't and I don't remember anyone telling me that the plan I had was poorly thought-out. On the other hand, I don't remember asking either, and there was no turning back for me then.

Iron-gray skies. Dark pine forest and the sweet smell of someone's wood stove burning dry birch logs. Dave and I had some fun. We spent our chilly November days talking hunting dogs and trucks, all the while working steadily, but not too hard. Oddly, maneuvering the logs wasn't much of a problem since no matter how big the log was I could manhandle it around with a cant hook and roll it up ramps into position. Things went okay and of course things that go well aren't very interesting. Go ahead, tell someone about a really great party and watch his eyes glaze over. But tell him about the party where one guy punched another or, even more interesting, assaulted the virtue of aunt Jane and watch his eyes open. In this case things generally went very well, we didn't punch each other. And as for sex I don't want to talk about it.

I was very aware then that my world had, by good or bad luck, compressed itself into one small, slightly hilarious constellation, consisting of myself, two beat-up vehicles, a bulldozer, a pile of logs, the footings for my house, Casey and Dave and myself. I don't remember being at all concerned and in fact was enjoying myself, though I probably should have been worried about winter, which was knocking at the door. Maybe one's guardian angel imposes some sort of mind anesthesia under these circumstances. I don't know. Whatever was going on, we worked every day and I was learning things so I didn't complain.

Some days we would go to town. When we went to town in my truck and I went faster than that, Dave clutched the seat and braced his feet against the firewall as if I was going to run off the road any second. Dave had had an accident with his truck recently and drove his own truck at about forty miles per hour. We would run errands, talk a lot, eat a cheap breakfast and then head back to my work site. It was fun, but Dave wasn't going to be around long. When I knew him, he was old and not in good shape. It was the hard fall of that hard year of '93, a northern winter was upon me and I was living in a little trailer designed for camping and not for two people. But Dave and I worked a little, and he showed me how to cut the logs and what to do until one day late in November, I couldn't afford him anymore and had no place for him to stay. So we parted company, but he had gotten me started and gave me a line for this book.

Speaking of friends, about this point I met a young lady named Beth and we went out for quite a while. She could cook the most amazingly scrumptious pastries. The other distinctive thing about her was her hair, which was orange, or more precisely, an orangey color. Her hair color was the result of some adventurous application of colorant, or so she told me. Further, her hair had a rather spiky aspect to it so that from a distance her head looked like a blaze-orange pineapple. Had her hair been a tad brighter, she would have looked like she was wearing her own organic blaze-orange hunting hat. Eventually she changed her hair again to a blonde color, which was less visible.

I liked her either way. She had a house and I gave some thought to living with her and working on my house from there. But somehow I knew that if I started down that road I might not finish my own project and, as I've mentioned before, I'm stubborn. So I stayed in the little trailer and continued to work on my house and saw her a couple times a week.

One night she asked me whether I believed in ghosts. I was taken aback. Way aback. One necessarily approaches this question cautiously.

"So far no," says I. "Why? Is there one here?" I said.

"No. Of course not. But the other night I saw a man and a woman standing at the foot of my bed looking at me," she said.

"This bed? What were they doing?" I said, resisting the temptation to smooth down some neck hairs, which had suddenly stood straight out.

"Oh nothing, just standing there," she said.

No ghosts appeared, thankfully, and we went on going out on weekends. And I discovered, eventually, that not all of her hair was orange.

At the Common Ground coffee house the lady with the music machine who sang religious songs showed up again. It had been a while since we had seen her. We thought her traveling show had just passed through and was gone.

Before I talk about her, I must stop right here to tell you that when I was young most of the people that I knew acted in a more or less dignified manner. Well maybe *dignified* is the wrong word, less demonstrative perhaps. Experience has rendered that conclusion laughable today, but it was somewhat true then. In the little town by another lake where I grew up, people didn't often get up in front of others and expose their feelings unless they were at a funeral, drunk or maybe in a fight in a bar, but of course that's different. I only suspected it then, of course, but there were certain, rather rigid rules by which people lived. And God help you if you walked outside of the dotted lines marking the boundaries of conduct.

Times have certainly changed, haven't they? Presently, not only do people seem to want to get up there and testify, it sometimes takes physical force to keep some of them from airing their psychic laundry. But let us not touch for the moment the question of whether this loosening of these social constraints is good or bad, and instead, speculate for a moment on the causes of this. One could of course perhaps ascribe some of this to the rise of the media in the latter half of the twentieth century. Thanks to the media, Americans have been exposed to much more acting, performing and singing, and this has awakened a lot of nascent performers. Well, nascent somethings.

Think not? Have you been to a Karaoke bar lately and listened to the bloody awful sounds emanating from the stage? Or watched some politician baring his very soul in front of the camera? Or perhaps watched some TV shows in which a person is paid to humiliate herself in one form or another? I could go on. Certainly these media forms contribute. Maybe the law of big numbers enters this picture. Perhaps out of the great mass of the people creep those souls who, wounded or suppressed in their lives, demand to have their latent, but obviously vast, talent released and who merely need to be given license to stand up and testify. One begins to long for some of that awful decorum of my misspent youth.

I mention this because one Friday the lady who sang the religious tunes came in with her machine, sang a couple of songs and stopped. This was great. No doubt she had learned the protocol for our coffee house. You may recall that at her first performance she had sang her religious songs until eternity seemed to be making an appearance on the horizon. Obviously, on that occasion she had been merely ignorant.

Ah, you innocents. Instead she picked this occasion to fill us in about her husband, who had been a high school teacher and who had been accused of sexual impropriety with his students. Apparently, while she was home practicing her religious songs, the proximity of nubile young females around him all day was too much and he let his fingers do the walking. She pointed toward her husband, John, who appeared startled, as if not expecting this attention. He was actually a rather pleasant-looking fiftyish man with thinning, somewhat lank hair. At the mention of his name, he smiled somewhat nervously and seemed to shrink in size, while she expanded and went on determinedly. "I want to take this opportunity to introduce my husband who was a teacher in southwest Minnesota and was falsely accused of sexual touching."

She seemed to add emphasis on the "sex" part of the word so that it sounded like sexual. "The terrible part of these sexual charges is that my husband, who is innocent, couldn't continue at that school. Our retirement is in jeopardy and I had to go back to work. These women run around with everything hanging out and then accuse my husband of some **sex**ual allegation which we have to defend ourselves against."

She went on like this for some time while the patrons of the Common Ground listened slack-jawed and her husband twisted slowly in the wind. Later they left and we never saw them again. Apparently she went looking for another tree on which to nail her husband's hide. I was twisting in the wind myself a bit and was looking with some trepidation toward December, which had come on me quicker than I expected. Still, how bad could December get?

Building Your Log Home, Part One

This isn't an instruction booklet on how to build a log house. There are plenty of these at your public library. Or, if libraries aren't your thing, you could spend a few bucks and buy a good book at a log home supply company. Look on the Internet if you aren't a Luddite. Schroeder Log Home Supply in Grand Rapids, Minnesota, is a good source for everything you ever wanted to help you build. Schroeder has an online bookstore, and that's a good place to start. There are probably others. They'll sell you anything you need and a few things you don't.

Planning Your House

I bought the book recommended by Schroeder. It's written by F. Dan Milne and is very good, even if he's a Canadian. The reason it is very good is that it has clear, easy-to-follow instructions and, best of all, pictures. The author apparently assumed, and here's the genius part, that the persons following its instruction had approximately the intelligence of your average chimpanzee. Considering the mistakes I made building my house, that assessment, if granting a bit too much intelligence to the chimp, wasn't far off. At any rate, for light amusement I've assembled some suggestions for your consideration. Most are pretty good, being based on skinned knuckles, aching muscles and bruises—particularly to my ego—when I finally examined the product of my labor. Still, read on, they might help and can't hurt.

One of the important things you can do is to research and plan your house. There are two simple reasons for this. With a little research you can avoid looking like an idiot, such as I did on certain occasions, and, most importantly, save yourself some work. A casual examination of the subject on the Internet reveals a flood of information on log homes, including several magazines dedicated to this subject. One site had seventy-four books on related subjects. There is a mountain of information available. Do research even if you're going to hire a contractor to build the house, since his or her interest isn't always yours.

But let's say you've decided to build your own. You can, of course, do as I did and get out your favorite napkin and begin sketching a plan. My house was large but simple. Picture a rectangle, forty by twenty-seven feet; with a ten-foot square chopped out of one corner. This alcove was eventually to be part of a porch. To be fair to myself, after I had developed an idea of what I was going to do and had committed it to the napkin, I did a considerable amount of investigation. And then being the stubborn sort, I went ahead and did it my way. I did it my way! A song. An idiot's lyric. People have been building log homes for a thousand years and I had to do it my way. Whole industries have been adapted to this and I did it my way.

Don't do it your way. Go and get a plan that someone with experience has built many times and build that. It's still you that's doing it, and that's the important part. Your way depends upon your needs and especially your equipment. If you have access to power lifting equipment, then you can pick a plan that uses longer, heavier logs. If you don't have a lot of equipment, use a plan with shorter walls and commensurately smaller lighter logs. It's simple.

You might, in the way of an experiment, go find a suitably heavy log of the length you are contemplating using and try maneuvering it around. You will find out soon enough what you're up against and what equipment you'll need. Don't get discouraged though. People have been building these things for a long time. If I did it, you can do it. And finally I might mention here that there are schools that teach log home construction. You spend a weekend or two and learn some of the techniques of log building by actually working under the tutelage of an instructor. I didn't go this route, but I think it's a good idea.

And get a plan that fits the housing needs of your situation. There's simply no point in building a mansion if you just need a summer cabin. (Besides, log mansions look ugly and attract ghosts.) Is it a summer cabin or a year-round house? The only caveat to this I would mention is that you know and I know that the "summer cabin" is a thing of the past, and any log home should be considered permanent. New construction, even it it's used only part of the year, is built to be permanent. Further, there are plenty of plans for cabins that are modular, which means the cabin can be added to in your, or someone else's, future. And besides, there is a quality issue here. With a little consideration you can build a house or cabin that has real value and that will appreciate in value over the years. And why go to the effort if it's not well done?

Peeling Logs

Building a log house is the process of getting a tree from where it is standing in a forest, minding its own business, to another place where it is piled with some other victim trees in such a manner that you can live within the confines of the assembled logs. The weasel and his relatives who took up residence shortly after my house was built don't care how it is piled. The human is not normally a weasel and thus requires some orderly arrangement of the logs. Once you have dragged the logs kicking and screaming out of the woods over to where they are comfortably resting on a pile with the other logs, you then have to make a wall out of them. This is a fairly complicated process.

First, one has to peel the thing. Logs don't come peeled. At least the ones I bought didn't, and while I suppose somewhere in the past people have built homes out of unpeeled logs, all of the pictures in the books entertained the peeled log. This was a bad shock. In case you didn't know this, peeling is best done in the spring when the sap is rising. In spring the bark comes off easily as if the log just wanted to throw off its clothing. Rather like humans. At least in the north, that is. In the south they seem to throw off their clothes at any time of year.

But I digress. Peeling is best done in spring, so naturally I started in late fall since I didn't want to wait until spring. By the way, amazingly, a felled and stacked log, so long as it hasn't been there too long, doesn't seem to know it has been felled and stacked and still peels easier in the spring. Don't ask me why. Trees, being optimists, apparently still think the sap is flowing. And I can tell you from experience that when you've been at this for a while, the sap really gets flowing, spring or no spring. One additional thing about peeling logs. It is best to peel them all at once. Hire some local teenagers to help you do this if you've got the dough or call up all of your friends and make a party of it; while you still have friends. Believe me, in the long run you'll be better off if you peel all of them instead of doing as I did and peel them as I needed the logs. Then when you have them all peeled, treat them all at one time with anti-fungicide to keep them from turning ugly gray, which they will do, believe me

Peeling is done with any metal thing shaped to remove bark. They range from the draw knife, which, so far as I can tell, is an instrument designed to discourage anyone from woodworking, to a bark spud which is any chisel-like thing with a handle that one attempts to slide under the bark to pry it up. For tough jobs I used a long steel bar, which originally had been a car axle. One end of this beast was flattened and slightly bent like the sharp end of a crowbar. It weighed approximately the same as a Volkswagen. But if you jabbed with this bar, nothing could withstand it. I used it for the tough jobs. Perfect, so long as you could lift it.

My main bark-removing tool I borrowed, à la Thoreau, from a friend. He didn't say it was the apple of his eye, but he still let on that he wanted it back eventually. It had a thin chisel-like blade and a short sturdy wood handle and, in total, was about three feet long. We are still friends, so the fact that I broke his peeler and then welded it back together didn't seem to affect our friendship. That could also have something to do with the fact that I didn't tell him about the broken blade at the time it happened. In the end he got his bark peeler back in working order, though not sharper. Still, intact isn't bad.

Types of Wood

When I considered building a new home for myself, I had only a vague idea of what sort of house I would build. Then gradually I began to think about building it out of logs. Log homes are common in northern Minnesota and recently many people have built them out of aspen, also known as poplar or, more commonly, popple. Popple is plentiful in our area, and, even better, I had a lot of it on my property. So at first I thought I would build out of these trees. Your basic popple is a soft wood and it shrinks a lot, but when peeled it is a nice cream white and when it cures it is hard and durable, so long as you keep it dry so that it does not rot. In northern Minnesota it is a big industry to harvest popple and turn it into pressboard and high-quality paper.

More importantly, a neighbor down the road had built a popple log home. I found his house nestled in some maple and birch at the end of a long driveway. He is a retired army soldier and, according to him, had built his house over the course of a summer and fall with the help of a friend and a tractor with a front-end loader. I use the present tense because he's still there, going for his walk every day on the county road, summer and winter, upright and vigorous. I visited him several times to talk about the good and bad aspects of building a log home. His house was large, rustic, warm and comfortable with a large fireplace, a furnace and one of those huge five-foot satellite dishes that are now about the size of a pie plate. It wasn't a perfect job. He showed me where the poplar logs had shrunk away from the fireplace. But all in all, a log home of some sort seemed to be just what I was looking for.

I also looked at a log home built by a teacher couple. Their house was built of large poplar logs, which they had allowed to cure, and then painted. It was a huge affair on two floors with very large logs in its lower courses. His wife was gone working and he told me he didn't have any time either and had to go, but as he rushed off he told me to have a look around. I could have plundered the place. Plundering not being on my mind, I looked around, impressed by the nicely fitting logs and the size and warmth of the teacher house.

I then visited several of the professional log homebuilders in the area to see how the job actually should be done. I could, it seemed, build my house of virtually any type of logs, including logs from my place if I had enough. Log homes have been built of almost any type of trees. You name it, poplar, which is very popular, yuk, yuk, not to mention oak, maple, chestnut and I suppose whatever local wood was available. Southerners have built them of yellow pine. My aunt Em, bless her departed soul, had a little log cabin of maple logs built at Prior Lake, Minnesota, in the 1930s. Maple was so plentiful in that area before the turn of the twentieth century that most of the trees were cut and hauled away for railroad ties to clear the land for farming. Her little cabin, with its fieldstone fireplace and screened porch, was used as a summer cabin. Later it was occupied year-round. It was still standing in the 1980s when it got in the way of modern houses and was torn down. Not many of those new shacks have its character. You get the point. You can build a log home out of any wood, I think.

In the end I didn't use poplar, but I still think that option a good one. In my case I had a forester come out and we walked my land evaluating my poplar trees. Most of my trees were too old to be used and so I began to lean away from using popple as the logs for my place. Then I got talked into using balsam, a nice pinewood that we bought from a logger. Balsam cuts well, is usually straight and seasons to a nice hard wood. It smells good, and the pitch gets on your hands and clothes until, when you've worked it some, you smell rather nice and piney, which is better than the alternative.

I should have visited a church. Actually, come to think of it, I sort of did visit a church. Or rather part of a church came to me. My front door, which is made of leftover pine floor joists, has very large hinges that came from a church that had been torn down. And, come to think of it, lots of churches have been made of logs.

Plumbing and Permits

Probably the single most important aspect of the planning you do is for the plumbing, heating and crawl space under your house. Plan for a suitable crawl space or basement with good access to your utilities. You don't have to put all of the plumbing in right away. But if you're going to go to the trouble to build a log home, you need to plan for the pipes, especially if you plan to pour a concrete floor of some sort. PVC piping is fairly cheap, installs easily and should be in place when the concrete is poured. The summer cabin outhouse is, or shortly will be, a thing of the past except as a novelty. Zoning codes regarding septic tank and evaporation systems are now used in every county. The heating and plumbing systems needed to heat your place and to transport effluvia outward require planning for a basement or a crawl space.

Another thing. I don't use my house all winter since I'm gone for a couple of months. And since I'm cheap and don't like paying for the heat during that period, when I leave I turn off the heat. To do this I have to blow out or drain all of my water lines. What a pain! Plan a water system that can be drained easily. Or you might plan for off-peak heating systems that keep the place from freezing but don't eat up your budget.

Which brings me to the subject of building permits. It will be necessary in virtually every case for you to get a permit to build your house. There are few if any places in the United States where you can build without a permit. Actually there are permits for most aspects of your building process. For example, no matter who does the electrical, plumbing and sewer system, you will probably be inspected for compliance with state building code. That's the good or bad news, depending on your view of the government. But I want to mention a couple of points, which may add a more positive color to the permit process. You need a plan anyway for all of the components of your site, including garages and your sewer system. To get a permit in most jurisdictions you need a reasonably accurate site plan so that the buildings are located at appropriate distances from your land or lot lines. In my case, for example, in addition to setbacks from lot lines, there was a minimum setback required from the lake. I was a professional planner and also sat for years on a planning commission. I've seen what happens when uncontrolled development occurs. It ain't pretty. So use the permit process to plan your driveway, house, garage, sewer and well location.

Most people, if they have money, will hire a surveyor to prepare a lot or site plan showing the location of the house, garage and sewer system. But if you don't have the money to do this, it is possible to simply measure these distances, make a scaled drawing of your site and use that to apply for the building permit from the county. Please note I didn't say this was possible in all jurisdictions, but it is in many, particularly in rural areas where the lot size is larger. In smaller city lots, with less room to plan your house, garage and sewer plan, a survey may be necessary. Plus there may be ordinance requirements for the use of a surveyor to make a lot plan for your home.

But surveyors aren't cheap and if the planner balks at you presenting him or her with a scaled sketch plan, then tell him to come out, bring his tape measure and the two of you will establish the setbacks together. The staff at the city or the county will usually be helpful and give you the criteria for lot line setbacks. Unless you get some officious idiot who thinks he or she is king or queen, you can use this process to have a comprehensive plan for your site at a low cost.

One additional small point. With regard to any important dealings with the city or county, make sure that you put your needs in writing. Normally city or county officials will be helpful, but a paper trail will help keep everything above board. Of course you are liable if your house is sitting on someone's property line.

Wall Lengths

I have no idea why it was that I did this (read poor planning), but I have one wall that is a lot longer than it should be. One of my walls is forty feet long. Why I ended up with such a long wall is still somewhat of a mystery to me. Temporary insanity, maybe. For the average house you shouldn't make the walls any longer than about twenty-four feet including the extensions, which stick out beyond the corner about a foot and a half. Obviously there are exceptions as in the case of very large log houses wherein larger longer logs are appropriate.

Everything goes easier when the logs are appropriately sized. Shorter logs are easier to handle, have less taper and are thus easier to fit. I should have shortened the long wall into three walls, two longer walls with one short corner. Since log homes gain strength from their interlocking corners, having more corners makes for a stronger house anyway. When log walls get too long, the logs taper too much and they are structurally weaker. In addition, the logs weigh too much and require heavier equipment to lift them. (Or more people.)

Log Sizes

You can theoretically build a log house with any size logs. But there are aesthetic and practical reasons for using certain size logs. A friend had been telling me about someone who was building a log house. He said it was going up fast. At that point mine was going up slow. I drove over to have a look. He was doing a good job, but the logs were about the size of fence posts! He said the thing that was good about this was that he could put the logs up by hand, without equipment.

Let me put this to you gently. The word log in the phrase log house implies something larger than a fence post. Aside from other factors, the known R factor of a fence-post-size "log" is too low. Of course there isn't any hard and fast rule to this and it's just my opinion, mind you, but he could have handled real log-sized logs, and it would have looked better. On the other hand, using gigantic logs for a small house looks ugly and they're awfully heavy and hard to manage without power equipment. Thus the logs should be proportional to the size of the house.

Usually eight- to twelve-inch logs are about right for a normal house. But of course huge logs have been used for larger houses.

Oh, several more points about logs. First, Americans can't seem to leave well enough alone. Ever since the first guy laid one log on top of another, people have been squaring, flattening, rounding (like telephone poles) and generally fiddling around with the wood to civilize it. I do not recommend the various squared, flattened, etc. logs. The charm of a log house is that it is made of logs. If you want a house that is of ordinary construction, go have Joe build you a stick-built (conventionally framed) house. A couple of caveats to this. Recently (actually as I was writing this) I found a house that was built in the 1940s of untreated telephone poles. It looked pretty good and had lasted sixty years. Someone had tried to put an addition onto the telephone log home, by using short lengths of telephone poles. That part looked ugly.

Another thing. Some people scribe the corners and then flatten the intervening surfaces of the log so that they lay flat on top of one another without scribing. Then they caulk the seams. Of course, one of the reasons for the Canadian method of scribing logs is that, in addition to fitting the logs together, you chip out a space along the bottom of the log, into which you put insulation. When you're done placing one log on top of the one below, you theoretically don't need caulking, since the space between the logs is now filled with insulation. The problem with this is that—at least in my experience—no matter the insulation, there is still some airflow through these spaces. These air leaks render the insulation less effective. In addition, various bugs find the cracks between the logs to be nice dry places within which to make a home. And no matter how tightly the logs compress, there are always places of entry.

I ended up caulking my place just prior to staining it. And so far I'm happy I did it. The house feels tighter and warmer in winter.

Thus I have come to conclude that scribing the corners, flattening the intervening surfaces and then caulking to seal the seams between the logs is okay. Since the insulation value isn't really there, why go to all that work to scribe a log if you're going to caulk and cover the nice scribing?

Advice Taking and Giving

Let me say a couple of words about taking advice, even mine, which is particularly good. I have an acquaintance whose theory of assembling things goes something like this. When you're trying to assemble something, you get a six-pack of beer and drink it while reading the instructions. Then you throw away the instructions and build it. That's not bad advice. I don't drink anymore, having leaned on the bar enough so that I'll leave that to others, thank you, but you should read everything you can about the process, then pick the best plan—considering your energy and your equipment—and then start. After all, you are building *your* house. You aren't building someone else's house. That other guy had other equipment and that other guy has other plans. Getting advice is natural, but you have to adapt your work and your life to the situation in front of you. Otherwise some situation that someone else found easy to solve will stop you. So take the advice, read the directions, have a beer and then build your house.

I have a neighbor who likes to have lots of people around. I only point this out because there are really two ways of building things, based upon which type of person you are. Both are good. The first is the quick way: you get a whole bunch of your friends or family together, and, usually with the aid of copious libations, you build the barn or shed or whatever. Having frantically worked at it for a day or a week, it's done and you go back to whatever you were doing when the insane idea struck you.

But building a house isn't a battle; it's a war. That rather dramatic statement is made to illustrate a point. Building a log house takes a while if you do it yourself, even if you have help. You can't get everything done in a day, so you have to adopt a more steady day-by-day strategy. In this way of doing things you have to accept what you get done every day and not be too impatient. There is fun in the doing and in the learning, too. I know many people who have built their summer home over many summers, coming to their lake places when the weather got warm and they had the money. Working and sweating in the sun is fun when it's your choice. Not that you want to spend forever doing it. Frankly, I had planned a much shorter process for my place. It didn't work that way and I wasn't hurt by it, but I still think it would have been better to eliminate some of the drudgery.

And finally a word about problems. Have you ever been confronted with the need to make a decision? Usually it's someone else's problem and they want you to spend your time and your energy (and money) solving it. The first rule of problem solving is do nothing. Don't make any decision quickly. Think about it for a while. A good night's sleep often helps. The harder the problem, the more someone wants you to make a decision quickly, the more time you should take. This particularly applies to any financial decision. Mulling things over for a while works too. I have a friend who mulls. He doesn't do anything very fast and instead mulls the problem over for a few days. Then usually the problem dissolves into the nonproblem it was to begin with. Of course, as they say, if you're up to your ass in alligators, it is not the time to think about draining the swamp. What they don't say about that little homily, however, is that if you'd thought about it a little, maybe you wouldn't have been in the damned swamp to begin with.

December

The road to hell is, of course, paved with questions such as, "How bad could December get?" December could get very bad. November had been the preliminaries, but December was the main event. It snowed every day now, with temperatures mostly in the twenties in the day and about five to ten above zero at night. From the time that Dave left, I worked steadily but I spent more and more of my time keeping my construction site and the driveway free from snow. I heated the little trailer for a while until I realized that I was using too much liquid propane gas, so I turned off the heat at night while I slept. I had an electric blanket that my mother had given me and that kept me toasty warm at night, all the while no doubt rearranging considerable portions of my genetic structure. I have never used one since, but in that circumstance the electric blanket worked wonderfully well. In the morning I would reach out and light the little furnace. A half hour later, the place would be tolerably warm and I would then get up and make my morning coffee. At full light, usually about seven, I would begin working, the usual goal being to get a log cut and into place.

In my trailer I had water jugs that I generally filled every few days in town. But if I had forgotten to get more, or had used it up, I would drill a hole in the ice and get water that way. The only problem with this is that eventually the ice gets very thick and the hole you drilled freezes shut. It's a lot of trouble to cut a hole every time you go to get water. Then I discovered that if I covered the hole with a board and then covered the board with snow, the snow would insulate the hole against freezing too quickly. The next time you need water you uncover the hole, break the skim of ice and fill up. Of course this assumes you haven't waited too many days and can find the place where you drilled the hole. I know, you think you'll never have to do that, but it's a good thing to learn anyway. One never knows.

I liked the sweet smell of pine bark when it burned, and I had a seemingly unlimited supply of the peelings, so most days I would build a little fire, put a small grill over it when it got going and heat water. I rather preferred coffee cooked on the fire since it had a nice pine-smoke flavor. Or maybe it was me that had the smoky flavor. When the water was hot I would dump in some Folgers instant coffee. In those days I didn't bother with good brewed coffee. When company came and I offered them coffee, they usually wrinkled their noses. Drinking coffee made from instant coffee didn't bother me so long as it gave me the necessary jolt to get going.

For breakfast I would usually have oatmeal. I would pour about a half cup of the old-fashioned kind of oatmeal into a bowl. To that I would add a small package of sweetened, processed oatmeal. Then I would dump some boiling water over it, stir and let the oatmeal sit for a minute. The unprocessed oatmeal gave the mix a nice chewy texture. To this I would add a large chunk of butter and milk if I had it. I was expending so much energy that the amount of fat and calories I was consuming did not concern me.

Once I got a bottle of homemade maple syrup and used several tablespoons of that every morning until it ran out.

Thus fed and having had my coffee, I would start my day and work until ten-thirty, when I would take a break and have another cup of coffee. If I had a sweet roll I would eat that with my coffee, sometimes smearing a thick coat of butter on it. Usually Casey would have shown up by now and we would speculate upon the red squirrels or some other weighty subject, while he did me the honor of sharing whatever it was that I was eating. I would then resume working and Casey would resume driving red squirrels crazy and guarding me from potential intruders. At about one o'clock I would stop and have lunch, which usually consisted of a couple of sandwiches and soup if I had it.

Every other day or so I would head into town on some errand. The snow began to make getting out of the driveway more difficult. In order to get out of the driveway, I resorted to putting several concrete blocks in the trunk of the Buick. I would then point the car down the driveway, rev up the engine and let her go. There's a long straight stretch before the driveway ascends some twenty feet and slightly turns to the right before intersecting the road. With snow flying I would get going as fast as I dared in the straight stretch, but not too fast since, if my velocity was too high, I would slide off of the driveway and over the bank into the brush on the lake side. Fishtailing up the hill I would try to make it to the top. Usually I made it, but if I didn't—and this happened not infrequently—I would have to back down the hill. Slippery wet snow made backing down the hill a treacherous maneuver, since one couldn't hit the brakes.

Sometimes it would snow a lot and I would shovel and sweep the entire driveway. This took several hours, and although not easy, it was more time-consuming than any-thing. Sometimes my neighbor Dale would come over with his plow on his truck and plow me out, but I didn't ask him to do this too much since I wasn't paying and I didn't want to prevail upon his generosity.

Actually the driveway was better the colder it got. When it's cold the snow has a slightly gritty consistency so the traction is better. In fact, when it is very cold, the ice on a lake develops a gritty surface upon which maneuver-ing a vehicle or even a large airplane is surprisingly easy. Then the neighbor with the cherry picker, whom I occa-sionally hired to set the heavier logs, showed me how ash from the wood stove is wonderful for traction, particularly on hard-packed snow or ice. He usually brought a pail of the stuff if he came over. I began to save it for use on the steep parts of my hill. With these means and as much velocity as I could muster with the Buick or the truck, I would usually make it to the top of my driveway hill. Having made it to the top, the next problem was stopping, since there was traffic on the county road and if I slid out onto the road there was a fair prospect of colliding with a car or, worse, getting squashed by one of the logging trucks that roared by every day. That didn't happen, thank you, Lord, and having then made it safely out of my drive-way, I would head into town.

Always interested in the little niceties, I discovered that I could get a shower at the YMCA for two dollars. The only bad part about this was that frequently I would be somewhat chilled when I got to town and was looking for-ward to a hot shower. And for some reason, which they never could seem to explain, the showers would be luke-warm. You cannot realize how dispiriting it is when you have a chill in your bones and are looking forward to a very hot shower and you get tepid water. I complained about it frequently. One of the ladies at the front desk said, rather snootily I might add, "I wouldn't know. I don't shower here." It's amazing to me that someone could be working as a desk clerk at some small-town YMCA and act snooty, but there it was. Finally, after complaining for some time, they let me shower in another part of the place where, apparently, they had routed most of the hot water.

Fortunately, to make up for this extreme hardship, there was a Hardees restaurant that offered fresh-baked biscuits and chicken or beef gravy and coffee, all for a dollar. It was sort of a tasty and fresh SOS (SOS is a thick gravy-like food served on toast, circa World War II, colloquially known as Shit-on-a-Shingle) with coffee. I was very grateful for this, since for one dollar you got as much of the biscuits and gravy as you could eat. I don't know how nutritious it was, but it was filling, loaded with carbohydrates and tasted great. Under the circumstances I would often eat two fully-loaded plates of this carbo-laden stuff. I was too embarrassed to ask for a third plate. A fair number of seniors, who weren't fed all that well, ate this affordable meal. And since there was usually a newspaper handy that I didn't have to pay for, I had a generous and I might say tasty meal complete with reading material. Thus fortified and errands finished, I would repair to my frigid disaster zone in the woods.

In December I wore most of my warmer hunting clothes while I was working, except for the blaze orange coat. If it was cold I would wear the wool pants over my regular cotton pants. This had the satisfactory effect of shedding snow and water. Cotton is a fine thing to look at and good for your yuppie town-living guy, but it's horrible when it gets wet because it stays wet and cold practically forever, whereas wool doesn't take in the moisture and dries fast if it actually gets wet. Also, I mostly wore my Sorel boots, which have rubber bottoms and leather tops and removable wool liners. I had several pairs of liners for the Sorels and would change them every day so long as I remembered. Finally, I wore full-length long underwear commonly known as long johns.

Thick warm gloves aren't very good when you have to feel your work so most of the time I wore leather gloves. I used leather gloves no matter how warm it was because I kept getting my hands beat up, particularly my left hand. Further, I usually wore out the fingers of the gloves, so I was essentially working in damp, mostly fingerless leather gloves, the snow falling and the temperature at twenty-five or thirty degrees. This seemed perfectly normal to me at the time. I wore out a half-dozen pair of leather gloves during my project, and since they aren't cheap I would resist buying new ones so long as it was above twenty-five degrees or so.

I might say, however, that working in the cold is hardly unusual in the north. Plenty of people do it regularly, although less do now since most of the equipment has a heated operating cab. Schroeder tells me that in the days when they were working in the woods, if it got too cold, twenty or so below zero, they'd head for the cedar bogs where it was slightly warmer. And of course when it's very cold there is mostly no wind. But they still worked. Those workers had a warm home to go to in the evening. Poor Mike had a bug trailer chained to a power pole.

A still, ice-blue, late December morning. I stop working, throw more pine bark on the fire, heat a cup of water for coffee and when it is steaming, sit on a log, holding the warm cup, sipping the coffee and staring at the little fire. Casey stops his poking around a log pile where he was sure a red squirrel was hiding to come over to see if we were eating. The pale sun, barely rising above the trees to the southeast looks down with little warmth. The lake is cold, gray-black against the white snow. In the night ice has crept far out from shore in places. Across the lake, the woods make a dark gash along the far shoreline. In Canada, the ponds, marshes and the big lakes are all frozen. All of the wild flying things, every one, has to move or die. The loons are all long gone. In the skies one skein after another of Canadian and snow geese fly over in ragged black lines, all eeking and onking to each other in wild talking voices. In the cold, dense air you can hear them coming for miles, the sound echoing across and far down the lake. Little black dots far off in the crystal sky turn into tight flocks of bluebills that come on in perfect formation, whooshing overhead with a sound exactly like the distant ripping of newspaper. There is no feeling sorry in those ducks, no need for compromise. Just exultant, sturdy bundles of energy, banking high up over the trees, hurtling in perfect formation as if there were nothing to it, down the cold air, some of them cupping their wings suddenly, dropping down, down and then flaring and landing far out in the cold middle of my lake, where they bob around like little living corks.

It is beautiful and here I am parked in the middle of a lonely mess of my own making. Suddenly the situation strikes me as hilariously funny, and further, how lucky I am in some amazing and slightly insane way to be able to be here to see this. Casey, who is a very businesslike and serious dog, and around whom I must not have laughed much then, comes over and looks quizzically at me as if to check whether I am okay. Or possibly he thinks this new sound might turn into additional food. But I just pat him on the head, laugh a little more and then I take a lesson from the bluebills, pick up the bark spud and head back to work.

In the interest of accurate reporting, I must tell you that I then slipped on the side of that goddamned little ditch I'd failed to fill prior to the ground freezing, fell on my butt, and my leg slid under a wheelbarrow, skinning my shinbone. Ow. Casey then thought I was playing, came running over and jumped into my lap. After that day, the lake froze and the work was about the same except that it began to snow more and stayed on the ground a foot deep. I was sweeping it off of the house every day now before I could work. I think I had about three courses of logs up by then.

This was the situation one day about the fifteenth of December when the propane guy showed up to drop off a tank of gas. I was working away at something and stopped to talk. You can picture the scene. A gray, cold, almost dark afternoon, bare poplar trees, dark pines and white snowy ground with one large black spot far out in the lake where it hasn't frozen over yet. Me standing there next to the little summer camper with pine peelings, logs, gasoline tanks and tools stacked in the open, snow drifting down in big fat flakes. I'm dressed in my beat-up woolen pants over cotton denims with rubber-bottomed Sorels, a dirty jacket, wet fingerless leather gloves and a dirty stocking cap. The only difference between a bum and me was that a bum would have had the good sense to catch the next train south for the winter.

I have never forgotten the look in his eye. "I thought you said you were heading south when the snow started falling," he said to me casually, in the tone of someone who had seen too many twenty-five and thirty-below nights to think I had much chance of surviving the winter. He, of course, would not be so forward as to tell you that you were nuts to stay there in those conditions, not to mention in serious danger. Most northern people operate on the theory that you have a right to make bad decisions and do any damn fool thing you want so long as nobody else gets hurt.

My benumbed brain thought about that look in the gas guy's eye for the rest of that weekend. I had never really thought that I would stay working for the months of January through March. Actually I just hadn't given it much thought at all, but the inclination to leave for a while was always there. Remember, I had spent one winter there and knew the conditions. Of course people have wintered here in a camper or less. In fact at the same time that I was building my house, I met a fellow who was working at the hardware store who had come up from Texas, of all places, to raise and run sled dogs. He and his wife were living in a tent while they constructed an octagonal log house. He had decided to get a job for the winter, since they needed money. It just happened that the job was warmly indoors at the hardware store while his wife froze all day out at the construction site. That was one of the worst winters for snow and extreme cold, but so far as I know, they made it. Those arctic explorers did it, so I suppose in a pinch they could have invited the dogs into their tent in a Minnesota version of the three-dog night.

At any rate I spent Monday and Tuesday cleaning up the place and getting ready to leave. On Wednesday I called a friend in Minneapolis and told him I would be coming down. I had little in the way of plans, but I knew that the work was done until spring.

At the Common Ground in December things were muddling along toward Christmas. We had been talking more or less seriously about how to improve the coffee house. The idea was that in addition to being a platform for local artists, the coffee house could invite outside performers who would draw a crowd, the intention being to make a little money for the coffee house. Lon was having no part of it. But here the equation had changed a little with Sally and myself and several others who generally supported this idea. And Tom was on the board of the art gallery, the organization that theoretically controlled our activities. So Lon could actually do little except sulk.

Still it was Christmas and I invited my girlfriend Beth, the one with the orangey hair hat, to the coffee house. When I had told her I was leaving for a while, she shrugged and looked away, but you could see she wasn't too happy. At the coffee house she was a great hit, and the good part was that with her practically luminescent hair, one could, in the dusky atmosphere of the coffee house, locate her head without a lot of bothersome looking.

Marilyn, the rather well-endowed woman with the pasty-faced husband, came in sans husband, looked around, nodded to me a little edgily and sat across the room at a table with a fellow I'd never seen before. He had a bushy but well-kept beard and neck-length hair.

Then Will came in with his button box accordion and sang some French voyageur songs. He is a sturdy, bushy-bearded guy who came in to the coffee house frequently, but not every weekend. He played the accordion and the guitar and sang in a rather old-fashioned, somewhat gravelly voice. He was unfailingly polite, extremely intelligent and very humorous, but stubborn, rather like some old Germans who farmed where I grew up. Once he got mad about something, he walked out and didn't come back for six months. As opposed to a lot of the others who frequented the coffee house, he had actually accomplished a lot in his professional life. He had been in the intelligence branch of the military, had once been a Spanish teacher and had, in fact, spent a year in Spain. But he just never fit into ordinary society, or so it seemed to me, and so he eventually retired himself cheerfully to a more or less ramshackle house somewhere in the swamps outside of town. He lived there with a pet weasel and a frog who wintered over in a well hole in his basement.

A little later a woman came in, sat a while, and then asked if she could read her poems. Of course, said someone, go right ahead. She said she was the retired editor of some rag. Her poems were edited to a fare-thee-well and she read eight or ten to polite applause. When she was finished and having a cup of coffee, I mentioned that I liked a couple of her poems. "Well, I'm so relieved. If **you** like them, I'm sure they're okay," says she, in a voice dripping with sarcasm. I conducted a strategic retreat.

Actually her stuff wasn't all that great but poetry is part and parcel of the function of a good coffee house. It is important for people to have a venue for getting up on stage and performing if they want. Actually some of the most heartfelt poetry, if not the best, came from the high school students who wandered in the coffee house regularly.

But of course there was a lot of bad stuff. One of the regulars was a professor who spent summers in the north. He was a decorous, portly, pleasant man whose poetry was full of loons and sunsets and other grand subjects which are great to begin with but which grow tiresome after just a couple of gorgeous sunsets and several loons. You can, of course, write poetry about loons and sunsets, but only if you kill the loon. At sunset. Who said poetry was going to be easy?

The evening hasn't been too bad. No one walks out in a huff. Must be the Christmas spirit. I notice Marilyn is now talking very animatedly with the hairy guy. She seems a little flushed. Probably the coffee. Later I look up and both of them are gone. I didn't think anything of it and neither should you. Besides I was talking with the nighthawk; the guy who lurked around gas stations late at night. I tell you he seems perfectly normal to me. That, of course, is hardly a recommendation one could take to the bank, considering my lifestyle at the time. He had a wry sense of humor and I enjoyed visiting with him. For a long while we had a joke going about Gogi Grant, a popular singer of the 1950s. We would usually ask players if they would play a Gogi Grant song. For some reason we thought that funny. I don't remember why.

Later we were all sitting around chatting when the LePlante family called to ask if they could come down. The LePlantes play bluegrass music on instruments they've made and are a bit of an institution in the area. Absolutely, says I, whereupon a whole bunch of the LePlante family showed up, instruments in hand, and tore the place up for a while.

January

I had talked to an acquaintance from St. Paul who lived in a big house and had an extra attic room. Unfortunately my acquaintance's girlfriend was under some stress then. She owned the house and turned off the thermostat when she went to bed at night and then turned it back on when she was up and out of bed during the day. Since it was winter the temperature would drop rather precipitously. By morning the temperature in the house would be several degrees above the ambient outside temperature. The male half of this couple, who was at least gainfully employed, apparently took no showers in the morning for fear of freezing to death. She didn't care, so long as the pipes didn't freeze, since she was fat and apparently impervious to cold. It sounds weird, since I was used to working outside, but somehow that cold house got into my bones and was very hard on me.

I got sick. I hadn't been sick a day since I'd moved north but I made up for it then. I got the flu or some such bug, compounded by an allergy to the bat droppings and dust in the room in which I was sleeping. Or maybe it was the horrible vibes in that place. I don't know. The allergic reaction had the effect of speeding up my system so that I thought I was going berserk. I felt so bad I decided to quit smoking cigars, which I usually smoked then. This made it worse. I had gotten a job at a food counter and tried to go to it, but gave up because I was coughing various substances.

Thank God for mothers. I left to visit my mother for the weekend. Since the temperature of her apartment was usually just short of your average sauna, it was perfect for curing what I had. So I sat there and baked while my mother fed me soup. During that weekend I talked to my sister in Dallas, and she urged me to come down if I wanted. This set me to thinking of a conversation I'd had several years earlier with my friend John, who said that if I ever got lacking for a place to go in winter I should head for South Padre Island in south Texas. He said you could camp out there for free. This idea began to appeal to me, especially when the word "free" was attached to it. So I gathered what money I had, and in the middle of that week, early in the morning, I headed south on Interstate 35W.

Naturally a blizzard showed up. The temperature when I left was ten degrees above zero and, unusual for that temperature, it was snowing. When it is very cold and snows, the snow is light and fluffy and blows around easily. In this case, it had snowed six or eight inches and was blowing hard, making a fair imitation of a blizzard when I turned the Buick onto the freeway and headed south. The only traffic on the freeway was me and some truckers whose slipstreams blew up huge clouds of cold, dry snow. If you found yourself near one of those trucks, visibility temporarily went to zero. Zero visibility, even your temporary zero visibility, just in case you are unfamiliar with the concept, is bad when you're driving. Upon entering your basic cloud of zero visibility one just holds the steering wheel of the car straight, hoping you don't end up dead when you come out the other side. The guardian angel assigned to shepherd me through this life and who, by the way, I think of for some reason as a former Jewish guy from New York ("What, I get stuck with this Schmuk again? What am I now, a miracle worker?! Look at what he's doing!") no doubt covered his eyes and applied for reassignment to someone with a more hopeful future.

The fluffy, dangerous, cold snow let up in southern Minnesota and by Des Moines the temperature was up to thirty-five degrees. Heaven! South of Kansas City my muffler started to make noise. I was passing through a town and saw a muffler shop so I stopped. The guys at that shop were the nicest bunch. They fabricated a muffler pipe section right on the spot and installed it for fifty bucks, all the while feeding me coffee and rolls and keeping up a pleasant upbeat chatter. I'm sorry that I don't remember the town or the business. That fact in itself is amazing to me now that I read what I just wrote. You remember every bad thing but not the good? Hmm... Maybe we'll take those lines out. I got on the road again and made the rest of the trip to Dallas in a rather exhausted, strung-out, nervous state. And then for some reason, no doubt related to my addlepated condition, I stayed only briefly at my sister's place. After a day or two I headed south again for Houston and the Gulf coast.

It is a long way from Minneapolis to Dallas. For that matter, it's a long way from L.A. to Denver, so let me add, it's also a long way from Dallas to South Padre Island, just in case you just had to know. I camped my way there. At Houston I stopped in a bar in a shopping center when I saw the word "food" in red neon blinking in the distance. Inside there was a lot of greenery and several hundred TV sets hanging on the walls disseminating news and noise and videos of men and women with large white teeth. I ordered a soda, a burger and some fries. A friendly female bartender seemed interested in me and for a bit I thought about trying to reciprocate, but my mind was a mile wide and not too thick so I scarfed half the burger and fries, glommed the rest and split for the coast. (I always wanted to say that.) At the coast I camped among some stilt houses on a spit of land as empty as the buzzing space in my head.

The next day I turned southwest through farm and ranch country with fat Herefords and round hay bales in the fields, through little towns in bright cool sunlight, people in cowboy hats and boots that they weren't wearing for fun or some parody of a dance. And then I came to the Brazos. The Brazos... I stopped at the sign on the bridge over the river. The Brazos was shallow and slow and muddy there. Something about this place, the name, made me lean against the hood of the Buick and watch a ways up the river where the current rolled a little. I stared at the river sign and the river and then, completely unexpectedly, I realized what it was.

It is this Brazos River and my old man and the Zane Grey westerns papa liked, and the horses he liked, and the war he fought in, and how friendly he was to everyone, and how he'd wave and I'd say to him those people don't like you why do you wave, and he'd just keep on waving, and how he'd laugh at the things I thought were embarrassing, and the musty, sweat-stained way he smelled and the smooth feel of the top of his maple walking stick, and how we'd walk and talk, and how he and I stopped in a rainstorm once and waited it out in a barn, and saw the rainbow of that storm together, and how he and I took the old shotgun out one day in fall and hunted upwind in a field and got a jackrabbit and then took it up to the big old house there on the hill and cut him up and made rabbit stew, and the...chunk...chunk...chunk...sound of him chopping wood for the cookstove out in the dark morning before light, and all of the stories on top of stories that he'd tell and how life gradually wore him down and how he was still cheerful to the end, and how badly I treated him and how badly I treated him and here I was at the Brazos, that Brazos of those Zane Grey westerns that he read dog-eared, and I was here now and the tears started streaming down my face and wouldn't stop, and wouldn't stop, and people drove by and looked, and I hoped they wouldn't see and the tears, they still wouldn't stop.

Not wishing that my flood of tears would overtop the banks of the poor Brazos and flood the surrounding environs, I headed out again. The obviously tragic flow of my own life led me to believe at that moment that perhaps I was just a tad, just a l-e-e-tle bit overtired. You think? So a ways down the road I found a campground, crawled into my sleeping bag and slept the sleep of the traveler, which isn't all that restful, now that I think about it.

The highway is a black strip to the horizon, the Buick purring along, eating up the miles. Brushy, brown and tan, cactus country, scrubby rolling hills now. Wandering, lonely, flop-eared cattle here and there. A plume of smoke in the distance. I can't see what from, but I smell it when I pass. I turn on the radio. Static. On the AM dial I get two preachers, some thick country-western music and a call in program. People call in about their financial problems and the radio guy abuses them for a bit before parceling out his advice. "Get real, honey," he keeps saying to a woman. "That's just stupid. You're an idiot if you think you can do that," he says to another guy. No one hangs up. They like it. Some of them fawn over the radio guy. "What an honor it is just to talk with you," says one guy. He is mostly nice to those people, offering fatherly advice. Radio off.

At a place on the Gulf I met some Mexican guys who were fishing off of a public dock in some place that I don't recall. They were big, solid and friendly, without being overly friendly, and shared some chicken they'd barbecued. They made it in a homemade cooker, sort of a large pipe about a foot and a half in diameter, split in half with a grill inside and hinged so one could open it. They used mesquite wood in the cooker and their own peppery tomato sauce. Wonderful. The rest of the trip to South Padre wasn't eventful or else I don't remember the events. I spent another night by the Gulf. I broke a fan belt somewhere south of there and fixed it. That and the muffler were the only repairs I made the entire trip.

The Padre Islands

The Padre Islands are a strip of sand dunes and ragged greenery that once extended from Corpus Christi south for a hundred forty-seven miles along the Texas/Mexico Gulf coast. Not willing to leave well enough alone, someone dug a channel through the island in 1962 so now there's a North and a South Padre Island. To get to South Padre you drive to the end of Texas and just before you run off the edge into Mexico you hang a left at the city of Brownsville. There is a bridge from the mainland to South Padre Island and a little town on the tip of the island. This patch of upscale development (see urban blight) looks as if it has escaped onto the island where it has taken root and is spreading. So if you cross the bridge there are hotels, fast food restaurants, various beauty pageants and other such institutions essential to a wilderness island.

North of this little town one could, and still can, I understand, drive to where the road ends in fat sand dunes, scrub greenery, harsh grass and other interesting stuff.

Beyond the end of the paved road there is nothing but seashore, dunes and whatever vegetation clings to the hard sand for fifty miles. The island varies in width from a mile or so to three miles with parts of the interstices between the dunes flooded on occasion. More of the island toward the Gulf is loose sand. The west side of the island runs more or less parallel to the mainland resulting in an inland waterway, most of which is very shallow tidal areas. When I was there you could drive north and pull over anywhere along the paved road and camp and no one would bother you. At least no one bothered me. The road itself seemed an imposition on the place. Sand constantly blows onto the road, first here and then there, and has to be plowed or scooped off. One's impression is that if no one maintained it, the little tongues of sand would creep out, at first tentatively and then en masse, burying this thing, this embarrassment, just like it had buried all of the other foreign objects in this place. With no maintenance, the road would disappear in a very short period of time.

That is, of course, the case almost anywhere, and certainly it's true back in Minnesota where, if you didn't drive on a road and maintain it, in a very few years the green grass and volunteer growth would quickly grow up through the cracks and, within a very few decades, that road would disappear. In Central America whole Mayan cities, abandoned by the people, completely disappeared for hundreds of years. In North America, if the people abandoned the cities, in a hundred years everything but the tallest buildings would all but disappear; in five hundred years one would be hard put to find a lot remaining except in the city centers.

Camping consisted of me pulling off the road onto some solid ground and pitching my tent, usually close to the car. Occasionally, if I didn't feel like pitching the tent for the evening I would sleep on the back seat of the car with my feet sticking out the side and the door open. Not a pretty sight. When I camped in the tent I used my extra sleeping bag as a ground pad. I worried at first about my personal security and brought a knife into the tent with me most nights. For a few nights I started at every scurrying thing that came around. Sometimes coyotes came around looking for food scraps or perhaps just to indulge their curiosity, and some mornings I could see their tracks in the sand. In a few days I relaxed a little and slept better. I realized that I wasn't going to get very much sleep if I was going to snap awake every time a sand crab or some other critter scuttled over for a look.

I loved the coyotes. They would materialize out of the dunes at dark, swirling around on the edges of my light. I would leave my food scraps for them for which they showed their appreciation by serenading me with their plaintive yipping and yapping and yowling at the mysterious moon that rose over the Gulf of Mexico. In a while I got used to the coyotes and the noises in the night and no one bothered me, so I relaxed a little, though I always kept some sort of a weapon in my tent.

Occasionally the local police would patrol the peninsula road. They looked at me but never stopped to check me out. I started no fires for cooking or camping. It wasn't necessary for warmth, and I had brought a small white gas cooker that I used to heat coffee in the morning and occasionally soup for lunch when I wanted it. My sister had prevailed on me to bring numerous packages of dried instant soups that were so, so tasty and contained a variety of chemicals unrelated to nutrition to boot. In general camping under these conditions was a lark since one was in no danger of being cold. The weather was heaven, about sixty degrees in the day with some kind of wind blowing most of the time, the ocean smelled good and the sighing wind was a sleeping tonic. So I passed the days and nights more or less in comfort.

On weekends elderly tourists would drive slowly out the spit of land, stopping and dragging themselves across the sand to stare briefly at the great expanse of the Gulf of Mexico. The Gulf stared back implacably and there was no communion. In a while the old folks would turn around and drag themselves back to their cars or fifty-thousand-dollar campers and creep off to the next major spectacle of their golden years. Once two elderly couples got out of their huge sedan to take the mandatory trek across the sand to the beach. When the couples were ten yards from the car one of the women noticed that the car door wasn't completely closed. "The door, Jim," she said, in a voice that left no doubt as to who was going to close said door. So while she kept on walking, poor old Jim toddled over dutifully to the car and closed the door and started back following her, his feet making little drag tracks in the sand. Someone please shoot me if I ever get to such a state.

During the week it was very quiet, the only people on the island a rather ragtag collection of campers apparently doing what I was doing, whatever that was. I didn't talk with many of them. Strangely the whole time seemed to have an empty-of-people quality. The place is chock-full of drunken students in the spring, but there were few people when I was there. I did talk fairly frequently with a Jewish fellow from New York who was traveling around the country in a truck with a camper on the back. He camped frequently in Wal-Mart parking lots, which, he said, were secure. He and I talked about investments and money, of which I had approximately none. I was interested in land as an investment, but he thought that stocks were a better thing. Apparently he knew whereof he spoke since this was at the beginning of the '90s, and, as it turned out, the beginning of one of the longest boom markets in the American stock market, which lasted until past the turn of the century.

Once I stopped in at a bar at one of the hotels with the intention of finding some... company. It was early and there were a grand total of three people in the bar: the bartender, who actually had some realistic reason for being there, and two women whom I looked at hopefully until I noticed that the one with the leather jacket had bigger biceps than I and was holding hands with the cute one. Since I don't drink, as I may have mentioned, talking with the bartender and getting drunk was not an option, so I left and went back to my camp with the coyotes.

On weekends, surf-fishermen drove their cars and trucks up the beach and stationed themselves along the shore to fish. I've never done it but I enjoyed watching them. They would rear back with their heavy rods and toss large chunks of lead with bits of bait attached far out into the water. There's something hopeful about surf casting for fish and it took me a long time to realize what it was. First, it's a social thing to fling that weight and the bait out into the great big ocean and then sit there on a section of beach contemplating the surf, next to some other guys doing the same thing. There was usually more than one guy fishing and that is, of course, the point. Even if you don't talk to the guy whose fishing down the beach a little, there's a connection from doing the same thing in the same place. Plus if you do catch some big honking fish or whatever, the other guy is there to see it. Part of fishing, a big part, is having the other guy see you catch that big honking something. And the second part of surf casting is the idea that there's something really big lurking out there and you might, just might, lug into it some day and drag it on shore. Of course they don't realize that some Japanese has already caught that big thing and sold it to some Chinese who cut it up and ate it. Or maybe they do but human nature can't admit it, so they keep slinging the lead. What I liked about it is that it is a hopeful activity. Okay, that bit about the Japanese and the Chinese already eating it already might not have been completely true then. But it probably will be by the time you read this. If you read this.

My daily pattern on Padre was to first cook a cup of coffee and then go for a long walk in the dunes. Later I began to go for a jog. The surface of the dunes was fairly hard in most places. I don't remember what I thought dunes were supposed to be like, but I found out they are substantial aggregations of sand and vegetation as well as other organic material and in many places have a nice hard surface, perfect for jogging. I would lope along through the dunes for a while and then head in to the McDonald's restaurant for breakfast. Most of the time I'd have to buy a newspaper since apparently no one there read, or if they did, they didn't leave the newspaper behind.

The first thing I'd look at was the weather. The weather map was color coded with blue being the coldest. And there most days, right over northern Minnesota, was that blue spot signifying temperatures cold enough to freeze the nether regions of a brass monkey. And me with my biggest problem being how to get the sand out of my shoes. I gloated. At mid morning or thereabout I'd make a sandwich, grab a bottle of pop or water and head out to explore. An exultant feeling! What fun! Time to spend and a new wild place to explore. And it was a wild place. I came to the island not really thinking about it, but began to realize that this place was wild when you got away from the places where there were tourists. It was possible to get yourself nicely lost by walking just a short ways north out into the dunes. On the sea side there was a lot of loose sand and less vegetation, but inland most of the dunes were hard sand and perfect for jogging or hiking.

Before sunrise I walk a long way north, find a place and sit on the top of a fifty-foot-high dune while the sun reddens the Gulf. Somewhere in the west a train whistle blows. Pelicans fly toward the Gulf. In back of me to the west the terrain is dark with grass and shrubbery. Vegetation hangs on to the dunes or the dunes hang on to the vegetation. In front of me a little bird scuttles into the vegetation and then to my left, suddenly, motion. A coyote trots out from behind some bushes and stands sniffing the air. I don't move and he doesn't move. Then as if the wind had blown a fluffy bit of dark rag away, the coyote folds into himself and the island swallows him. Thus do the coyotes and I spend our time.

February

There are deer here. One day as I was walking on the inland side of the island where most of the vegetation was, I began to notice little hoof prints. Goats, I thought, without thinking about it too much. Deer, someone in town told me. Deer? I had to see them and so began to get up early to find out where they were. Actually they were where all deer hang out (no, not in your garden), namely in places where there's food and water. Water? What do they do for water? They can't exactly belly up to the McDonald's for a drink. How could they be here? I had to see them, and so I began to assiduously track them along the west side of the island. Three days later while I was walking slowly upwind along a low blufflike line of dunes, I found them. Three little grayish deer, about two feet tall, rather like oversized jackrabbits, got up from in front of me and took off like little rockets through the shrubbery, around a dune and were gone. What fun! It turned out that if I was careful and worked upwind, I could see them fairly regularly along the western dunes and shrub areas.

I never did find out how they got water. It was very dewy in the morning so perhaps they got water that way or with the vegetation they ate. Or maybe there are pools of water somewhere. They were very small, so perhaps they didn't need a lot of water. Maybe they swim to the mainland. Don't laugh. A local guy told me he'd once seen five of them a mile out in the inland waterway, making for the mainland, another mile or so away. Maybe they were going over for a drink and a visit. That same guy said they know when a hurricane is coming and head off to the mainland. It was a mystery to me, and there was no way I had enough time to find out. No doubt several Ph.D. papers on this very subject have been written.

I didn't try surf fishing, but I've been a fly fisherman since I was about fourteen years old and had fished a lot of places prior to having to suspend those activities for the year in northern Minnesota. Someone told me you could catch redfish in the shallow inland tidal areas. As an afterthought I had brought along my fly rod and I began to venture cautiously out onto these areas. Once I followed a track made by some vehicle for a long way across a dried mud flat, angling northwest and then doubling back a little until it ended in the water.

There is a rich, muddy, prehistoric smell to the air. The bottom is firm. I looked at the water for a while, and then waded for a quarter of a mile to the west out onto the tidal flats to where I was thigh deep in water. I was then standing alone, far out in the shallow bay, the dunes a long way in back of me to the east. A boat slid across in front, the only moving thing I could see. Here and there the water swirled a little. Schools of small fish I suppose. I floundered around for a while flapping my fly rod, not having the slightest clue as to how to fish these waters. But what fun! I waded around fishing here and there, not catching anything and then started back. At shore I stopped, found my lunch safe from the coyotes and sat on top of a low dune next to some shrubbery, slowly chewing a salami, cheese and sliced onion sandwich and chasing it down with water. Yum, yum.

I tried fishing that water several more times but didn't catch any fish. No matter. I knew that if I had time I'd figure out how to catch them. I just felt good doing it, and fishing with my fly rod put back a piece in my puzzle that had been missing for a while. I had previously fly-fished quite a bit in the United States and bonefished in Belize in winter. When my fortunes had slipped, I had stopped fly-fishing for a while. I had forgotten the things that I liked to do. And right there I rediscovered something I'd temporarily lost. Let me say to you that nothing is so important as doing the things that make your life enjoyable. Model airplanes, trains, working with dogs, your work, collecting this or that knickknack, whatever. It's important to keep your hobbies, because when the cold winds blow, which they inevitably will, your hobbies and interests keep you from blowing away.

South Padre Island looks pristine from a distance but the place was full of garbage. Plastic bags, medical debris, food wrappings, shoes, almost anything you could think of was decorating the island and bobbing around in the water waiting to come ashore. Everyone had a different opinion as to where this garbage came from. There seemed to be two general theories. Most people blamed it on the Mexican cities dumping garbage into their rivers. The garbage would then would float out into the Gulf and eventually wash up on the shores of the pristine USA. The second theory was that it came from ships off shore. Wherever it came from, there was garbage everywhere.

The locals don't like the garbage on the beaches because it isn't good for tourism. They even send crews around to clean up the beaches a little. Some garbage though is okay with them. They realize that this old place has a way of hiding unsightly objects. A few months, a year or two at the most, and the corrosion eats, the sand covers and whatever bothered you is gone.

But the litter bothered me. So one day I took a garbage bag along on one of my morning walks and on the way back picked up garbage. I could have filled it easily on the beach but contented myself with picking up garbage from further away from the beach so that it took a little longer. In town I had breakfast at the McDonald's and then stopped at the city hall to ask where I could dump the garbage. I felt good. Like a saint. Saint Michael of the Garbage. I fairly beamed with a light from above when I told the staff at the city about my activities and asked where I could dump the garbage I had picked up. A stolid, somewhat stumpy-looking man behind the counter fixed me with an opaque expression.

"So where did you get the garbage?" he asked.

"On the island," says I.

"Oh well," says he, shrugging his shoulders and upturning his fleshy palms in the direction of God's own sky. "The island's not in the city. It's not our garbage."

"Where," I ask, "could I deposit the garbage?"

"Don't know. Not here," said my municipal friend.

There was some more tedious bantering of this sort, but the upshot was that he looked as if he would not be opposed to tossing me in his barred dumpster and letting the garbage go free. I got the hell out of there, but this situation irritated me. So every day I picked up garbage on my walk, headed in to town and tossed it into the dumpster behind the McDonald's, figuring that old Ray Kroc wouldn't mind.

Fats

Most of the tourists would show up on weekends and some would try to drive on the sandy areas. After you were there a while, it was fairly obvious where the hard and soft sand areas were. But some of the tourists would get stuck. They'd spin their wheels for a bit, get out and walk around their cars, then back in and spin their wheels some more. Sometimes several would try to push. Occasionally this worked. Mostly no. After a while they'd get out again and look up and down the beach helplessly. They would look at the Gulf, and even from a distance, a look of suppressed anxiety could be seen on their faces and you knew they were remembering that video. You know, the one of the car swallowed up by the raging ocean, even though, right in front of them, the Gulf was purring like a well-fed cat. Then by some magic that I don't pretend to understand, except that these guys had mapped out all of the good places, a fat guy in opaque sunglasses in an old salt-spray, brown-colored, four-wheel-drive Dodge sedan, the one with the high wheelbase and oversized tires, would slowly drive toward the victim like a crab scuttling toward a nice piece of meat. With one fat arm out the window he'd sidle up and turn to pretend to have a look at the situation. "Stuck?" he'd ask, not even deigning to lean even slightly out the window. The victim was of course stuck in more ways than one.

After brief negotiation, some money, usually twenty dollars, would pass hands. Then Fats, or some equally laconic minion, would get slowly out of the four-wheel-drive car, hook a twenty-foot-long elastic tow cable to the stuck car and instruct the driver to put his vehicle in drive but "don't spin your wheels." When the stuck tourist was hooked up, Fats would drive slowly toward the road, his car on the solid hard sand, the elastic cable would stretch a bit and the tourist car would come free with a yank. In a bit the minion would get out and unhook the tourist, and Fats would slowly head off to another place where another tourist was stuck in the sand.

I liked the days on the island but I loved the nights. After supper, which usually was sandwiches and soup and some sort of fruit, I'd walk the beaches. In the evening, at just about dark, the coyotes would come out of the dunes to hunt the beaches and to see if the tourists du jour had left anything to eat. They came close at night and I liked them very much, although the moment I say that I can almost hear you recall how they ate someone's pet or worse. Sometimes I would leave parts of my sandwiches for them. They would flit around in the growing dark and the wind would blow around between the dunes and the coyotes would perform their formless dance, like dark filigree on a very low clothesline whipped around in the wind, moving, sniffing, playing and then gone, back into the glowing dark dunes.

Some nights I'd walk a ways, sit for a while on the highest place I could find and wait while the western skies grew dark. The wind would come sighing all about me, ruffling the shrubbery. To the west, lights on the mainland would glow and wink a little. Somewhere off the coast I could see the lights of a ship. In a while the stars would come out above, clear and bright on some nights, hazy on others.

Then one night in late February when the breeze was stirring and the stars were blossoming high on high and I was sitting on a hard sand hill in the dark, I thanked all of the lucky stars above me that I'd had enough sense to come down here. And I also knew without question that it was time to start north.

March

I left the island one chilly, sunny morning and pointed the Buick toward Dallas. I drove all day and in late afternoon took some paved county roads, driving through very pretty, mostly green ranch country with budding groves of trees here and there. The air smelled fresh of middle spring and growing things. Late in the night, finally exhausted, I tried to catch a nap in a city park, but I was uneasy and after a while I drove on. The only significant thing that occurred during this long drive was that I gave my spare sleeping bag to a hitchhiker. He was small and didn't say much, a little light adrift in a sea of bright lights. He was heading west and seemed rather unconcerned about being out on the highways on a cold night. I let him out on the edge of Dallas at a cloverleaf. I only mention this in case my name comes up for sainthood. I stayed with my sister again, and in the middle of March we headed north in warm spring-like weather, through green Oklahoma, arriving in bleak, cold Minneapolis a couple of days later.

Anxious to get working again, I headed to northern Minnesota the next day. At my place the snow was two feet deep, the driveway plugged shut with snow. So I put on my old working togs and took up my snow shovel. After two hours I had dug out a place for my car at the end of the driveway. I had quit smoking when I was south and when I entered the little camper trailer, it stunk so badly from old cigars that it took two days to air the place out. In a couple more days I got the driveway plowed out and the site cleaned up. Then I started back to hacking and hewing. In a day or two Casey showed up, whining and wiggling his greeting, and looking around for a squirrel to harass as if I had never been gone.

Then the Witch decided I needed a welcome home so she brewed up a slashing, tree-bending, wild storm that started with a moaning wind and ended with eight inches of wet snow followed by temperatures in the teens at night. No problem, I stayed put for a day and then shoveled and scraped my way out of the driveway. And just to show she was making one of her icy jokes, when the snow had melted so that there was just thick ice on the lake, one morning she covered everything in a white wedding dress of thick hoarfrost. I got my camera and wandered out on the ice of the lake to take some pictures of the shoreline. And there in the icy garden of her lake, she had scattered thousands of the most beautiful white frost flowers, some three inches across, complete with petals. I lay on the ice (crushing about ten of them) to take a picture of one, amazed and thankful to have been there. They were gone an hour later.

One day shortly thereafter, I was working as usual on the walls of my house. Snow covered the ground but the late March sun was very warm. Heat from the sun made the balsam bark smell pitchy and sweet. I was wearing my Sorel boots and wool pants, but on top I had stripped down to an old sweatshirt, cut off at the elbows, a stocking cap and my usual mostly fingerless leather gloves. There was no sound from the white frozen lake, just chickadees celebrating spring and a woodpecker drumming somewhere in the woods. I could hear a car on the county road for a mile or so away coming and coming and then with a tearing sound, whooshing past and fading into the distance. Sometimes a logging truck loaded with popple logs, so long the slender tips looked as if they were dragging on the highway, would come roaring down the county road. When it got to the hill by my place the logging truck would gear down with a clash and a bang, and the engine would roar from spinning up and then gradually the sound would start to die away and die away, until in a while the quiet would return and I would be there again working in my island of silence. Casey was poking around looking for something to annoy. I stopped and sat in the sun, drinking a cup of coffee, looking at my Buick and my old truck and the driveway that was still deep in snow.

Suddenly, right there on that morning, just as clearly as I'm talking with you right now, I realized that some important point in my life had passed. The winter equinox was several months behind me, but in some way that I do not understand, I knew that the equinox of my personal fortune was past and it seemed to me, consciously, on that day, sitting under that sun, that the downward swing of my fortune had stopped and I could make it go the other direction. As bad as my situation looked to an outsider, I had time to finish my house so long as I wasn't injured. I wasn't going to starve or freeze to death. I had two vehicles and could fix both of them. I didn't have a lot, but I owed no one anything and no one could take anything from me. There was plenty of hard work ahead, but I had all summer and fall to do it and it would be finished. The warm March sun beat down and Casey eyed the sandwich I was munching on, leaned against my leg and examined me with soulful, calculating eyes. I tore what was left of the sandwich in half and tossed part to Casey. He gulped it down in one bite, and I picked up the slick and went back to work.

Naturally, to make up for the above self-congratulating, I promptly ran the truck off the steep side of the driveway. The brave and hardy truck had roared to life more or less promptly after having been left neglected in the cold and snow for several months. On that day it had snowed several inches, and I needed to take the truck to town to replace a couple tires. So I rattled down the driveway, zigged this way and that, and then halfway up the hill, with no further ado, zagged off the driveway. I couldn't back anywhere, much less down the driveway, and Dale was nowhere to be seen, so I got out the come-along, some chains and other paraphernalia and slowly cranked the truck back onto the driveway. I then slowly backed down the hill to my house where I threw more concrete blocks and other weight into the back and let her rip again. This time I made it to the top of the driveway hill with rather more velocity than was required, and being naturally reluctant to reduce speed, I found it difficult to stop on the slippery snow and almost collided with a fully loaded logging truck on the county road, very nearly squashing my personal equinox as well as the rest of my solar system right then and there.

I then staggered off to breakfast with Tom and to attend to the deplorable state of my tires. The tires on my truck were bald and I didn't want to spend a lot of money on them, so I stopped at Acheson Tires in Grand Rapids to see if they had any used tires. At Acheson Tires there are hammers banging, air whooshing, workers rolling tires, prying on tires, hammering on tires, all midst the dust and a rubbery smell of new tires. And all of this activity is overseen by the inestimable Acheson. Tires aren't the cleanest things to work on in the cold of the winter or the heat of the summer, but his workers bustle around, their clothes and hands dirty, and somehow they are both proficient and good-hearted. When I explained what I wanted, the businesslike and genial Mr. Acheson himself looked through stacks of used tires to find me some serviceable tires for my truck. He somehow imparts a certain good atmosphere to his workplace, which is reflected in his workers. I have seen a lot of other businesses with squeaky-clean work environments whose owners aren't the good businessman Acheson is. For fifteen dollars per tire mounted, the brown truck was shod with some serviceable tires and I trundled off to seek my fortune.

In the interest of accurate reporting I must say right here that my relationship, such as it was, with Beth had ended. While I was gone she had gotten seriously ill and, in fact, had spent more than a month in the hospital and had almost died. I had called her from Texas several times and couldn't get in touch with her for obvious reasons. By the time I returned she was out of the hospital. When I finally got in touch with her she acted very angry. She had good reason to be mad, I suppose. I liked her and was very sorry she had gotten ill, but I was never sorry that I'd headed to Texas.

I showed up at the Common Ground coffee house on Friday, the prodigal son having returned. Tom greeted me enthusiastically, but the rest acted as if I'd left the week before. Lon, who had reached the peak of his enthusiasm for me when he was assessing whether I was his kind of guy back in the previous spring, acknowledged my return with a wave of his hand and went back to saying something important to his little knot of followers.

A gloomy balding fellow is sitting morosely in a chair by the front door when I arrive. He is a Vietnam veteran and is haranguing the other patrons about the war and its unsalutory effects on him. He is a good guitar player, but writes songs within which metaphor, simile and any other indirect alliterative mechanism are not extant. He sings several of these songs to an obligatory smattering of applause. Lack of response doesn't bother him in the least. He seems to expect it. He packs up his guitars and sits with some group at a table. Gloom follows him around.

At one of the tables two people are arguing about the height of a tower in town. Russell the smart kid hears this and pleasantly offers them the answer. They stare at him for a moment and then ask him how he knows that. He then offers them an explanation based upon some calculation, which he has done in his head. They change the subject.

Then Len, that sturdy product of the Norse, comes in and the atmosphere improves. Lenny is an amiable local guy who seems to bring a little sunshine to the group every time he comes in. Plus he plays the guitar very well and can accompany almost anyone on the guitar or mandolin. I once mentioned to Len that a girl in my high school had sung the song "Moon River" in a quavering voice. He then produced a perfectly quavering version of the song. I tell you tears came to my eyes. This night no quavering, but Len and some other player start playing some tunes and we had a good time.

One of the writers in the area came in one night. Several of the attendees at the coffee house are writers. She writes mysteries and enthusiastically produces one manuscript after another. I had gotten to know her fairly well and we talk for a long while about her writing, or rather she talks and I listen. After knowing her for a while, she had let me read several of her manuscripts. They were long, but seemed to lack life and had a certain mechanical quality. She was part of a local writers group, I wasn't, and so she rightly discounted any other critiques of her work. The central theme of her latest story included much material about various poisons. She had investigated these poisons extensively. I have a lot of respect for anyone who writes and so, since she had asked, made a few gentle comments about her latest story. Nothing really. She didn't seem pleased about these comments.

The next week the mail carrier said I had a package. It was a box of caramel popcorn. There was no return address on it. Then my writer friend called and asked how I liked the caramel popcorn she had made for me. I wasn't in the habit of turning down dessert in those days, but I decided, in light of the subject of her last mystery story, to err on the side of caution and dump the popcorn out. Then I thought better of that course of action, thinking Casey, or at least some of the birds, might eat some of it. Eventually I burned it and that was the end of that matter, the only upshot of it being that I no longer look at other people's manuscripts.

April

April is an ugly month in the north. In southern latitudes spring has arrived and bright green garden things are poking up toward the sun. At my place sometimes a cruel, keening, sleet-driven wind blows for days off the frozen Canadian wild and down across the lake. In April the Witch wakes up the sleeping earth, and she isn't happy or gentle about it. Cold rain and lightning lash the face of the earth, the bolts stringing down from the frowning lines of her storms. But then the big spring sun comes out warm and yellow, smiling, and the Witch retreats sullenly to her lair in the north. As the month goes on, the ice on the ponds melts and the spring peeper frogs start peeping a little in the warm sun but then stop when the temperature drops, as it frequently does. How they manage to come out at all is a mystery to me, since the water they are in is just above freezing.

In April the frost goes out and the gravel roads and driveways turn to mud. In the old days all of the schools used to let out for "mud vacation." It's not as bad as it used to be now, since more of the counties' roads, including mine, are paved. But my driveway, which wasn't that good to begin with, was virtually impassable for a week, so I parked the truck and the Buick out by the road until some local—who was even worse off than me, if that was possible—tried to break into the Buick, couldn't and decided to break off a mirror, possibly for a souvenir. Fortunately, and considerately I might add, the vandal broke off the one I didn't use as much, so that worked out okay.

The Bear Wakes Up

It was a day such as happens in awful April when I went looking for my neighbor Dale. I hadn't seen him since December. And come to think of it I hadn't seen the bear either, which of course wasn't surprising. He hadn't used the bear den, so I figured he had just headed off into the woods and parked himself there for the winter. A wild cold wind was slashing down from the north across the lake, making a lonely rushing sound through the pines and whipping the tops of the trees. Broken branches lay here and there on the path. A cold rain was threatening to turn into snow. I loved it. I stood in the wind, some old ratty stocking cap on, no gloves, my coat half open, looking for a while at the darkening ice on my lake and watching three or four crows dance exultantly in the wind. I stopped next to some huge white pines, listening to the wind moan in the pine tops, leaning on one of them. It was humming and vibrating in the wild wind as its top swayed with life.

Dale was small but physically strong with a curious quickness of movement. He was subject to periods of mild euphoria and then depression. I had met most of his family, some of whom had personalities rather like con men and others who seemed straightforward and honest, but all had a kind of knotty, Appalachian intensity. His father had bought the resort many years earlier. Then his father had a stroke and was more or less incapacitated. Most people would have had him institutionalized, but Dale and his mother took care of the father themselves. Year after year Dale carried his dad to the dinner table, to the bathroom. Then his mother passed away and Dale had wintered over in one of the cabins. When I got back from Texas I was busy with things for a while working, and then one day I had some reason to be at Dale's place.

I found him unshaven, alternately staring at the TV and moving boxes of things from one side of the room to the other. It seemed that most of the rest of the family wanted to sell the resort. He thought he had to move out. I told him that was nonsense; I encouraged him to get an attorney and said that no one was going to kick him out any time soon. After I'd talked for a while, he seemed to brighten a little and then got up and looked out of his window for a moment. "Look at this," he said, calling me over to the window. And there was the Big Long-Legged Bear, or at least there was his big nose and part of the rest of his head, sticking out from under one of Dale's cabins, sniffing the air and waking up. The bear had spent the winter not one hundred feet from the dogs and Dale. I suppose the bear figured he might as well stay close to his main food source.

Of course Dale didn't have to leave then, but I got enraged every time I thought of the rotten deal he got. And eventually that set me to thinking about what I was going to do when my time building the house was over. But for the time being I put it away in the back of my mind.

Moose Lake was still completely frozen on the fifteenth, though the ice was darkening. When it broke up, the wind blew blocks of beautiful white ice four or five feet high along the shore. It was spring! The days were long now and no amount of rain can really dampen the feeling that things were on the upgrade toward summer. At night the sky was alive with wild cries of migrating flocks, and during the day ducks and geese were everywhere. While the lake is still mostly frozen, he lake was unfrozen in places along its edges. One night I heard a loon calling and somewhere across the lake another loon answered. Of course the gnats and mosquitoes came out as soon as the temperature got above forty degrees. These I kept at bay by the use of bug spray and a smoky fire of balsam peelings and punky cedar wood.

The work went on and the days were long now. The logs that I was peeling had figured out that it was spring and the bark came off like clothing at a nudist camp. When the sun did happen to come out it was wonderfully warm. My body was getting used to the work after the winter's laying around in the happy south. My hands got very strong again, not surprisingly, since I was working every day with the slick and the chain saw. Once I was standing at the bar in a local place and a person who didn't wish me any good stepped up next to me. Apparently not knowing what else to do he stuck out his hand. I shook his hand and practically crushed it. This dissuaded him from whatever he meant to do, and he made some small talk and then left.

For some unknown reason I was impatient and testy then. On one occasion I took along three or four chain saw blades to have sharpened at one of the hardware stores (not one of the good ones). The proprietor of this store, a rather spongy, money-grubbing clerk, looked me up and down and told me rather abruptly to leave them and that they'd be done in several days. A certain buzzing heat rose in my head and I was suddenly struck with the overwhelming desire to whip him across his pudgy soft white face with the chain saw blades then dangling from my damp, no-fingered, leather-gloved hand. The image of blood flowing from his face was, at that moment, very gratifying. I moved right up to him, a pressure growing in my chest, thinking to put this impulsive plan into effect promptly. Seeing something in my face, he backed away. Luckily for both of us, the phone rang and he went to answer it. The moment passed and the overwhelming desire to whip him across the face with the chain saw blades was surpassed by the overwhelming desire not to spend many weeks in jail. I left slightly shaken and half sorry I hadn't finished the thought I'd begun. When I got home I related this incident to a neighbor who burst out laughing at my reaction to that particular hardware guy. He motioned in the general direction of my chain saw blades. "That woulda been some sight, you'd hit him with those tings," he said. But then he added, "Hey, old Krantz over t'other side of da lake used do them chains." So I went over to old Krantz who came tottering out, old and dry as a maple chip, but still spry, bright-eyed and cheerful. The rest of the time I was building my house, for two bucks apiece, he sharpened my blades until he got to where he couldn't anymore.

One cloudy, misty day in late April, I was getting ready to go to town and as per usual, was in a hurry, since I was going to meet Tom for a hearty breakfast of freshly made biscuits and chicken gravy. The wall was about six feet high. The weather wasn't bad enough to stop me from working, but I never got up on the log wall when it was moist since the logs get extremely slippery in that condition. On that morning I had to get something off of the wall and climbed up to get it. Suddenly my feet went one way and I went the other and I fell to the inside of the house, where six feet down I landed flat on my back on the frozen ground.

I lay for a moment, checking out my various parts and getting my breath back. Amazingly nothing was broken or even strained. As luck would have it. I love that phrase.

They say it a lot out east. Anyway, all winter I had left various chunks of wood inside and around the walls chipped out of the scribed portions of the logs. I was lazy about it and only thoroughly cleaned them up about once every two weeks, instead kicking them into piles here and there. They were everywhere along the walls, perfect for falling from a great height onto and breaking one's neck. But as luck would have it, the previous day, sick of the clutter, I had picked up all of the chunks, put them in the wheelbarrow and piled them for later burning. When I fell, I landed on an area that I had cleaned up. Apparently, my mother was right, it pays to be neat. Having checked out my parts and finding no serious injuries, I slowly picked myself up, staggered out to my truck and then drove to town.

Fish and Turtles in My Lake

When I first came north I said that I was going to try to fish every lake around. There are more than fifty lakes within twenty miles. I did not fish all of the lakes and only developed a passing knowledge of my lake, mostly by passing over it in my boat. The following is what I know about fishes in my lake. In the lake at present there are populations of bass (large and small mouth; my brother caught a huge small mouth of about seven or eight pounds, but it got off the hook, which is too bad because we realized later that it might be a state record), northern pike (lots of those), walleyes, muskies and crappie (my nephew caught one so there must be more). There are big fat yellow-bellied bullheads that you can catch in the mud flats in the spring, and rock bass that you can catch in any patch of weeds, particularly in the evening. There are also tullibees in the lake, although Deer Lake across the road has more of them. I guess because it's deeper. The tullibee, if you've never seen one, is a pretty little fat silver fish. They are a favorite food of the muskie I'm told, and so full of fat that the story was you could put a wick in one and light it for a candle.

Once of an evening at the end of March evening when the temperature and a big yellow moon were on the rise, I was out for a walk and saw a fisherman way out in the middle of Deer Lake. It was still light and warm, being about forty degrees. There were water puddles here and there on the ice, and a very slight fog in the air, though you know in that country a mist in the air, puddles on the ice and forty degrees in March is only a sign of spring, not the real thing, and winter is lurking in the woods out back. I had my camera along and walked out to see what he was doing way out there all alone. It was an old guy, Norwegian, I think, he standing there quietly in the twilight, next to his hole in the ice, a red plastic sled and a bucket next to him, with his parka up. His fat old golden retriever wagged at me as I walked up, but stayed leaning against the old man's leg. The fisherman jigged his short rod with a practiced little wrist motion. He was fishing tullibees fifty feet down and hadn't caught any yet. We talked a little, though he didn't seem much for the gab. I asked if I could take a picture of him and the dog with that big moon in the mist as a background, and he said that was okay. Then he turned and looked up a little at the moon as if seeing it for the first time and then looked back down at his hole. His wrist had not stopped jigging.

There are snapping turtles also in the lake. Some of them are very old. People eat them and you can get a permit to catch them. When I was a kid an old man on another lake caught them by putting meat in wire traps. The turtle would swim in the funnel-shaped entrance to get at the meat and couldn't get out. I haven't seen this here and

I have not caught turtles here. I am told it is done by getting on the lake in a boat at night just after the ice goes out in the spring with a strong light. They then go around and probe the bottom with a pole. The snapping turtles spend the winter in the mud, which is in itself an amazing thing. They are not, after all, fish. They breathe air normally, and somehow have adapted to shutting down their system for six months or so. Once the ice is on, they can't come up for air. It must be related to the water temperature. At any rate once the fishermen locate a turtle, there is a hook on the other end of the pole with which they grab the torpid turtle under the front edge of its shell and raise it slowly to the surface.

Once I asked a turtle hunter how much he got for his turtles. "A hundred," he answered. I gave him the hundred and he gave me all of his turtles, some seven or eight, including one brute of about twenty pounds or so. The captive turtles were in gunnysacks. I let them all go and the big one I let go in my lake. At one lake, two fishermen who realized what I was doing gave me dirty looks and grumbled something, which I ignored. The big one tried to bite me, which if you get bit by a twenty pound snapping turtle, you stay bit. And then it swam off, plowing through the weeds like a bulldozer, without saying goodbye. Ah well, karma, Mike, karma.

There are big fish in my lake. All the neighbors talk about the huge muskies and other even larger fish. Thus I swear that the following story is the God's own truth.

An acquaintance of mine who is a great fisherman, by his own account, came up for a few days. He had brought his canoe and spent many happy minutes paddling back and forth through my weed bed and around the shore of the lake. Being the reckless sort, he brooked no stopping for any obstacle and plowed along happily, scattering various wildlife and fauna. This was the situation when in midstroke he realized that he had paddled the canoe onto what he assumed was a sunken log. The canoe then hung up on the log, balancing on its midpoint, while Bob whistled a tune. He didn't tell me which tune, but certainly it wasn't "Nearer My God to Thee." Suddenly the log began to move, carrying the canoe and Bob with it, so that now the canoe was moving sideways.

This irritated Bob who knew instinctively that the canoe was supposed to move forward and not sideways, no fool was he. Bob then, in order to get the huge fish's attention and to perchance get his canoe off of the great fish's back, swung his paddle at what he supposed was the head. The huge fish, apparently being irritated at having its nap interrupted, then twisted around and bit a chunk out of the paddle. This enraged my acquaintance, who then jumped out of the canoe onto the back of the great fish, which being frightened, sped off sans canoe. Now my friend, being used to canoeing while wearing his cowboy boots and spurs, dug his silver spikes into the side of the beast who accelerated greatly, turning toward the middle of the lake. This, Bob knew, was not good as he could barely swim, and not at all with his boots on. Not knowing what to do and not really wishing to relinquish his spur hold on the fish, Bob dug in harder and struck the fish a blow on the side of its head, turning it toward shore and shallow water. As luck would have it, after the blow to the fish's head, he found that by merely touching the fish on one side or the other of its head he could guide it around with alacrity. Alacrity, he and the fish thus went this way and that through the shallows. Further by digging in with his spurs he could induce the fish to greater speed. Thus Bob did turn back and forth for many minutes until he found himself back at the starting point by his canoe and did jump off, none the worse for wear. He then gave me the paddle with the chunk bitten out of it, and I hung it on the wall. It hangs there to this day and I bring it out to chase off door-to-door salesmen or Republicans.

Some people have questioned the veracity of the above story. I understand that, and frankly feel sorry for them. Some tales are long and some short, and Bob's fish story achieves the impossible. It is both short and tall at the same time.

At any rate I haven't caught any huge fishes and only a few of the little fishes in my lake, though I did once hook a muskie on a streamer fly with my fly rod. As soon as the muskie felt the hook, he decided that he wanted to go to some other part of the lake and left me with the line and the rod while he kept the streamer. I don't know the lake any better than when I first came. That is all that I have to say about the fish in my lake.

Weed Beds

The area of the lake in front of my land is very shallow. In summer it is totally covered in bulrushes. These round, segmented, willowy plants grow in the water and on shore. They are not the dense green weeds of other lakes but instead grow thinly spaced but widespread in the hard sand bottom. It is relatively easy to walk through them. Sometimes, usually in spring when the waves are rolling in from the north, I take the casting rod and a weedless spoon and wade a long way out through the bulrushes to cast for northern pike. Once I caught a small muskie there, and many times northern pike have followed my lure in, only to hold for a moment like shadows in the water and then turn back out into the deep.

My weed beds are about eight hundred feet long and extend about fifty yards into the lake, including all of the areas in front of my land. These weeds die in winter and begin to grow again in spring, poking their green heads up, until in early summer the whole flats area is covered with the thin green stalks. They are very fibrous and tough, and they bend in the wind and waves, and in fall they begin to die and turn a tan color. In late fall the tips of each stalk dip again and again into the cold water and little ice bells form there. In the quiet cold of late October and November days, if you are quiet yourself and listen, you can hear the whole bed of weeds clink and tinkle in a slight wind.

There are also substantial weed beds in the rest of the lake, but in many places people have removed the weeds in front of their docks. One fellow told me that he made a game of it with his family when he was first on the lake. He and his family would pull some weeds each time they went swimming. It doesn't take much to get rid of these weeds. Some weed removal comes from the back and forth passing of boats. In previous days (and maybe now) people would drag around an old bedspring to yank up these weeds. Since the sand bottom is fairly sterile, they would soon have a nice sandy clean bottom. These weeds do not readily regrow once they have been pulled. So far the weed beds in front of my land are largely intact. In other lakes, including the lake that I grew up on much farther south, the weed beds are mostly gone except the nuisance weeds, which are growing with even more vigor.

Clams

There is a large clam bed in front of my place. If you put on waders—I prefer shorts and old tennis shoes—you can wade out and look at them. When I was working in the hot August days I would often wade out into the flats, swim a bit to clean up and cool off and then wander around for a while. Hundreds of broken shells litter the bottom. Among the broken shells are the empty open shells of the clams that have presumably died of old age. Here and there are live clams attached to the bottom, doing whatever the lowly bivalve does. I don't know whether the clam bed is thriving or dying. I'm told or I read it somewhere that clams live a very long time, assuming they aren't eaten. Once I had a notion to mark the live clams with an indelible marker, and since one assumes your clam is not a noted traveler, I would count them from spring to spring to see how many lived or died. I never did this. Too busy. Also I couldn't figure out how to mark them clearly. Somebody should do this on my lake.

Otters and mink eat clams. In early winter the otters pass along the shores of the freezing lakes heading for the places where the water stays open year-round. I have seen their large footprints and the places where they slid on the snow. On several occasions I have noticed small mounds of vegetation on the ice. Upon investigation I found many clam shells, the vegetation and a frozen-over hole in the ice. It seems the otters have used the hole to feed on the clam beds and the vegetation to prevent the hole from closing once they got it open.

At the Common Ground coffee house we finally were able to put on a show to raise money. Spider John Koerner, who is alleged to have had some influence on the Beatles, was the entertainment. He was a big hit and a good crowd showed up. Shortly before the program was to start he asked Sally, the helpful, energetic Finnish woman, if there was a bar close by, apparently being used to having a couple of bumps prior to the start of the show. Sally pointedly indicated that there was no alcohol nearby; no doubt she was thinking the demon rum would send him astray if he was allowed a drink prior to the event. Spider John seemed rather startled at this rejoinder and stared blankly in my direction. I pointed him to the closest bar several blocks away, whereto he promptly disappeared for twenty minutes. He then returned and put on one hell of a show. Let me add here that about a year later I met Koerner at another bar he was playing. He vaguely remembered me, but clearly and somewhat indignantly remembered the gig at the Common Ground as the place where that woman tried to keep him from having a drink before the show.

A fellow whom I call the Voyageur came in one night. He is a good-looking, strong-shouldered man with longish hair and is fascinated by voyageurs, those hardy little men who plied the waters of Canada and the northern United States in pursuit of furs. Once he came to the coffee house in mukluks, footwear appropriate to very cold conditions, not room temperature. Hot sweaty feet aside, apparently he thinks he was born too late and would have made a good voyageur. He wasn't born around this area but instead moved here to live in the woods.

When I tell him that my family originally was in the fur business and that my great grandfather was a voyageur, he seemed skeptical and slightly shocked. "You don't look like a voyageur," he said, examining me. He is right. I am tall, voyageurs were powerful but little men, supposedly each less than five feet eight inches, the better to fit them in the cargo canoes.

"Me saintly mother was Irish," said I blithely, "blame her." This doesn't seem to help. But I have proof, I tell him. I have a copy of my great grandfather's handwritten (in French) voyageur contract. The fur trade was a business, essentially a franchise granted in the new world by the kings of France and England. Part of my family came to Quebec from France very early in the nineteenth century. They plied the waters of Canada, gradually working their way around Lake Superior, south and west along the rivers of that area. Eventually they reached that great waterway, the Mississippi, and the French became the dominant foreign force in this area. The Mississippi valley was a French area until the Americans showed up. But by the time my great grandfather was in the business in what is now Minnesota, the fur business was essentially dead. Trading went on, but beaver were gone and the trade was in the lowly muskrat.

Your voyageur was essentially a hired mule. They were hired to lift and tote. If a mule could have paddled a canoe the owners would have certainly used them. And they were expendable. It is said that each voyageur routinely carried two *pieces*, each *piece* being a bundle of furs or goods weighing ninety pounds. If the voyageur acquired a hernia, a condition not unusual, or became otherwise ill, there was little help. They got well themselves or died. And if they died they were buried out in a vast, dark, lonely wilderness, away from their lively, warm French families.

But he is right about the romance of the Homme du Nord (men of the north) in one regard. They were French and while the fact of their being French, not American, doesn't seem to register with him, it is essential to the romantic vision of them. Despite the drudgery and the danger, the mosquitoes and often lonely death, these little Frenchmen did bring a joy to their work. It was an exultation born of the simple fact of survival and a little joy of singing out long days spent paddling huge canoes in a cold, mostly joyless and unforgiving wilderness. And like our coffee house, it was a simple, very French characteristic of sociability. The French, as opposed to the stiff-backed Protestant Americans, loved a good time, music, fun and visiting. So for these Frenchmen, isolated in a vast wilderness, getting together once a year at the "Rendezvous" to talk and argue and drink and fight and enjoy music was life-giving. In this regard it was just like our coffee house.

But alas none of this made any difference. I could never seem to get on the good side of my erstwhile Voyageur and we didn't talk about it again. It's just as well. One of the little sins that the better angels are constantly on guard against is the sin of stomping around in the middle of someone else's dream with the muddy feet of reality.

Then the Veteran came in and morosely sat with his guitars and songbook. The book is full of songs he has written. The songs are about being misunderstood and treated badly when he was in high school and the great injustices people do to each other. He plays and sings, then finishes to the obligatory smattering, which he ignores. His guitars are very nice. (Gibson's, I think.) I ask him if I can look at one of them. He declines. "People get sweat on them when they pick them up," he says, a deadpan expression on his face.

A little later a woman of about thirty-five or so with flaming red hair sauntered in, carrying a guitar. She said that she was from Duluth, played the guitar pretty well and wrote her own songs. She played a few songs for us. You could see she'd played some in public. She shifted her long legs sexily, flashed her pearly white smile and was gone. But I knew she'd be back. She couldn't keep away from us; from me. She was the stuff of Wednesday night dreams, not to mention a couple of the other nights of the week.

Building Your Log Home, Part Two

In thinking about building my log home I came to the conclusion that I would try to pay cash for it. Not that anyone was rushing forward to loan me large amounts of money. I was not sure at that time how my life would go, but one thing I was most certainly sure of was that I wanted to be in charge of such life as I had left. And a big part of that life would be the freedom that comes from not owing anyone anything. Sharing ownership of my house with a bank or a mortgage company was not what I wanted.

These days most people acquire a home by borrowing money. That's the American way. I borrowed the money and I made a lot of money on this house, people say. And it's true, borrowing money to purchase a home is part and parcel of the American dream. People in this country are presently availed of the opportunity to buy homes on a scale not seen previously. In the period after World War II, various federal programs gave millions a home-buying opportunity they might not have had. They borrowed the money for their little homes, gradually paying off those loans, improving them and building up equity toward their retirement. Actually a lot of the early houses were fairly basic and the owners would build garages or additions when they had extra money.

Now most people borrow the money for a finished home. Practically no one builds something on his or her own now. The reason for this is that before they have a chance to think about it, most people are busily at work, paying for the house and new car that they drive to work. People accept this without question, and pile headlong into their working life doing the same things that others have done. Before very long, many of their decisions in their lives are dictated by banks and the credit card companies.

It occurs to me that it is a very strange thing that anyone would subrogate his or her life to a house. Not that I haven't done a considerable amount of subrogating myself, but I think we are looking at the question of how to live from the wrong end of the problem. When people are young they are seldom asked to consider the effect of indebtedness on their lives. Usually they are just relieved that someone thinks they are creditworthy enough to get a loan for a house. It's not so much a bad deal as it's a proposition in which you are given the chance to get nice things, all you have to do is to narrow the choices in your life.

People now have too much debt. I knew a couple who had a house and twenty thousand dollars in credit card debt. In total they had accumulated a hundred thousand dollars in debt to finance the husband's law school studies. Perhaps in their case it will work and his career will generate enough income to justify that debt level. I doubt it. Of course most people have a mortgage and some debt and usually they have equity in their house and other assets. The banks have apparently figured out that this was a vast untapped source of money and they worked to translate the unsecured credit card debt into secured debt by tapping the equity in people's homes. If that was their strategy, it worked partially. Lots of people have used up their home equity. Except that they still have the credit card debt! It may seem strange to say this now, but historically, people suffered from lack of credit. That is they were hindered from helping themselves because they couldn't readily get money, at least not at good rates. Now they suffer from too much credit.

You don't have to do what others have done. I know a couple who adopted the strategy of actually saving money when they were first married. Shocking, isn't it? Then they bought a lot on a lake with that money. After that they bought a house that was to be demolished by the highway department and had it moved onto the lot. They and their family improved the place and lived there for more than twenty years, until they finally sold that place and bought a small farm. Of course not everyone can do this type of thing, but it goes to show that it can be done. No debt equals freedom. I felt that if I could acquire a house without debt I could then extend that process to other aspects of my life. Assuming, that is, I ever acquired a normal existence again.

I follow two simple rules. The first is I won't borrow money for anything that doesn't make me money. You don't have to be ridiculous about this. Most people have to borrow to buy a house and a house has traditionally been a good investment. Buy a house if you can afford it and if it makes your life more free and happy. And I use a credit card for traveling and to buy things that are going to be shipped to me. As a practical matter, one can't travel without a credit card. But I always, repeat always, pay the entire balance off upon getting the bill.

The second rule I follow is that it absolutely doesn't matter what others think when it comes to your finances. Sometimes that means you have to get by with a used car instead of a new car. It is nice to have new things, but it is nicer to be free of debt. This way is harder, but the result is freedom.

Tools I Used to Build My House

All of the good log home building books will show you how to use the principal home building tools. And the catalogues have good descriptions of the tools needed to build your house. Or you could stop in to an actual site where a professional is building a log home. The professionals are usually friendly and happy to talk about their craft. These ideas in mind, I humbly present a few comments of my own here regarding some of the tools I used to construct my house.

The Adze

An adze is an axe-like tool except that the blade is turned so that you cut the wood in a chipping motion by swinging it between your legs. It is used for hewing, hopefully wood, not your foot. There are numerous types of adzes, each generally adapted to a specific use. And just to confuse matters more, there are right-handed and left-handed adzes. This tool has been used for several thousand years in the building of boats and other woodworking jobs. If you don't know what it looks like, look in one of the catalogues for the log homebuilders. When you have finished scribing a log, you cut the log along the scribe lines laterally and then kerf-cut the piece you're cutting out. Kerf-cuts allow you to cut short pieces out of the long lateral cut. Then in order to get the scribed part out, you straddle the log, swing the adze between your legs and chip out each chunk. At least that's the way I did it.

The only exciting part of this chipping is that you have to swing the adze pretty hard to get the chunks to split out, and they sometimes lift off in the general direction of the family… jewels. I never got hit precisely in those environs, thank you, Lord. Dave, the old gentleman who helped me for a while, told me he knew someone who did and said that the fellow subsequently spent time curled up on the ground. Naturally I used my adze a lot since it was needed on every log that I scribed and cut. When I got it, the adze was sharp enough to shave with. I was more afraid of that tool in the beginning than anything else I owned.

Come-along

A come-along is a ratchet-driven pulling tool. It functions exactly as it is named. It is commonly used in the north to firmly tie down large loads and for so many other functions that it is impossible to list them all. It is sort of a poor man's winch. If it did anymore things, it would be a poor man's wench. I kept one in my truck in case I got really stuck, whereupon I would loop a chain around some other object and slowly yank the truck out, or, if I was stuck too badly, yank the object toward the truck. Which reminds me of a friend who purchased a new jeep with a power winch and drove into the wilds on a logging road with a friend. How could they get in trouble? They had four-wheel drive and a winch. Of course they got stuck, buried to the axles. Not to worry, out came the winch. Whereupon they proceeded to pull down every sapling and tree within range of the winch. Luckily for them, a logging crew with a cherry picker was working nearby, and they were plucked from their swampy resting place soon after they had plucked forty bucks from their wallets and had given same to the logging crew. Of course a tool doesn't substitute for good judgment, but a come-along can do a lot. It is one of those tools that you may not need for several weeks, but when you need it, you really need it. Get one.

Chain Saw

I'm not sure just how they built log houses prior to the chain saw, and just in case you feel like telling me, I don't want to know. It sounds like too much work. My chain saw saves work and can be used for all kinds of jobs, not just cutting logs. I got so I could very accurately cut a scribe line on a log, board or sheet of plywood. I had used a chain saw some before I went north, but it was in the north that I became pretty good with one. And even though I don't use one regularly now, I still can use my chain saw skillfully. Most of the chain saws that are produced now are pretty good. As opposed to the old days, the modern ones start easily and run pretty well if they're taken care of. I had a Stihl model saw first, and now I have a Jonsrud. Both work just fine.

Here is the first point that I want to make. The chain saw is one tool that will work the best for you if you take good care of it. Fill it every day with fluids and, most importantly, cut with sharp, properly tensioned chains and you'll get the best results. I know, I know, this seems obvious. But it's easy to get sloppy about this. My second point is that the more I used a chain saw, the more I realized how quickly the chain saw could hurt you. Practice caution *all* of the time that you are using one. Please note the emphasis on "all." If you're tired, stop. Take a break. And always, repeat always, wear safety glasses. Once I was using my chain saw and stopped to fetch something. I then picked up the saw to cut the base of some brush, a few seconds work, and I would be done. I had put my safety glasses on a stump a few yards away and didn't get them since I would be done quickly and was going to cut no more that day. When I cut the base of the bush, a dry stick that had been lying there got caught by the chain, flew up and hit me rather sharply on the left cheek. It just as easily could have been my eye.

I might also add that when you are around power equipment such as a chain saw, bad things generally happen in two modes: very fast and very slow. When I was going to college I had an acquaintance who was wonderfully smart, a mathematician and a very humorous guy to boot. So far as I know he did very well in his life. But once, one time, he was working on a construction site and a splinter from some wood he was pounding on flew up and put out one of his eyes. He wasn't wearing safety glasses. Of course in those days most people didn't wear protection unless the job was really dangerous. One accident when he was twenty, and he had to live the rest of his life with one eye. Ain't worth it.

Accidents happen slowly too. Consider an acquaintance with whom I went to high school and who for many years had a tree-trimming service. He and his associates handled chain saws virtually every day. In addition to that, he was around operating machinery most of the time. So far as I know, he was never seriously injured during his work. Apparently, however, he didn't wear hearing protection early in his career as a tree trimmer, because he is virtually stone-deaf now. There is absolutely no reason for this. There are plenty of cheap forms of ear and eye protection available.

Of course, as they say up north, "shit happens." This rather colorful phrase illustrates that there is always the possibility of accidents, no matter how much you protect yourself. Taking risks could end your life, but it's better than dying of boredom. A few years ago I read an account of two men who were cutting trees for firewood. One was running a chain saw and had equipped himself with a helmet and built-in ear and eye protection. He had everything. Except that he didn't see his partner felling another tree and couldn't hear the screamed warnings whereupon the end of the tree squashed him. The squashee could hear nothing over the sound of his chain saw, due to his excellent helmet, eye and ear protection. He had excellent hearing and good vision when he died.

For those of you who do build a log home and thus use a chain saw for a considerable period of time, I would bring up one more thing, a grisly phenomenon apparently first noted in the northwestern United States and Canada called white hand syndrome. Apparently the vibration from the chain saw will, over a period of time, damage the nerves and small capillaries in one's hands. You do not notice this damage until it is too late, and it is not repairable. It is necessary, therefore, if you're working for any length of time with a chain saw, to have vibration damping on the handle. I'm not sure, but I think most of the new chain saws have the vibration damping accessories available. After I had been working with mine for some weeks, I cut a piece of fairly stiff foam (from those tubes that you get to protect pipes from freezing) and duct-taped it to the handhold. This vibration damper made a big difference to me. It was more comfortable with the larger handhold and my hand didn't tire so easily.

Breathing Protection

Did I tell you that I'm allergic to dust and molds, particularly molds? Well I am. Furthermore I didn't figure this out until I was an adult, a state, by the way, which a couple of former girlfriends have contended I never have achieved. I have two words for them. Niyaaaaaa! Niyaaaa! One late winter afternoon I arrived at the house to do some flooring work. I had a high-speed cutter, sort of a high-class table saw, with which I was to cut black ash flooring. I had cut lots of wood with power saws inside and out before, so without giving it much thought, I set up in the kitchen, put on my safety glasses and started cutting. I used no breathing protection, and I continued for about an hour until I started noticing that I was a little light-headed. Then I was a lot light-headed and was having trouble breathing. I stopped working and stood outside. Being a little hungry, I decided maybe that was the problem and so went to a restaurant to get something to eat. After that I felt a little better, but my body felt as if I had taken a double dose of speed, rather like I'd drunk five cups of strong coffee. Not pleasant. Thinking I was overtired, I lay down to rest. My body continued in its over-revved mode until late that night, with me lying there uncomfortably. Finally somewhere in the night, it began to subside and I managed to fall asleep.

The next morning I felt okay and began to work again. I did not move the cutter outside, nor did I put on breathing protection. Remember, I'd done a lot of cutting before and just didn't think anything about cutting some boards. Within ten minutes I felt weak and breathy. Finally I decided (am I brilliant or what?) that something was wrong and packed up and left. While driving I thought about it and stopped to get an antihistamine. I took one, and within ten minutes I could breathe more easily. This beneficial effect lasted for two hours whereupon I took one more antihistamine. When I got home I realized that my throat was swollen. This lasted until the next day, when it subsided. I had a medical checkup scheduled and when I described my experience and the symptoms, the doctor suggested that I had anxiety. I changed doctors.

It turns out that black ash, a fine wood that makes a beautiful floor, by the way, has toxic molds and who-knows-what-else in it. When these toxins enter your system, your body wants to get rid of them and speeds up to do so. The high-speed cutter spewed nice, fine dust into the air in the enclosed kitchen area, wherein I breathed it. After this experience, I do my cutting outside, no matter the material. And I wear breathing protection whenever I think there's any dust. A dust mask costs two bucks (and that's for an expensive one). Cheap to avoid the aggravation. Use a dust mask.

My Old Brown Truck

Speaking of tools, I hope the reader will pardon me for getting a little misty-eyed over my 1977 Chevrolet truck. Gee, this could be a country song. It is gone, long gone now, replaced by a succession of vehicles, including a new truck parked in the garage. But during the years I was building my house and could not afford alternatives, it worked with a minimum of complaint. It started when it was parked in a plywood and plastic shelter at thirty below zero. It bounced up and down my rutted driveway in mud and snow. It hauled gear and building materials. By chance it had heavy-duty springs in back and could carry a lot of weight. Through all of my construction it ran with practically no maintenance except to fill it with water, antifreeze, gas and oil and to occasionally clean the spark plugs.

Sometimes in winter when it was extremely cold (below minus twenty), I had to watch the temperature gauge because the water–antifreeze mixture in the radiator would sometimes freeze. This would happen because there was a very slow leak in the radiator and I would add (mechanics, avert your eyes) water to the fluid in the radiator. When the radiator froze the engine would overheat since, amazingly, the engine block was then being deprived of flowing coolant. When the engine temperature got somewhat hot, I would turn off the truck, and the heat from the engine would thaw the radiator enough so that the antifreeze mixture would become liquid. Then by adding more antifreeze the radiator would totally unfreeze. Do not try this at home.

The brown truck hauled many loads during my project and never failed once. Four or five times I loaded the truck high with black ash flooring lumber from a sawmill seventy-five miles south of my place. This lumber I later had planed for my floors. On several other occasions I loaded the truck until it wheezed, with pole rafters, which stuck out fore and aft, green leaves trailing in the wind. I looked like a moving greenish pole pile creeping down the road toward my house. My neighbors were greatly amused.

If I had to, I could fix almost anything on the truck. Once, the truck began running badly. Noticing the dramatic increase in fuel consumption, I, with some help, determined that the floats in the carburetor (a mechanical device for getting fuel into the engine) were stuck. I then disassembled the top of the carburetor and installed new floats. Presto! The truck ran well again.

In another rather dramatic illustration of the fixable nature of my truck, prior to starting my house I was driving on a busy thoroughfare in the Twin Cities coming back from a fishing trip. I pulled up to a stoplight, and a fellow in a truck next to me waved and asked me if I knew my truck was on fire. Just at that moment smoke began to emanate from my engine compartment. Being if nothing else, a master of the obvious, I concluded this was a bad sign. I then pulled the truck into a convenient field and got out. (Actually "bailed out" would be more accurate.) When I lifted the hood, a considerable part of the left side of the engine was engulfed in flames. I assumed the game was up and the truck was doomed. Still, I didn't want to give up, and I happened to have a large plastic bottle of carbonated water in the truck, and this I shook up and sprayed on the fire. Amazingly the fire, which had been fed by a crack in a fuel line, went out! I was much relieved but the left side of my engine was a mess. All of the spark plug wires and the hoses as well as part of the air cleaner were melted. As luck would have it (here we go again) there was a large shopping mall across the highway. I went to the mall and purchased new wiring and one new hose. I then replaced the wiring, taped up the cracked fuel line, started the truck and drove home. As luck would have it indeed.

Speaking of old trucks, once a friend and I were headed to Montana on a two-week fly-fishing trip. We had another old truck that worked fine, although it was rust-eaten and had a hole in the passenger-side floorboard. The hole in the floorboard was such that one could see the highway whizzing past underneath. Prior to leaving, my friend expressed the fear that his lungs wouldn't hold up well at higher altitudes. He had been a cross-country runner when young, but he had taken to smoking cigarettes (and a few other things) in that old Vietnam War, and now rolled and smoked his own at a fair clip. I thought he wouldn't have much problem with the altitude, but suggested that if he was that concerned, he take up chewing, which is simply nicotine in another form. He brightened at this idea.

Thus did this friend buy several containers of chewing tobacco (I think it was Wintergreen) and forthwith stuck a small wad of the chewing tobacco into the space between cheek and gum. Whence to Montana we did repair, the trout to catch. En route, however, my friend noticed that it was messy to spit out of the window. He was nothing if not concerned about appearances. He then hit upon the notion that he could spit out the hole in the floorboard, which, one must admit, was conveniently close at hand. Which he did, and to his credit, hit the hole the vast majority of the time. Thus did we pass two weeks, fishing and eating a meal of trout every evening until the two of us and the truck with the hole in the floorboard headed home, whereupon he went back to smoking. He said that chewing was too disgusting for his teaching profession. He could teach for a couple of hours and then sneak out and smoke virtually at will, but spitting was out.

Tools to Lift Logs
(Or How to Make Do Without Them)

It is of course better to lift logs using power equipment such as a cherry picker or a front-end loader. But it's amazing to me even now just how large a log one can lift with absolutely no power equipment. I once got a forty-foot- long log from the ground up onto the third or fourth course by myself. This log was green and weighed at least fifteen hundred pounds. I felt like an Egyptian. Of course they had it easy since they used slaves. There was no help for moi. I was the slave.

Anyhow, back to the log that I got up onto the wall by myself. It had snowed a foot or so. It wasn't cold, mind you, just a heavy, wet, slippery snow. There was not much moving. I couldn't even get Dale going, and for some reason I was hot to get that particular log up on the wall. So I did it myself. Now here's the way that I did it. Using my cant hook, I rolled the log so that it was parallel to the wall. Then I made a ramp for the thin end of the log and rolled the thin end of the log up the ramp so that it was on the wall, holding it there by inserting a suitably sized pole into the angle formed by the wall and the log. I continued to roll the log up onto the wall until it balanced on its midpoint. Now you have a fifteen-hundred-pound log balanced on the wall. This is a dangerous moment, just in case someone needed to tell you. So whatever you do, try not to let go of the log and instead keep maneuvering it until you get the log to lay across two of the walls, where you can leave it temporarily while you collapse in exhaustion or go for a cup of coffee or, alternatively, a glass of water and a Valium for your jangled nerves. The upshot of all of this is that you should either have good equipment to lift and reset the logs or you should have smaller logs.

Log-Scribing Tools

A scribing tool is any device that translates one irregular surface to another surface. Actually it's a cool-looking tool designed specifically to make you part with a considerable amount of your hard-earned money. Or you can make one for diddly-squat. Dave claimed he used a block of wood with a stylus at one end and a marking pencil at the other. Whatever you use, if you place one log directly over another log, you can theoretically transfer the irregular surface of the lower log to the upper one by means of this scribing tool. Then when you cut along the line on the upper log, it will fit onto the lower one. Now isn't that clear? Get the book. The one with the pictures.

Some fool somewhere, in appreciation of his own vast skills, got it into his head that one should transfer these marks in one continuous flowing line. And then the same guy apparently felt it necessary to publish those views in a book and everyone since has felt the need to follow those instructions. You don't need to do that. It is far easier to hold the scribing tool level and make a series of short marks. A level scribing tool is much more important than continuous lines. The books don't tell you this. Oh, one more thing: the smoother the logs the easier this process is. It's easy to get sloppy about this.

Organizing Your Tools

One naturally uses a lot of tools when building a house, some of which are actually useful. It is possible to separate tools into different categories. For example you could list your regular tools and brute force tools, the ones you resort to when reason and nice talk fail. As I have mentioned somewhere previously, for this purpose I used a car axle as a log peeler. It also worked as an all-around persuader for recalcitrant machinery or heavy logs. I also had several mauls. These are useful tools and deserve to be considered. One tool that you should get if you do any construction, even home improvement construction, is a tool belt. Carry essential tools in it. Along with a collection of screws and nails, I carry in the tool belt a hammer, pliers, chisel (which I sometimes use to pry things with), pencil, tape measure and screwdriver (which I also use sometimes to pry with). If you don't have a belt you'll be leaving things all over the place and driving yourself insane trying to find the tool you left in the other room. By the way, you don't need some huge belt. I use a simple one hip tool holder.

Having said all of that, I will conclude tools with my list of the three most useful tools and my reasons for listing them thus. You can, of course, make your own list.

Most Useful Tool #1: The T Bevel

My first nominee, a rather simple and seemingly insignificant tool, turned out to be very useful to me. When I was first doing a lot of cutting, I found it difficult to estimate and replicate angles other than ninety-degree angles. Many of the angles one cuts when building a log house are oblique or acute (or whatever the other one is). One day I got so frustrated about this—remember, I am not a professional carpenter—that the thought suddenly occurred to me that I could make a tool to measure and replicate these angles. Which I promptly did with two short strips of oak wood fixed together at one end. Voilà! With this tool no angle would confound me. I had invented a working tool. Why, I asked, hadn't anyone thought of this? A friend considered my blathering about this great discovery somewhat owlishly over a stack of pancakes, hoisted a considerable portion to his mouth and said, "It sounds like a T bevel." I was crushed. Of course. The sliding protractor is one of the oldest tools in the world. It was probably invented prior to the Egyptians and shortly after a cave man attached a handle to a rock and tried to put a dent in his neighbor's head with it. I used the one I'd made until I broke it, and then bought one made of plastic and steel at the tool store. The store-bought one doesn't work any better than the one I made, though.

Most Useful Tool #2: The Shop Vac

To me one of the most dispiriting aspects of any construction project is dust and dirt. When I read that statement, I realize how funny it is, since dust and dirt are practically the definition of a construction project. But this is especially the case when the project goes on for a long while and my project went on for years, not months. One can only clean up so much with a broom and dustpan, and these tools generally raise a lot of dust. When the job is outside, this isn't so much of a problem. But when you move inside, dust and sawdust collect in places where it is difficult to thoroughly clean. Now I'm not a neat freak. You couldn't do what I did and survive if you were. But I do like things as orderly as I can get them, and for inside work neatness counts. At least it counts toward one's mental health. Such was the situation when I purchased my first shop vac.

The effect of this tool on my job was amazing. At the end of each day or every couple of days I could thoroughly clean up. Floors, walls, corners, anywhere, dust, sawdust, pieces were but grist for this baby's mill. My outlook brightened wonderfully with the use of this tool. I realize here that you'd think any idiot should have thought of this. Well, this idiot didn't. So I'm telling you, if you do any kind of building project, get one. It saves a lot of aggravation, and since aggravation-saving is one of Maslow's basic needs of life, I recommend the shop vac as one of my three most useful tools.

Most Useful Tool #3: The Power Orbital Sander

When I was building my house, most of the things I read about logs related to protecting them, but not necessarily making them look better. Practically anything a person did to the poor log could damage it, and one didn't want that. Which I might say is a good thing because lots of damage can be done by an amateur such as myself, and I did my share. By the end of my house-building project, the logs had accumulated a lot of dust, dirt and mold. At that point I was heading down to the finishing stage of the project, and various people suggested ways of cleaning the logs prior to finishing them. Human nature being what it is, usually they suggested whatever they had done. Power washing seemed to be the most popular method of cleaning logs. Sandblasting or blasting with corn (yes, this is done and it has the beneficial effect of attracting wildlife) are two other ways of cleaning and preparing the logs for finishing.

Then one day I stopped in at a site where some log-building professionals were working. One of them was using an orbital sander to smooth some scarf cuts on a log. This stuck in my head and when it came time to sand things I went to the sander store and bought one. When it comes to rough woodwork, the orbital sander can make you look good, and what, I ask you, is more important than looking good? I have previously mentioned how I used the sander. You install one of those hard rubber heads on it and use appropriately rough sandpaper and then you can sand anything. Just remember to stop before you sand your neighbor Ray. He's rough and wants to stay that way.

Thus endeth the tools section. The following sections do not concern tools. Life is tough; read them anyway.

Crawl Spaces and/or Basements

Which brings us to basements and crawl spaces. You need either a generous crawl space or a basement. Of course this depends on the water table and the type of soil at your site. My site was not suitable for a basement. Had I dug one, it would have been a swimming pool before long. In the north, if you want to get below the frost level, you need to excavate to a depth of four or five feet. Or deeper. Since you're doing that, some argue that you might have well built a basement, particularly if the site allows for a walkout. And I might add here that lots of houses are built as slab-on-grade. Violent storms and tornadoes are not foreign to much of the country, and it has been demonstrated that basements are the best places to be during these events. At the very least I suggest several feet of crawl space. A friend of mine who doesn't have a basement has a four- or five-foot crawl space with a cement floor, within which he slides around on one of those auto mechanic's wheelie thingies. But of course I used a crushed rock footing with several courses of reinforced blocks on top of the crushed rock. I've said it before and I think it's worth repeating that this footing has worked extremely well. It has not visibly shifted in very adverse conditions.

I should certainly have provided for more of a crawl space. In fact you could say that I removed the "crawl" from my crawl space. My heating consists of a wood plenum heating system in which a downdraft furnace blows heat under the floor. Vents in the floor then allow the heat to flow up into the living area where it is recirculated back into the furnace. The advantage of this system is that there are no heat runs needed under the floor. This is good, since in my case there isn't enough room for heat runs. The whole area under the floor is one sealed plenum. This system is described in a lot of the old carpentry instruction books. At any rate, don't do what I did. You need room under there in case you need to work on pipes or perhaps hide from a tornado or your wife.

Site Preparation

For some insane reason when I was finished with the footings, I did not backfill right away, so that for a while there was a ditch around the house. Then it rained and froze and there I was, stuck with a frozen ditch for the winter. It wasn't much of a ditch, but a ditch nonetheless. I didn't think anything of it, but Dave, the old guy who helped me in the beginning, was continuously stumbling over and around this ditch and generally slipping and sliding. This he didn't like. What with the house in the middle of it, my site was limited in area for maneuvering equipment, and that ditch didn't help. While it was easy to work on two sides of the house with power equipment, the other side might as well have been in China. You couldn't drive to get to the other side of my house unless you wanted to drive in a swamp.

So allow plenty of room around your house and grade it flat. I guarantee everybody will be happier. Assuming you have power equipment, you will have to maneuver said equipment around and if you're picking up and placing logs, this requires considerable room. You can always landscape when you are done and replant trees.

May

May, glorious May! Marsh marigolds pop up and sprinkle the swamps and ditches bright yellow. The warming air smells of life itself and hums with insects. In every pond the spring peeper frogs reach full peeping chorus while the bigger, deep-voiced leopard frogs grunt out their desire. All around, everywhere, thousands of tree frogs begin trilling and trilling and trilling to a crescendo, and then they stop… while the peepers and the leopards keep on. And then the trilling starts again, rising and rising until the very night is filled with a constant trilling, grunting and chirping chorus. Out on the lake the ducks are gabbling and the loons frantically call up to a night sky filled with stars wheeling back toward summer. There is a wonderful exultant urgency in the crystal air and it's all about… sex.

May was so wonderful that I don't remember what I did that month. Maybe some alien took it. Maybe I was so relieved to have made it through the winter and its extension April that I slept through May. Certainly the frost was gone early and with only a little backbreaking labor, I managed to make my driveway passable. I do know that my brother and nephew came up for the fishing opener. We caught walleyes out in front of my place in the evening and cooked them over an open fire in the dark. My nephew said these were the best fish he had ever eaten. They were pretty good, though usually how good the fish is is a function of how hungry you are. No doubt I worked very hard in May, but rather than talk about my heroic efforts, I'm going to talk about birds at my lake.

Birds

At least four or five pair of loons live on Moose Lake. In late April and May, when the pairs are establishing or re-establishing their relationships, the nights are filled with a cacophony of their wild cries. The rest of the year, they usually cry out to each other every night just at sunset. Normally they go about their business, which is to catch minnows or fish and avoid boats and eagles. Loons on my lake tolerate the boaters, merely moving out of the way when the boats come along, occasionally protesting the fact that they have to share the lake with such loud, obnoxious creatures as humans. But if an eagle flies over they all begin crying out to each other a warning. Eagles will attempt to catch the loon chicks, I suppose. They don't usually succeed because the loon parents are always alert and have extremely good vision. If you hear loons hollering in the middle of some hot summer day, it is usually a good indication that an eagle or an osprey is flying somewhere overhead.

There are no osprey nests on Moose Lake that I know of, but there is an eagle nest on the peninsula, next to the swimming beach. It is, as usual, in a large white pine and is difficult to see in summer. You can actually see the nest more easily from the bay toward the public beach, which is on the western side of the lake. The eagle nest is well known to everyone and no one bothers it, but when I was first on the lake I looked for it in vain. Moose Lake is a fairly large lake, being about eleven hundred acres, and it's surprising how eagles, which are big birds, live here without being noticed, except by the loons. When the wind gets to blowing hard from the north, as it does frequently, an eagle will sometimes hover over the south end of the lake, patrolling up and down the shore. I think this is because the wind blows the warmer surface water to the south end of the lake and roils up the shallow water. The fish come in to feed, and occasionally the eagle can pick up a meal there.

When I was growing up it was extremely unusual to see an eagle. I did not see one in the wild until I was hunting in northern Minnesota as a twenty year old in the mid 1960s. When I was a kid, people shot raptors. I shot a sawwhet owl when I was about fifteen years old and didn't think much of it. When I showed the little bird to a young biologist acquaintance of our family, I got an earful. I can still recall the injured look in his eye when he asked me why in God's name I'd shot this poor animal. But I was in the majority, not the minority then. There ain't no way to put a finer edge on it: hawks, owls, eagles, people shot them all. It seems ridiculous now, but that's what they did. In Minnesota at Hawk Ridge by Duluth and at a mountain in Pennsylvania, and no doubt at other places, hawks and other raptors, happened, by a freak of the winds, to annually fly by certain locations. People would gather every fall to shoot migrating hawks there. In Pennsylvania a biologist found his way to the site by the sound of the shotgun fire. Down the mountain he found numerous dead and wounded birds. Does that get your blood boiling?

But people mostly stopped, thank God. And I would point out that this change in people's habits is something that has occurred relatively recently, in my time. Around

1900, interest in the environment and wild places began the modern conservation movement. This movement expanded by fits and starts, accelerating in the late 1950s and particularly the '60s, culminating in various legislation in the late 1970s. Others have written more or less interminably about the environment, and of course in a lot of cases they've overshot the mark and now you can't touch anything without some sort of permit. The point is that this is a great change after several hundred years of blasting away at anything that flew. However much shooting of raptors was done, I am told that the real culprit in the reduction of raptor populations, particularly eagles, was DDT, an insecticide, and by the way a very good one that helped control malaria in the early years. Unfortunately DDT also had the habit of getting into the food chain and weakening the eggshells of the raptor. The shell would then break and thus no raptor. But it certainly didn't help that every adult and kid who was old enough to hold a shotgun or rifle thought it normal to blast away at hawks or eagles.

There is a short stubby little hawk, a broad-winged hawk, I believe, that frequently takes up a perch on a tall basswood tree at the end of my driveway. Mice, birds and, less likely, chipmunks (I wish) are the things he or she is interested in. I don't know if it's the same bird. Probably not. Hawks migrate, and the end of the wooded lane that is my driveway is merely where a broad-winged hawk likes to sit while he contemplates his next meal.

Numerous woodpeckers inhabit the area around my house and the periphery of the lake. The lake edge is woodpecker heaven. The lake is presently surrounded by a band of tall standing mixed deciduous and conifer trees, and there are a lot of tall standing dead trees that are favored by woodpeckers.

Three or four pileated woodpeckers regularly patrol up and down the shoreline wood past my house. They are impressively large birds, and one hears their cries fairly frequently at Moose Lake. They must be somewhat territorial. One summer I saw two pileated woodpeckers noisily fighting up and down the side of a tree. At least I think they were fighting. I'm not sure if they fight much, but they didn't look as if they were enjoying themselves. They certainly didn't look as if they were making love. I think one male was trying to chase off another male. Another pileated, presumably the female, perched in a nearby tree, pecking casually at the odd bug.

Woodpeckers drum on trees year-round, but as the winter gets on into spring the frequency and intensity of their drumming increases. They select certain dead resonant trees for this activity. Or they select anything that resonates. Such as your roof. I once had a steel antenna stand, about twenty feet tall, which I had stood up on the side hill and tied to a tree. On top of this steel stand I put a small triangular piece of plywood so that I could place the TV antenna on it. A downey woodpecker figured out that pecking on the plywood made a nice resonating sound magnified by the steel frame of the steel antenna. He happily drummed on this for several years until I didn't use the antenna stand anymore, and eventually it fell down.

Woodpeckers are not exactly the most sociable birds and don't associate with each other once they're grown. I had a nest of hairy woodpeckers in the woods next to my driveway. Have you ever had a family in your neighborhood that just couldn't get along? Well that's what these hairys were like. Bitching, pecking, complaining in loud voices—about the food, no doubt. Finally the young left their nest hole one day and I had juvenile woodpeckers crash-landing all over the yard, hopping around, chasing grasshoppers and other bugs for their first meals on their own, and then flying awkwardly back to the trees to scream and yell for food, while their parents flew frantically back and forth.

I can't leave woodpeckers without mentioning one rather amazing behavior, which took me a long time to figure out. On birch trees one often finds rows of little holes on the white bark sections. Often there are twenty or thirty little holes. From a distance they look like hash marks. When I first saw them I assumed they were from woodpeckers looking for bugs. This didn't seem logical since the trees were healthy and your average woodpecker looks for bugs and larvae in dead trees or on the heavily corrugated bark of large adult trees. I saw many woodpeckers hunting for bugs on other trees, but I never saw them making those rows of peck marks. Further, I seldom saw fresh peck marks in late summer or fall. I finally figured it out, or rather think that I figured it out, one late spring day when I saw an adult woodpecker carry a bug up to the hash mark sites and, after fiddling around, mash the bug into one of the little holes. Then the bird flew off. I thus assumed the hash marks were for storing bugs for future consumption. As I stood there a juvenile woodpecker flew up to the hash mark site on the tree. And then it seemed clear. The adults make the hash mark sites about the time the juvenile birds are going to leave the nests. The juveniles, who aren't that good at finding food, quickly learn that they can get food at these sites. The nice thing about this is that the adults don't really have to have that much interaction with their progeny, and the juveniles learn that bugs are found in holes in trees.

Yes, there is balm in Gilead. Actually, this is a northern tree known by the interesting biblical name balm of Gilead. I first heard this name from a timber cruiser who was looking at the standing timber on my land. When he said balm of Gilead, I remembered in my childhood a topical balm of the same name that came in a jar. It seemed to me that this medical miracle was white, but perhaps I am imagining that. The timber cruiser didn't know. The tree grows to a very substantial height and frequently is a foot or more in diameter. But it doesn't grow straight, isn't sellable for pulp and, further, it is a soft wood so you can't burn it for long in a stove. It is generally despised by the timber people as being useless. When I rubbed the leaves of this tree together, I immediately remembered the peculiar smell of that salve of my youth. Try it if you ever get north, assuming you can figure out which tree is which. Rub the green leaves together. You can smell the essence of balm of Gilead.

All this is, I know, just horribly interesting and you can't tear your eyes away from the page, but what I wanted to say about the poor old abused balm of Gilead tree of northern Minnesota is that woodpeckers *love* this tree. The bark of the balm tree is deeply corrugated and apparently hides bugs of every sort. And because they are very large trees, bugs have lots of places to hide. So woodpeckers assiduously hunt for their lunch up and down the verdant slopes of the balm of Gilead, but all people think about is that this tree is worthless and needs to be cut down.

I know two things for certain about owls. First, there are lots of them in the woods around my lake, and secondly, I don't want them calling my name. So far, so good. In the fall and winter, particularly on cold nights, one hears them hooting and hollering and laughing about the last guy, off in the cold woods to the southwest of my house. But there is one owl call that I recognize immediately and that is the saw-whet owl. This is a very little owl that people almost never see because it spends the day sleeping in thickets and the night hunting. One warm, late summer night, when the moon was full and I was reclining in the plush luxury of my trailer, I heard an intense bzzzzzzit, bzzzzzzit, bzzzzzzzzzzittt. This little bird uses this noise to aggravate small mammals out of their hiding places and then locate them so that it can fly down and invite them to lunch. This particular sound was coming from the trees above my place, but it was hard to tell since it seemed to come from everywhere. How nice, I thought, a little saw-whet. Bzzzzzit, bzzzzzzit, bzzzzzit went the little owl. I nestled back into my bed contemplating one of nature's little wonders and what a wonderful fellow that I was and how my mother was right, I am special. Bzzzzzzit, bzzzzzit, bzzzzzit. Hmm, what a penetrating sound that is. Gee, I wonder how long he can go on like this. I chuckled.

Sixty seconds, two minutes, five minutes. I hope the reader can appreciate just how piercing and quickly irritating this sound can become. On and on. I covered my head with a pillow. The bzzzzzzzzzzit, bzzzzzzzzzitt pierced right through it. I rolled around. Bzzzzzzit, bzzzzzzit went the little owl. Finally, at the point that my sanity was about to fly away, the little owl got one mammal to move. Me. I got up and went out with the flashlight and the little owl flew away, apparently after coming to the conclusion that I was a little too big to swoop down and invite to lunch.

Hummingbirds are plentiful around my lake. They arrive in May and most of them are gone by late August. By that time the adults have nested and have put on enough fat, but the juveniles haven't built up enough body fat to leave. The juveniles usually stay until September. They are very common in the lakes area in summer. All you have to do is put out a feeder and you'll have several of them buzzing around. It is still very strange to me to see this itty-bitty little bird sitting on a branch like other birds.

They are nice to have around, but they aren't nice to each other. They chase each other relentlessly, and the big ones bully the little ones away from the feeder. More than once I've seen one of them chase a smaller one under a table or, in one case, a chair and dive-bomb the poor victim. To a hummer my place is a bad neighborhood and only the toughest survive.

When one realizes that every year these little birds fly from here to Central America, head north again with just barely the time to feed enough to get strong, mate, nest and then head south again, one understands why they're aggressive and tough little birds and wonders even more how it is that they maintain their populations. Maybe they don't. The common thing that goes into the feeder is sugar water fortified with red dye #3. When one considers the hazards of a two-thousand-mile journey every single year, to some location where someone has hacked down their winter homes, it wouldn't take much to tip the population down. Someone ought to do some sort of a census so that over the years one could figure out how they are doing. I would but it's so hard to get them to sign the census registry.

There are crows in spring, summer and fall and ravens in winter. Most people don't like crows and I know why. Crows are just like humans. They are social birds and hang around in groups, yakking and gossiping about humans (except for when they are nesting). Once I saw a group of them on a cold windy winter day that had figured out that the strong wind was hitting a building at just such an angle to create a strong updraft. Crows were happily flying into the column of uprising air, riding it up a hundred feet or more and then getting off and diving back in down below. This went on for twenty minutes before the rumor of an owl or a hawk to harass took them elsewhere.

In the bigger cities crows have figured out that they are relatively safe and have moved right in like some unwanted obnoxious cousin. After all, cities have everything a crow needs: plenty of lawns where they can hunt worms—a favorite entrée for le crow—plus plenty of dead animals on the roads, not to mention the odd french fry from your favorite fast food parking lot. Crows are prey for owls, but lucky for the crow, not many owls frequent cities anymore since humans have generously removed the old forest nesting places for the owls.

Crows eat almost anything with food value—seeds, carrion, fruit, worms (especially worms). If it looks edible, your crow will give it a try. They have extremely good vision and can see you or something that might be edible for a long distance. When I was a kid growing up on what passed for a farm I had a pet crow. In summer this crow would find a certain large green slug in the lawn, leap upon it like a starving man on sirloin steak, and then after munching the thing back and forth in its beak to kill and tenderize the thing, it would then swallow the slug with a look of birdie ecstasy. But one has to dine according to the season, so on summer mornings on our county road there were inevitably numerous frogs lying squashed on the road. The crow would wait until the sun got high and the frog carcasses got nice and warm before flying down and dining. Don't tell me crows don't have taste. Crows also have a taste for little birds and once they have learned to do so, will rob another bird's nest and eat the contents. Once I saw the crow that I raised carrying a pathetic cheeping victim, followed by a posse of twenty or thirty enraged local bird citizens.

Which brings me back to Moose Lake and one old female crow. After I'd been there a couple of years, I began to recognize her, since she was bigger than the others. At certain times of the year I noticed that she was carefully working her way through the brush and woods along the shore. Then one day I found out what she was looking for. Nests, preferably duck nests. There was a mallard nest in front of my house. She found it and before long had eaten every egg in the nest. In fact once she found the nest, the mallard seemed to understand that the other eggs were doomed and abandoned the nest. This old female crow had lived for years there and had many strategies for feeding herself and her progeny. And, of course, so do the mallards who are very careful about where they nest. One smart mallard successfully raised a clutch of eleven eggs about twenty feet from my house next to a rock pile.

Once on a cold, gray, snowy day in March I came home to find some crows in the yard. Upon seeing me, they all flew off except one who sat hunched on my porch and didn't move much. Obviously it was sick or injured and too weak to care about me. A shocking condition for a crow. I had leftover bones from some chicken I had bought in town. These I put out in the yard. The weakened crow hopped down from the porch and ate some of the meat left on the bones and sat very still for a long while. His family or friends flew around making snide comments. Mercy is not known in crow society. Then I noticed the crow was missing one eye. When I left, I put more food on the picnic table. I hope that crow made it, but I doubt it, and besides, sympathy is wasted on a crow.

And then one day in late November or early December it is too cold and crows are forced south to places where the pickings are better. Then ravens come down from farther north and spend the winter patrolling the roads for roadkill. Most people wouldn't notice they have arrived, but if you live in the north for a while, one day you hear the ravens croaking when the days get cold. Then the crows have gone.

Others have, no doubt, dwelt at length in flaming lines of praise at the disposition of the chickadee, which, at twenty degrees below zero, is flying around cheerfully, acting as if the world is perfect. Which, of course, for the chickadee it is. But I mention this little bird because at my place the chickadees will eat sunflower seeds out of your hand. To hold this little bird in the palm of your hand is an amazing experience every time. "You can feel them push off when they fly away!" a friend exclaimed. I hope when you read this the chickadees at my house are still eating out of your hand.

At the Common Ground the woman with the flaming red hair and the come-hither look came waltzing in trailing her boyfriend. I don't remember much about him except that he had greasy dark hair, a tattoo and tried to play the guitar, which he couldn't. I swear I wasn't jealous. Really.

On the weekend after the Koerner gig, none of Lon's group came in. Someone said they were getting together somewhere else. Someone else said Lon was mad and was talking to other art board members. Spreading rumors apparently. One of the rumors was that we were making a lot of money and keeping it.

A woman came in leading a severely retarded man. They come in fairly regularly. She earns part of her living caring for him. Whatever she earns, it isn't enough. She isn't the only one; there seems to be a substantial local industry in this sort of thing. It is hard to tell how old the retarded man is and I don't know whether the music and talking have any effect on him. All of the normal cues that one uses to measure these things don't seem to be available when I look at him. They usually sit, have coffee and a snack, listen to the music for an hour or so. They seem to fit in fairly well. He sits quietly, occasionally drooling, once in a while making some noise that the woman seems to interpret. In a while they leave, he stumbling along, she with her hand on his arm.

My friend the woodtick showed up again one night. I asked him how he wintered. "Good,' says he, looking at me with that goofy grin, "though you know the winter is getting a little long when you start trying to change the channel on the wood stove." And then be darned if he didn't start reciting poetry out loud to a lady, from memory. His poetry was quirky as one would expect and pretty good. I wasn't sure whether to be shocked that it was good or surprised he did it at all. This romantic flair must have worked; the two of them later left together.

One night after the coffee house wound up I was cruising along home in the Buick at about eleven o'clock, my mind occupied with some momentous subject unrelated to driving. I was thus unprepared when I came over a small hill and standing on the highway were three deer. Trying to avoid these deer I whipped the wheel to the right. This was a bad idea since I still hit one of the deer, and further, after a certain about of swerving and out-of-control maneuvering too predictable and tedious to describe, I exited the highway. That tattered and exhausted angel assigned the seemingly impossible task of guarding my fortune was apparently on the job that night, since the place that the Buick and I left the highway was a low, swampy cattail area. The huge Buick sailed into those cattails and came to a stop with hardly more strain than you'd incur parking at the local shopping mall.

I wasn't injured or even shaken up. Further, just in case I happened to be injured in any way, the guy behind me happened to be a paramedic on his way home from work The concerned paramedic, having seen the rather dramatic gyrations of my car and my unplanned departure from the road, stopped and offered me a ride home. It turned out that my personal guardian angel, tired of attending to me, arranged things so that the paramedic was going past my house.

The next day my neighbor Dale and I went down to my stuck Buick and dragged it backward, up the ditch, until we found a place to yank it back onto the highway. I am more careful about deer since that incident, and I try to be careful in the low areas where they cross the roads and in the evening hours when deer are active. In the long run, however, if you drive in an area where there are a lot of deer, eventually you're going to hit one. But I won't swerve abruptly to avoid a deer anymore. If I'm going to hit the deer, so be it, I'm real sorry. I was fortunate that time, but a lot of injury accidents happen because people react, swerve and go out of control. And besides, my guardian angel is sick of having to bail me out, so I have to watch it.

June

Casey positively hated the Big Long-Legged Bear. Which you would think would mean nothing to the bear. This was my opinion also until one summer evening. Casey usually went home in the evening when his owners returned from work, but on this evening, for some reason he stayed. I hadn't seen the bear much lately, except for a few tracks in my driveway. I didn't think anything about it. He'd been lying low all spring, what with all of that fifty-mile-walk-home bear abuse. Who could blame him? Also there had been a fair amount of fishermen at Dale's. The pickings probably had been pretty good so he didn't have to roam around and get into trouble. And then one evening Casey and I met him.

We were fooling around, working on the driveway, I think. I don't remember at what. But I do know that we were down the driveway a bit and it was twilight. It was probably my imagination, but I felt that I could tell when the bear was around. When he was close, things would get very quiet. Bears, particularly big bears, have an undeniable presence. Perhaps it was timing. He usually showed his nose about dark, and that is the time when it often gets quiet. And showing his nose is an accurate description of what you could see of the bear. He was exactly the color of a shadow, and in twilight was very difficult to see, except for his face and huge nose. Further, the bear, while a huge animal, could move through the brush along the side hill very quietly, though in the night he usually used my driveway, it being easier.

At any rate Casey and I were down the driveway when it suddenly got very still. I was always glad to see the bear so this didn't bother me. Anyone could see that I was unconcerned by the way I sprinted for the safety of my house. Just kidding. I certainly wasn't thinking about Casey who, being the chicken that he was, I knew would stay close to me. Suddenly I heard a low growling next to me. As soon as I started breathing again and the hair on the back of my neck stopped standing straight out, I saw that Casey had turned himself into a tense little growling bundle of energy. Before I could grab his collar he shot off for the bush. I feared for Casey's life. Casey was small, the bear very large. Further, you have to understand just how quick a bear is. Despite their roly-poly look, they are lightning fast with their claws. One quick swipe could kill or badly injure a dog or a human, for that matter. As for Casey, the bear could swat him into the next county. The dog running headlong into the bear in the growing dark could have only one result, and that result was not good.

So you can imagine my surprise when the bear, who brooked no nonsense, began legging it frantically through the brush, crashing along with Casey yapping, and one supposes, nipping at his heels. Soon a husky from down the way, hearing the ruckus, happily joined the chase. Shortly thereafter the bear selected an appropriate tree and clambered up into it. The two dogs yapped at the bear for a bit and then the husky, having done his duty, went home. Casey, I suppose, not knowing the difference between a red squirrel and a bear, probably tried to mesmerize the bear by staring at it. But it was dark by then and bears are slow thinking and don't mesmerize easily, or at all. So all went home and I went inside since the mosquitoes were bad.

In June I became more careful with the work on the logs. Which is a rather strange thing to report considering the fact that I'd been working on my house since the previous fall. But it is true and no doubt due to the fact that any novelty associated with my project had long since passed. Or perhaps it was because the days seemed about twenty-eight hours long. Certainly I was sick of working, though I think I'd passed the sick-of-working stage some time back. Once you're beyond that, you begin to focus on doing the job well, or at least better. In the fall and early spring I had been in a hurry, but now I could take the time I needed to place each log. Whatever the reason, I had slowly come to the conclusion that if you took care to debark and clean the logs more thoroughly, it made the scribing and subsequent cutting process a lot easier. It's a Zen thing, you know. This, of course, seems obvious now, but it wasn't to me then.

Also, the long days allowed me to clean up the place every day. Naturally, with all of the construction, the place had begun to look like a dump; or rather more of a dump than it had been before, so I spent more time cleaning things up. I began to make this cleaning a ritual every day in the evening when I was done working. I would collect the tools and get them under cover and gather up the detritus from the day's work. Also in late spring I'd finally managed to get that ditch around the house backfilled so I now had a level working area around the house. This made it easier to maneuver equipment so that when I collected the wood chunks at the end of every day I had a reasonably clean working area for the next day. I did it with the memory of that incident in the spring when I'd slipped off of the wall and tried to rearrange my sacroiliac. When everything was straightened up, I'd wash up in the lake or go for a swim and then have a hot cup of coffee and cook dinner. My, but isn't this interesting. Rather like life at the local hobo jungle, don't you think?

By this time the walls were up six courses, and I was beginning the seventh course. The height of the walls was becoming a serious problem, particularly when it came to putting up longer, heavier logs. It was possible with strenuous effort and a little assistance to get these logs up on the wall and once they were there I could manage them, but it was easier to have my neighbor with his cherry picker come to set the logs. But waiting for him to take the time to show up was frustrating and cost money. It isn't really necessary, but having some equipment around all of the time to put the log into place, mark it and then remove the log to the ground to cut it is a lot easier than marking, cutting and recutting the log in place. It's safer, too. Just in case I hadn't mentioned this, the logs often don't fit exactly right the first time you put the log in place. When you have proper equipment, it is fairly easy to put the cut log up on the wall, mark the places where the log doesn't fit and then take it off the wall and recut it on the ground. In my case I didn't have lifting equipment standing around, so the log would be put up on the wall, whereupon I would check and remark it and then roll it over and make any adjustment cuts while standing on the wall. I suppose I need not tell you that one has to be careful walking around on top of a log wall, but I had no choice since I didn't have scaffolding. I got so used to walking around up there that I didn't think about it, but having scaffolding and proper lifting equipment would have been a vast improvement.

Casey was over most days during the week, and he left when his owner came home from work in the afternoon. I liked having his company but worried about him going home on the county road where traffic sometimes went pretty fast, particularly on weekends when there was more traffic and weekend people were up. Some days, not infrequently, I would load him into the truck and drive him to the road leading to his house. Very quickly he got on to this taxi service, and in late afternoons, if he hadn't left, he would whine and look at the truck. Often I would then load him up and take him to his road, whereupon he would get out and trot on home without so much as a look back.

There were good days in June and a few bad ones, and since the good ones are mostly boring, I'll tell you about a bad one. Rain was a nuisance more than anything, and I would work right through most rains unless they were very heavy. I couldn't get up on the walls when it rained, but there were plenty of other things to do. The truck and the bulldozer, just to mention two examples, needed constant fiddling to keep them happy. On that day I was working on the bulldozer and had removed a bolt from the clutch housing for some reason that I no longer remember. What I do remember was that as I was handling it, the nut for the bolt dropped between the housing and the clutch. Dropping parts is not unusual and had happened numerous times before on practically every repair job I'd ever done. On this occasion after dropping the nut I crawled under the bulldozer to retrieve it. Not there. I searched around. Not to be seen. There were very few places where the nut could have fallen and be hidden. Yet the nut had disappeared somehow. I searched several more times. Then I noticed a two-inch-long slot in the clutch housing which was just a wee bit wider than the nut if you looked at the nut edge-on. It couldn't be, could it? You guessed it; the nut had somehow managed to exactly hit that hole and went into the clutch! I stared at the hole for a long while trying to calculate the odds of this happening or perhaps hoping the nut would come crawling back out of the hole of its own volition. It didn't and in a while I went and got a magnetic probe with which I fished around inside the clutch for an hour. I was unable to retrieve the nut, though I did manage to bark a shin on one of the sharp edges of the bulldozer. A thin trickle of blood ran down my leg.

I then quit in frustration and was heading toward my trailer for a cup of coffee when I happened to look up. Up in the air heading straight in my direction was a blue heron. Have you ever glanced at a situation and knew, just knew, exactly what was going to happen? Well I looked up and in that particular split second I knew that the heron was going to do exactly what nature designed it to do, aside from flying. The heron, in the event you weren't aware of this, has the habit of reflexively, oh how shall we put this, "lightening its load" when it is startled. This, of course, is so that it can avoid its enemies or perhaps make interesting designs on the ground. Whatever its intention, the heron flew until it was above me, suddenly pretended to be surprised, squawked as if startled and then cut loose a long stream of heron effluvia. I'm not sure whether the heron compensated for the wind, but I assure you his bomb load was headed straight for moi. I'm happy to inform you that he didn't get me or at least mostly didn't get me. Moving more quickly than I had all day, I dodged under a handy tree while the ground around was splattered with whitish heron stuff.

These events should have confirmed the notion that some days one should stay in bed. But I am stubborn and have never followed that logic, and so I stuck a bandage on my barked shin and went back to working. There was no way I was going to take the bulldozer apart. I started the bulldozer to determine if it would work. The clutch, not surprisingly, made strange noises and engaged poorly for several weeks. I was making a few strange noises myself just about then, so this was no problem. I continued to use the bulldozer and every time I did, the image of the clutch being ground into pieces entered my mind. But they must have made that bulldozer of very stern material because it never stopped working. Then one day the nut must have worked its way to the bottom of the clutch, since the bulldozer suddenly began working like its original self again.

Bugs

June is the month for bugs. In the warm hazy evenings, the very world seems to vibrate with a humming as if some great tuning fork had struck a tone of buggy life. There are a variety of bugs at my place. These don't all come out in June, but I'll try to mention some of them here. There are mosquitoes, naturally, but also alder flies in the alder bushes along the shore, crane flies, damselflies and occasionally stoneflies. Pine sawyers are my favorites. They weren't built for flying. They're able to fly just enough, it seems, to get into the air, buzz around blundering into things and finally crash-land. They remind me of Mr. Magoo. By the way, speaking of bugs, it's an interesting thing that the minute (even before that minute) you get a log house done, a small army of bugs and other unidentified creatures start tearing it down. They will eventually reduce the place to sawdust. I think you have to get used to that idea, and besides, you'll probably be dead and long gone before they get the job done. Now isn't that a cheery thought?

There are three types of bees at my house. The most noticeable are the bumblebees who take up residence anywhere it is warm and dry. This is rather alarming at first because to get stung by one can be a serious proposition if one is allergic to the poison. I'm not, and soon figured out that the bumblebees aren't very aggressive and mostly bumble back and forth from their food supply to their home in my logs. By the way, it may well be that I have more bees because when I planted what passes for a lawn, I included clover in the grass. The clover grows very well at my place, and the bees feed on the clover flowers. When my house was closed in, but not chinked and finished, the bumblebees found the insulated spaces between the logs perfect for their living quarters.

The problem was that some of them got in the house and there died since they bumbled around and naturally couldn't figure out how to get out. They were trapped, enraged and panicked, and they buzzed and bumbled until they got dehydrated. I found them dead on the floor. I didn't give this much thought at first, but as it happened fairly frequently, particularly at certain times of the year, I began to catch the trapped bumblebees and let them out. Just in case you find one and don't want to kill it, you catch it by putting a jar or a cup over it and then sliding a sheet of something under it. Also just in case you might be the stupidest person on the face of the earth, it isn't a good idea to pick a bumblebee up with your bare hand or even let your hand get close to an enraged bumblebee.

Then one day I found a big one that was dying on the floor. I picked her up in a cup and brought her outside. (I'm assuming it was a she.) She didn't look strong enough to fly away so I watched her for a little, admiring her black and yellow coloring, feeling not a little sorry for such an impressive thing expiring. Then it occurred to me that she might just be dehydrated, and I put a few drops of sugar water from the hummingbird feeder into the cup to see if she would drink some. The big bumblebee got the water all over herself, in a helpless fury, but then finally her little proboscis extended and she began drinking or doing whatever a bumblebee does to take in water. She drank for a good long while. I then set her down in a sunny spot and she sat there warming. Finally she buzzed off to resume her bumblebee destiny. After that, I put them out if they were merely trapped and tried to feed them if they were weak.

There are also yellow jackets at my place. These, I'm told, are imports from Germany. I didn't have any experience with yellow jackets prior to building my house. Then one day I was up on a ladder and felt something buzzing around my head and in my hair. I gave no thought to this, but waved at the offender as I worked. Whereupon having warned me, the yellow jacket attacked. You know, it's quite amazing just how intensely painful it is when a yellow jacket stings your neck, which one then did. The only redeeming aspect of this is that the intensely painful part doesn't last long.

Thus did begin my education concerning the yellow jacket. Now, I don't dislike your yellow jacket. But they are like some obnoxious and dangerous neighbor who insists on taking up residence just where you don't need him. While a bumblebee merely ignores you unless you sit on one, yellow jackets act as if they ought to live anywhere and you better not mess with them. Actually they don't attack at once, you know. They usually just buzz around a little, and then if you stay in their zone of influence one will eventually attack. Once a group of the little delinquents took up residence in my front door jamb. I never was stung by this particular family of fiends, but having them greet me at the door was too much, and I resolved to get rid of them. It took two days of water and chemical warfare before they were gone.

There are carpenter bees and carpenter ants at my place. Carpenter bees and ants are aptly named since they leave little piles of sawdust, which look to me like the garbage heaps of some diminutive civilization. They spend their lives drilling holes in and otherwise tearing down that which you have assembled. I have treated my logs but you can't get all of these bees and ants, and no doubt they will reduce my place to a pile of sawdust before I finish writing this.

Then suddenly one day hordes of very large (three-inch-long?) dragonflies follow me around when I cut the grass, picking off the mosquitoes and hovering in the hazy evenings in the thousands. I love these things. They are all eyes and mouth and wing. In good years there are thousands upon thousands of these and many thousands are killed on the county road where they hover in the heat over the asphalt. They are wonderful fliers but the speeding cars kill them. Cars are going faster and faster and more dragonflies die. I would only point out that this didn't happen as much in the days of slower cars and not at all, one presumes, with the horse and buggy.

In June fireflies are everywhere and mayflies begin hatching. Mayflies and fireflies are, of course, notorious for lust. Fireflies too, but for them, it's a cold sort of lust, mostly flash. At my place, the fireflies show up in late May, and in the warmth of June, the nights are full of them winking their little cold lamps on and off all over the wetlands and along the shores. Disgusting. It's sex, you know. But the mayflies make up for the calculating flash of the fireflies with their lusty columns of aerial mating. There are numerous (I was going to say four or five, but I really haven't counted) hatches of mayflies on the lake each spring and more as the summer goes on. They hatch on and off all summer but most of them hatch in June. That's why they're called mayflies. Of these, the most visible are large mayflies, *Hexagenia limbata*, I think. Hexs for short. These very handsome mayflies are the largest and hatch at the end of June and July. Along many lakes there are so many millions that the dead ones cover the roads and sometimes create a driving hazard. Around my lake the tourists and the drunken locals are the driving hazard, not the mayflies.

Once I stopped to get some coffee at the casino by Mille Lacs Lake. At the entrance to the casino the sidewalk was so covered with dead and dying mayflies that the gambling public was squashing them on their way in and out. And wandering around midst the people in front of the casino was a female dog, who obviously had puppies somewhere, and she was carefully lapping up the dead squashed mayflies on the sidewalk, while the casino patrons walked by ignoring her. Hey, she needed the protein and you take it where you can get it. I was never so desperately hungry to eat one, but it's a good thing to remember, just in case.

By the way, the Hexs are the biggest, but they aren't the prettiest. That honor, in my opinion, goes to a beautiful medium-sized mayfly commonly called (I think) in fly-fishing lingo the pale evening dun. These creatures sit like little beautiful, erect, yellow-gold jewels, part and parcel of nothing but themselves and their destiny, and you are nothing but an ugly human.

Then suddenly, for a few days, and especially nights, the bushes are full of big mayflies. The spider webs along the eves vibrate with struggling mayflies and the spiders get fat. In the tall trees along the rivers the cedar waxwings and other birds know that the hatch of these huge mayflies is on and wait expectantly. Why they don't get into the bushes and get them is beyond me. I suppose they want the large females with eggs. When mayflies are out you can't do anything without a couple of them riding along on your clothing. If you walk down to the shore on those days, you end up with dozens of the huge Hexs hanging on you like living ornaments. They don't seem to be much alarmed at the prospect of you squashing them. If you put your finger close to one, she merely raises her front legs. Then maybe she'll fly away, but more often not. It's a numbers game with them. There's millions, and a few thousand more or less won't make much difference.

On rivers and some lakes the trout go wild when these big chunks of protein hatch in late June. My nephew and I fish them in the hot sticky dark on a certain river in Wisconsin. We stand in the dark and swish, swish, swish, cast huge flies to the aggressive splashes of these fish. The normally elusive big brown trout suddenly become aggressive feeders, and the dark is punctuated with the "guuulps" and splashes of the big-bellied browns. If you manage to put the fly right and the trout takes it, there is a strong yank and the brown sulks on the bottom of the pool shaking its head, trying to get rid of the hook and get back to feeding.

I don't like to kill mayflies, no matter how many of them there are, so I try to carefully pick them off by their wings or, more usually, shake them off, whereupon they flutter off to the bushes to wait. When evening comes, the air is suddenly full of them, fluttering and disconcertedly bumping into your face in the gathering dark. And then they fly up in great columns of buzzing, humming, wildly living orgies of mating life. And down below the fireflies wink their lights and cheer.

Because there are insects, there are lots of bats at my place. The minute I had my log walls high enough, the local bat civilization decided that the spaces between the logs would be perfect as homes, apparently because these spaces were dry and had nice comfy insulation. I have had them ever since. Once while using the chain saw on the end of one of the logs, several bats staggered out of a hole, stared frantically around and one by one flew rather raggedly off in search of another place to hang for the day. On another location, while working on the roof I ripped up some tar paper and a bat that had been sleeping away the day fell out of the tar paper and rolled end over end down the roof for a couple of feet. I then picked up the poor bat with my leather-gloved hand and put him in a space between the logs. He was gone when I returned. By the way, bats are another instance wherein there has been a change in people's attitude during my life. When I was a kid we generally killed them and thought nothing of it. A badminton racket or other such instrument was generally used to kill bats. Then people began to realize that the bat is innocent and, further, catches a lot of bugs. Now many people put up bat houses in their yards. People still kill them, I suppose, but less than before. Of course one has to be careful around them; some have diseases. If a bat gets in your house, either pick it up using gloves or throw a thick, soft towel over it and return the bat to its mosquito-catching duties.

At the Common Ground coffee house, after the gig with Spider John Koerner, we could afford the coffee we drank and the cookies we ate and we built more tables that could be disassembled. With red-checkered tablecloths and candles on the nights when we had entertainment, the place looked somewhat like a nice coffee house: tables, candlelit atmosphere, a small stage and a lot of bad art on the walls.

This personal assessment of the quality of the art and my big mouth were the ingredients for the beginning of a simmering pot of trouble, as if we needed more. One night we were sitting around just prior to starting the coffee house with some of the members of the gallery board of directors. One of the directors, a lady who thought of herself as a great artist (actually she wasn't that bad), said we had to remember to turn on the security system for the gallery when we closed for the night. Apparently my mind was busy elsewhere and my tongue was left unattended. So without thinking about it I said, "Security system? Who would bother to steal this crap?" After the furor died down, we managed to get on with the coffee house for the night. But some of the board members didn't forget this remark, and it had bad consequences later.

Later the Veteran came in and sat at a table with some young women, describing to them the torturous artistic process of writing songs. He then got up and sang several, which reflected this torturous process.

166

To make matters worse, Lon gathered his little cadre of followers over in one corner and sulked for most of the night. Tom tried to get them to participate, but it was obvious that Lon wasn't going to be the center of attention in the new scheme of things, and he didn't like it. They started playing some music, and when we asked them gently to play up on the stage, they refused. One of the board members came in. He was a guy who actually was a good guitar player, although he played alone mostly. He went over and sat with Lon's group. This, I suggested to Tom, wasn't a good sign.

As if to cap off the evening a lady with a fairly bad drinking problem came in. She wasn't a regular but came in once in a while. She had showed up on her bicycle with a six-pack of beer, which she stashed in the alley and visited frequently. When she was sober, she was a good blues harmonica player and would play along with Lenny or one of the others. After Lon began his sulk in the corner, she showed up, almost fell over a chair and then stumbled around slurring her words. She tried to play along with several people, to no avail. Eventually she sat down in a dark corner weeping a little, muttering to herself and occasionally waving her hands in some imagined conversation with one of her demons.

The Bars of Grand Rapids
(and Other Topics)

In the 1820s, or so the story goes, the Anishinabe (Chippewa) found the slightly nutty and certainly flamboyant Italian Count Giacomo Beltrami floundering along, dragging a canoe up some mosquito-infested river in what would eventually become Minnesota. The count had started out with others in search of the headwaters of the great river, the Mississippi, and had abandoned them or perhaps they had abandoned him, tired of aimlessly wandering the unending ocean of forest, rivers and lakes. One imagines the Anishinabe, with their wonderful sense of humor, to have been greatly amused by our valiant and outrageous Count, he struggling along, perhaps singing Italian opera to preserve what was left of his sanity. Our hero came close but never did name the source of the Mississippi. (The lake he named as the source flowed north.) Or perhaps he did, but it wouldn't have been proper to credit it to a crackpot Italian. Whatever, he eventually went home to obscurity, and, in return for the amusement afforded by him, his name would eventually be attached to a Minnesota county.

I speak of the Count because that great river, the Mississippi, is the principal reason for the beginning of Grand Rapids. Timbering and mining and railroads and highways came later but the river was first. If you're looking for Grand Rapids all you have to do is follow the Mississippi River almost to the end of its northern reaches to find the city. Rivers were the highways of the early nineteenth century and the bigger keelboats and later steam-powered paddle boats could navigate up the river only as far as the place the French had named the Rapids Grande; the large rapids. The rapids was a stopping point, and it was here the city started.

Economy and History

Today Grand Rapids's image is of a small, squeaky clean, thriving city straddling the Mississippi. The great blue Blandin Paper building, hard by the river and belching white clouds of steam, dominates the landscape. Grand Rapids is the county seat of Itasca County, the word Itasca being a contraction (minus several letters) of the Latin veritas caput, which, if you spend the winter here, caput is the condition you may feel you have reached along about February. (I'm just kidding, the phrase actually means "the true source or beginning" as in the true source of the Mississippi.) One Mr. Schoolcraft, who is credited with finding the lake that is the source of the Mississippi, didn't like the perfectly good French name Lac la Biche (Elk Lake) used by the Chippewa who had guided him there. So he changed it, and since the whites wrote the laws and most of the history, it is Lake Itasca today. Oh, one other thing. Itasca County has hundreds of lakes, but Lake Itasca, the alleged source of the Mississippi, isn't in Itasca

County, it's in Beltrami County. What?! Just remember, it's the Mississippi they were looking for.

When I was building my house, there were three main hardware stores: Cole's, which was the one I liked the best; the L and M store; and the other one, which I didn't like. The Wal-Mart store generally marked the southern boundary of most of the city's commercial development on highway #169. To the east the community college established the boundary of development then. To the west commercial development extended a mile or so, finally petering out in the woods and swamps in the general direction of Deer River. There was a newspaper that purported to write the news and several nondescript radio stations. And of course there was the art gallery that held our coffee house, numerous bars and more numerous restaurants catering alternatively to the locals in the winter and, more lucratively, to the tourists in the summer. There was a library, half a dozen churches and a YMCA.

Grand Rapids feels that it is different in the sense that it never has been a town that was based solely on one of the three basic economic legs of traditional northern Minnesota: timbering, mining and tourism. Grand Rapids people have always worked in mining and still do, but today the economy is more based on the timber and pulp-processing business and tourism than at any time in the past. It seems to look upon itself as sort of the prosperous western, white suburb of the Iron Range.

Grand Rapids's history is inextricably linked to the timbering of the late nineteenth and early twentieth centuries. Most of the land upon which that timbering took place was stolen fair and square from the Native Americans, a story that, though interesting, is too long for even this diatribe. The white pine timber, deemed inexhaustible by certain newspapers of the day, was soon exhausted by the enthusiastic timber barons, who used the proceeds in very worthwhile endeavors, such as becoming drunks and building big mansions on the tops of hills in cities some place where the carpet wasn't rolled up at dusk.

Speaking of loggers in Minnesota, once in about 1980 in British Columbia, I was driving along, going who knows where, and up ahead saw an old man limping briskly along the road. Don't be ridiculous; of course you can limp briskly. We were about ten miles from any town, and he turned to watch me coming, so I stopped and offered him a ride. Said he lived on a homestead five miles from the road and was heading into town to pick up a few things and to go out dancing. We got to talking and it turned out that he was eighty-five and had worked in the pineries of northern Minnesota in 1915 until a log rolled off a stack and crushed his leg. This convinced him that timbering in Minnesota wasn't for him. He went back to BC and had lived his entire life there farming and apparently dancing with a limp.

Actually that snide remark about Grand Rapids rolling up the carpet at dusk isn't true. Grand Rapids, at the turn of the century, apparently consisted of the essential functions of a county seat, plus innumerable bars and other purveyors of liquid spirits, most of which stayed open late into the evenings. They certainly needed their recreation, such as it was, since the timber cutters existed in a very harsh environment. Many of the men who came to cut the timber were city guys and were neither dressed for the cold nor up to the conditions in the woods. Timbering was done in winter when the winter roads were frozen, and the colder the weather the better. Work started early on the dark mornings and it was no joke if, out of destitution, a person showed up without warm shoes or mittens. Many of the companies wouldn't supply the workers with even the most rudimentary winter garb such as warm boots or "shoe pacs" until the men had earned enough money to pay for the gear out of their wages. If you didn't want to work, that was your problem. Get out, and you had to get out on your own power.

So these men could perhaps be excused for their predilection for cheap whiskey and a little semi-violent fun at the local watering hole. But it is their descendents that I want to talk about now.

The Bars of Grand Rapids

I don't drink, having given up sloshing down the booze somewhere back in the '80s, but I very much enjoyed stopping into the bars in town on occasion. After trying a lot of the bars, I settled into stopping at a bar on Fourth Street more or less regularly. Please note I'm *not* talking about one particular bar here. The descriptions that follow are generic.

The bars in town serve the usual social functions of meeting friends and acquaintances, drinking and listening to live music. The music on Fourth Street ranges from fairly good to execrable, with execrable generally winning out. Most of the music is rock and roll or country, and the bands tend to make up for a lack of talent by the simple expedient of playing loud. To get an idea of how just how loudly the bands play, I can only describe it like this. If you stand outside in the parking lot in the winter, you can hear each song in detail without straining your hearing. You could, in fact, freeze to death out there and hear bad rock or country music the whole time you're freezing, so that your last memory might be the off-key strains of some country song. A nice thought, eh?

Occasionally there are bands with real talent. In these cases the audiences respond enthusiastically, although a good deal of the enthusiasm is due to the consumption of alcoholic beverages. Usually band members drink while they are playing, so that as the audience is getting drunk, the band is getting somewhat lubricated also. It occurs to me that one of the attractions of playing in a rock band is that it is the one occupation in which you can legitimately drink on the job. I have seen certain band members drink and enjoy themselves, but I haven't seen anyone get so drunk that it affected his or her music. Of course for most of the local bands, it would take a lot of alcohol to have a deleterious effect on the music.

The bar that I stop in has changed ownership since I first stopped there. Originally it was a traditional working man's bar to which locals repaired after work, most still in their construction duds. It was virtually identical to the bars in the town that I grew up in. These bars were there to serve the working men of the town and essentially were stand-up drinking establishments. Social activities in those bars were limited. Most have changed so that now bars cater to more diverse groups, particularly the very young crowd and women. Most have followed the lead of other bars, which have plugged cable TV, electronic games and other media forms into the bar. They cater more to the social instincts of their market, with drinking as the lubricant. There are differences between the bars. Two bars on the south of town serve the younger crowd and several others, such as the Legion, serve an older clientele.

Aside from that, there isn't much difference between bars, really. They look the same and smell the same because, generally, the same activities occur. They may start out with a nice bathroom, but in a while the bathrooms slowly degenerate into soiled and smelly little rooms with broken toilet lids and graffiti-laden walls. At their best they are utilitarian places, although sometimes the utility is a bit confused. A waitress told me she had to go to the bathroom one busy night and discovered a man and a woman standing up in a stall, fully engaged as it were. The guy's pants were visible under the door, on the floor around his ankles! The barmaid had to go badly, and having no particular concern for the niceties of the situation, yanked open the stall door and ordered the drunken couple out so she could relieve herself. The man, being jammed into the stall with the woman, had difficulty bending over to reach his pants and almost fell into the space between the wall and the toilet, before regaining his equilibrium and slinking unrequited out of the bathroom.

Speaking of bathrooms, much of the graffiti on the walls concerns sex or allusion to sex, occasionally with illustrations of male and female sex organs. Oddly, quite a lot of the graffiti also refers to one's place of origin, as if that were of some interest to the general public. This is apparently because Grand Rapids is a big tourist area and also a point of transit for travelers. Having gotten to the wilds of Grand Rapids, certain parties feel the need to record this fact. Allusion to sex in the graffiti isn't unusual, but what is interesting is how amazingly, boringly rudimentary and mundane most of it is. One would think that with all of the information available about sex and the sex act, this graffiti would be somewhat elevated in style and content, but it isn't. Of course that is likely the nature of graffiti the world around, so I suppose one shouldn't be surprised about it at home. Originality isn't one of the principal characteristics of the purveyor of graffiti in these bathrooms, but then it isn't in bars, either, because no matter how they start, they eventually look the same. .

There are two rooms in the bar that I go to. The front room has the bar and offset kitchen. Most of the bars serve food, and in my bar the kitchen serves hamburgers, steaks, salads, pizzas and other dishes. The quality of the food, I might say, is not bad, and it is even better if you're drunk. I ate there once, and then I saw the cook and haven't eaten there since.

The front room of this bar has half a dozen dartboards, a foosball table, a game of electronic golf (of all things) and, more appropriate to the twentieth century, an electronic race car driving game. It also has two pool tables and I have wondered why this is so. True, the pool tables are very busy most nights. The players take the game seriously and some are skillful until they imbibe too much alcohol. But the pool tables take up a lot of room, and it would seem they don't make the bar that much money. Further, the pool cues represent at least the potential for use as a lethal weapon, though I have never seen that. I suppose there is some business reason, but maybe it is just that one of the owners of the bar likes pool. Or perhaps they are a holdover from traditional bars that I grew up around. Still, one wonders whether the pool table will be around in the future. It occurs to me that a simple reason for the attraction of pool tables in a bar is simply that with the tables people have something to stand near or stare at, a focus for their attention.

In the back room of the bar there is a bandstand with stage lights, a small dance area and an area for more tables for dining. This space is essentially just a large room with tables and the small stage on one end. The atmosphere, such as it is, is created by turning down the lights so that it becomes a darkened area full of tables. On each table there is a round glass globe for a candle, which is lit each evening and left to burn. These candles are a nice touch and contribute, along with the turned-down lights and incessant smoking, to the atmosphere of the place. On a busy night the oxygen level, not to mention the visibility, shrinks considerably, though strong duct fans and filters do remove some of the smoke. One really wonders whether those candles will be around in the future. I hope so.

The dance floor is busy most weekend nights. More women dance than men, and the woman are the more enthusiastic dancers. If there are groups of women and if they can't find a man to dance with (or don't want to), they dance with other women. Often there are four or five or more women dancing in one group. They certainly do seem to be enjoying themselves and letting off steam, but they are usually more energetic and enthusiastic than good at dancing. Every once in a while one sees a good dancer with a natural rhythm, and I have seen several couples dancing the Lindy (I can't describe that) very well. But most dancers move jerkily like the actors at some over-sized hyperactive puppet show.

To quote one of the lines of a popular song of a few years ago, it's only rock and roll, but I like it. On a good night the bar is jammed with people, the band is blaring and clashing, like a demented bear in a tin can factory. There's usually a nice comfy haze in the air, the warm smell of popcorn, food cooking, sweat, stale beer, cheap women's cologne, cigarette smoke and lots of loud laughing in a mini sea of red faces. All in all, not bad.

But there is also a pervading sense that things could be a lot better. This is because in Grand Rapids the bars are the principal option for socialization. More specifically for the type of socialization that might result in one's pairing off with someone who could heat up the blood. And only a portion of the population wants to go to the bars. It strikes me that in many respects the innocent socials, dances and church functions of earlier times were better at putting men and woman together in a such a way as might generate more little Finlanders or Norwegians.

Drinking Habits

During my life, the drinking habits in these bars have changed. In the last twenty years or so there has been a serious increase in the crackdown on drunken driving. This has, without doubt, caused rather serious changes in the size of the drinks served, not to mention drinking patterns of the patrons. In the old days you could go to the bar, get drunk out of your mind, drive home and probably no one would stop you. In the hometown of my youth, the police would often merely give the drunken person a ride if they knew him. This doesn't t happen now. In every case the drunken driver will get hauled off to jail. Further, getting arrested for drunken driving most likely will deprive you of your license, not to mention a lot of money. Locals try to put a somewhat macho spin on getting arrested for drunken driving by calling them "whiskey tickets," as if they had just gotten a ticket for doing forty in a twenty-mile-per-hour traffic zone. In fact, I talked to locals who still drive after their licenses are pulled. One of them, a swarthy, chunky guy with a full beard, had inconveniently lost his license due to driving while drunk in front of some local police. This didn't stop him from driving. He would drive all the way from Grand Rapids to Hibbing on gravel back roads to visit his girlfriend. He just drove like a bat out of hell. They call these back roads "whiskey trails."

The dram shop laws, which increased the liability of the bars, were a big factor in the change in bars.

Previously, many of the bars would serve large strong drinks. It wasn't unusual in the municipal liquor store bars of my youth for the bartender to fill the drink glass full of whiskey and then just top it off with a drop or two of water or whatever you added to make it a mixed drink. When I was in college we would often stop at the muni and have a couple of drinks to get a buzz on, prior to heading out to the party or whatever damned fool thing we were into. After a number of persons had gotten blind-drunk and had killed others, and the bars had gotten sued successfully, the state passed laws regarding the bar's responsibility to the patrons. No more getting people so drunk they would fall off of the stool, as I've seen several times. Darn. But these laws were needed and they have saved a lot of lives. Not enough, however. When I was a youth in my town a fellow got extremely drunk after work one day and then tried to drive to his home a mile or so away. En route he ran head-on into a young man who was driving home. In those days no one used seat belts if they had them, and air bags weren't available. The young man died there. Naturally the drunk didn't get hurt at all. He served six months in jail.

Smoking

Most people in Grand Rapids do not smoke now, but practically everyone in the bar smokes. There is a trend now toward nonsmoking in the rest of Minnesota, pushed by the health lobby, but that trend isn't in effect yet in the bars of Grand Rapids. Personal health doesn't enter the equation for most people who frequent the Fourth Street bars. If you want to smoke you can buy cigarettes in the bar dispensed from vending machines. At current prices you insert four paper dollars and yank on the knob of the particular brand to get a pack of your favorite poison. To prevent juveniles from sneaking in and buying cigarettes from the machine, the bartenders have an electronic clicker to release the cigarettes from the machine. Thus the present dispenser is a combination of the old and the new—a mechanical dispensing machine that is partly electrical. I doubt these things will exist in the future.

Incidentally there are free paper book matches in containers at the bar. I know this fact is huge in its insignificance, but I'm curious how long bars will offer free matches. Who in fact knows how long smoking in bars, and thus the paper matches, will be around? Frankly I rather like the fact that one can acquire the means to burn something down right at the bar. I think we are seeing the last of the paper matches and that is the reason I want to mention them. Even if smoking in bars doesn't last, most people now use plastic disposable lighters, which have become cheap, usually under a dollar. When I was a kid a lighter was a shiny metal thing one had to fill with lighter fluid. Often people decorated their lighters and most people hung onto them like some valuable bauble, which, in a way, they were. Everyone smoked. At that time, it was common at parties in the suburbs to put out a large serving bowl of cigarettes. A guest merely had to take a cigarette from the bowl to light up. Apparently if you were going to die, you were considerate enough to want your friends to go at the same time. Smoking is an addiction, and they didn't used to call cigarettes coffin nails for nothing, but it is also a social phenomena. This can be illustrated by the fact that if you happen to be sitting at the bar and light up, others suddenly, and one supposes unconsciously, also get out their cigarettes and ignite.

As for my predilection for the tobacco leaf, I started smoking a pipe when I was twenty years old and continued to smoke various forms of tobacco off and on for many years. Finally a girlfriend got me smoking cigarettes (I blame her), and when we stopped seeing each other I continued smoking cigarettes for a year. Then I quit and now no longer smoke. It is a very difficult addiction to lose, though, and even after several years, if I go to the bars and see someone light up, the urge to do the same suddenly rises from the synaptic depths of my brain. I quit permanently when I met a gentleman (who's now smoking in ethereal realms) who could barely talk and was on constant oxygen, and also saw numerous older people dragging around oxygen tanks. Not smoking is hard, poor me, and no fun to boot, but of course emphysema and lung cancer aren't fun either.

Women and Men

There are a lot of good-looking women, even beautiful women, in Grand Rapids, but on Fourth Street the women are generally more robust than beautiful, and that's being generous. Any moderately good-looking woman is in demand. There are a lot of Finnish people in Grand Rapids. Most of the Finnish women are sturdy and stubby, built like inverted triangles. Rounded hips seem mostly nonexistent on Finnish women. They are generally intelligent, cheerful and durable, though, which they had to be to survive in this area.

On Fourth Street there are more men than woman. As with the women, the men in Grand Rapids are generally good looking though they tend to be on the beefy side. Thankfully the guys who really work outside tend to be of moderate and cheerful temperament. They come into the bar in their work clothes to drink and smoke and socialize. Many work in the woods, but the number of people who actually work out in the big woods is miniscule, since mechanization allows one person to do a lot of work, compared to earlier times when work in the woods was labor-intensive. Most of the people who work in the woods are independent contractors who feed the great paper- and pressboard-making machines in Grand Rapids and other places. Essentially they are factory workers.

The fact that the local guys tend to be on the beefy side seems to result in their being impervious to cold. One fellow who drove a truck basically wore no coat, a shirt and sort of a furry vest for the winter. He was perfectly comfortable at ten above zero (Fahrenheit) and could have worked indefinitely at lower temperatures with nothing more than the addition of gloves and a hat, which he generally eschewed. One rather stolid person who plays pool on Fourth Street drives a bulldozer and works at it in the open air most of the year, warm or cold.

Fortunately, most of the locals are fairly good humored, even when they have imbibed quite a bit. Winters are long and cold and summers can tend to be wet. Though the construction workers are hardy and resourceful, this area isn't an easy environment to work in and the men could be excused if they liked a little rough fun. And after tangling with whatever I was doing during the week, I wasn't interested in going a round or two at the bar.

Waitresses and Bartenders

If it's busy, the waitresses (I've seen two young male waiters in all of the time I've gone there) are bustling around. When it's not busy they're bored and, more importantly, not making any money. Some of the waitresses are good looking and a few are really pretty, but most are plain. Some work as a waitress to augment their income and a few are going to college, usually the community college. Many of them work for a few weeks or months and then they're gone and another young eager girl takes her place. They pass their time waiting on tables and talking and, when they can, lighting up and smoking. If they work on Fourth Street for a while, they assume a bored demeanor and acquire a pallid complexion, like someone who hasn't been out in the sun enough.

It is understandable that they are bored. If you are like most people and head for the bar on weekends, the bar is usually a somewhat pleasant social occasion, even if one goes there every Friday night. But if you're working in the bar from mid afternoon to one o'clock every night, and see mostly the same tired people, nothing is novel about the experience. Oddly, though, in their days off, the waitresses generally show up at the bar. Apparently the application of liquor renders the atmosphere interesting enough to spend more time there.

Practically all of the bartenders are women, and it's unusual to see a man tending bar now. When I was young, it was assumed that only men could handle the fights that occurred with some regularity. That has changed. I mention this because one of the reasons I kept going to the bar on Fourth Street was that I seldom saw a fight there. This was an attractive feature of the place, since it's hard to enjoy yourself when you constantly have to be alert for the prospect of a tangle with some massive slab of beef commonly known as a local. I related this fact to an acquaintance who claimed that she visited bars infrequently (the drunken sot), but whom I happened to meet there one night. She said that as soon as I left, a huge brouhaha broke out or erupted or whatever happens when a brouhaha is occasioned. The fight, as with most fights in bars, was over very quickly, but there was much blood and yelling. Once in another bar, I saw an obviously drunk man hall off and punch his significant other, laying her out on the dance floor. Now you must understand, that civilization having advanced considerably, the law is that in such a case, the cops are suppose to be called and the guy is going to jail. But no, the bartender merely jumped over the bar and indignantly told both of them to leave the bar if they were going to act that way. The couple then left with the woman holding her head, the man presumably looking for a place where he could punch his wife in peace.

Alternate Impulses

There are gay people in the bars on Fourth Street. This shocking observation is only mentioned because it seems to me that it would be interesting to come back in fifty years to see if there were more gays acting out the type of semi-sexual activities straights act out. They aren't obvious about it, but it's becoming less hidden, and I don't see any particular response—negative or positive—regarding it. Once I saw two women holding hands and fondling each other in a darkened corner of the dancing area. There is little overt activity of this sort although dance-floor flirting and occasional fondling is fairly common. Once I saw two men actually dance together. They are known to be gay men and generally tolerated, if not accepted. I've never seen it but if two men kissed in some dark corner that would probably not generate much attention so long as they didn't make a habit of it. If two men started kissing at the bar, I'm sure the action would suddenly change. If it were two women, however, most of the men would… cheer. (Kidding.) Actually I think there is much more bisexual female activity in the recreational mode than is obvious. Or possibly I'm hoping.

It is interesting to note that until relatively recently, say up through the '80s, the sources for prurient stimulation in places like Grand Rapids were relatively limited. A few girly magazines, some books at the library and, if one wanted, one could hunt the big cities for such literature as may get the blood boiling a little. If one were really adventurous one might perhaps head for Minneapolis or Duluth and procure a prostitute. Stimulation for woman was limited mostly to some rather tame novels or such banned written material as could be quietly gotten hold of. As with the rest of the country, most people in the north had relatively little exposure or chance to act out on their, shall we say, alternative sexual experiences in their formative years. In general the Protestant view of the world held sway in Grand Rapids and the rest of rural America.

The Internet and satellite and cable TV have permanently changed this. This is a recent and gigantic change. Since the net, the general population has been exposed to an explosion of anything (and I do mean anything) related to sex or anything else, for that matter. Want to learn something about necrophiliac bisexuals? Want to look for housewife swingers who only do fat black men? Look on the net. Cable TV, video movies and especially the Internet, all of which can be watched in the privacy of one's own boudoir, have given people ideas. With the prospect of pregnancy not much of a threat because of the pill, and the only other constraint on human behavior being the threat of various socially transmitted diseases, people are free to try things unfettered by previous social constraints. Throw in a little booze and people will, rather more commonly than is thought, try out the things they've seen on TV. Most people might try a same-sex experience once or twice and then drop it because they don't get much kick out of it. But some continue, and there are more bisexual and homosexual activities than previously. The action on Fourth Street hasn't changed that much that I can see. Still, even with the increased exposure to alternative sexual ideas most people mainly head out to the bars when they want a little social jolt.

I knew someone who came home unexpectedly and found his wife in bed with a girlfriend, trying out a few alternative sexual ideas of her own. This ego-shattering experience resulted in him walking out and not going back. Good for him! I didn't inquire as to what happened to the woman. Probably nothing. She likely just went on with her life after a little fun in bed. Of course some more flexible and adventurous men would have jumped in with the women in a Grand Rapids ménage à trois, but perhaps the shock of finding his wife in bed with another woman was too much for him.

In a mildly sexual early example of use of the Internet, I am familiar with a person who had a good knowledge of the Internet and a blonde wife. His Nordic-appearing wife dressed up in sexy lingerie and then assumed her best innocent, come-hither look. He videotaped her and set up a business on the Internet selling lingerie. He had the world as his market. A simple and, I might say, brilliant idea. Apparently the world has an appetite for scantily dressed blonde women, since this effort was very successful and his wife now drives a Mercedes. The mind reels to think what she's wearing under those heavy northern Minnesota clothes while driving that thing around. This fellow found economic salvation in technology, and lots of people, including me, have had their lives improved through the use of computers and the Internet.

Gambling

There isn't much gambling on Fourth Street, or rather there is a lot of low-level gambling. The most pernicious form of it presently is pull-tabs, which are basically numbers gambling. It wouldn't be a problem if the people just bought a few pull-tabs now and then. The problem is that people come into the bar after work to enjoy themselves, get drunk and spend a considerable portion of their paycheck on pull-tabs. Their prospects of making anything is virtually zero if they play any length of time. Some of the money from pull-tabs goes to the State, and thus pull-tabs are a tax on the people who work.

Cliques

Grand Rapids has the usual small-town cliques, and locals seem, naturally, I suppose, to differentiate themselves from tourists and other outsiders. Years ago, when I was first in Grand Rapids, I was talking to a man in a restaurant and during the course of the conversation he asked me where I was from in the Cities. Since I wasn't dressed materially different from him I wondered at the time how he knew I was from the Cities. Believe me, it's easy. Tourists are the easiest to spot, not that they give a rat's ass about that. One blonde woman with whom I was talking and whose occupation is that of a hairdresser looked me up and down for a few seconds and pronounced scornfully, "You're not from here!" in what amounts to a sentence and permanent condemnation. I was heartbroken. The fact that she is a dumpy, aging, small-town hairdresser whose social life consists of heading out to a dirty smelly bar seemed not to limit the finality of the sentence. Now, now, Mike, your scars are showing.

Entertainment Outside the Bars

Reading over what I have written so far, I see that one gets the impression that not much else goes on in Grand Rapids. Many younger locals might agree, but to be fair there are many things to do in Grand Rapids that don't involve alcohol. The city has invested a tremendous amount in facilities for their citizens. For example, there are many athletic facilities and events, particularly through the public schools. There is the art gallery, a semi-public facility, of which not every town has. The community college has excellent facilities for theater and music and is very generous in making them available to the public. There is a good community theater and, in the summer, a riverboat theater. Also during the summer, the annual Judy Garland festival is held, the best aspect of which is that it occurs when Grand Rapids looks clean and green. Not that Judy actually spent much time here. I don't know what got her family to Grand Rapids, but apparently the shock of spending part of a winter in town convinced her that sunny Hollywood was the better place for her. This shows a great deal of sense.

Then there are the fairgrounds, the site of concerts, foot races and car races. The LePlante family puts on a bluegrass festival every summer at the fairgrounds. People gather for a long weekend, camp out and play music. It's free and lots of fun.

Native Americans, Immigrants—and Others

Whites and Native Americans constitute the two principal racial groupings in Itasca County. Most local Native Americans are Anishinabe, more commonly known as Chippewa. In recent history (since whites arrived) they have lived on reservations in what amounts to a modified, American-style apartheid.

Movement of the Natives to reservations occurred across the county and was intended by whites to get the Native Americans out of the way while whites exploited resources. In Grand Rapids and Itasca County the issue of jobs and resources was settled early in the century and hasn't changed a lot. Whites exploited the forest and controlled and exploited the enormous mineral resources of the county. The better-paying jobs in the county are virtually all held by whites, although there are many people with some Indian blood in them. Presently the major employers in the county are the Paper Company, the county itself and the cities and other governmental institutions, including the State of Minnesota.

The Chippewa have managed to survive very well on and off Minnesota reservations by hunkering down in a corner (in this case in the woods) and making do with what they have. Recently the growth of casino gambling has changed the situation somewhat. In Mille Lacs County and other places the casino is the largest employer. This has also changed, to some degree, the way Indians see themselves, and it will be interesting to see if the growth of casino employment has a significant impact on the overall assertiveness of the Anishinabe.

Immigrants

When the ancestors of these locals—immigrants—came to northern Minnesota, expectations were simple. Most of them came thinking that with a lot of work in the place they would live well, if not get rich. Most were farmers, and the prospect of getting 80 or 160 acres of good land in a new country when they came from an old country with little bits of worked-over land must have overloaded the circuits of their imaginations. They did pretty well. They built their saunas and log barns and houses, cut down a lot of trees, picked more goddamn rocks than there'd been in the old country, planted their gardens, sent their kids off to little schools, laughed together at the weddings and cried together at the funerals.

It didn't last. Clearing the land for farms in northern Minnesota was hard, grinding work and the land under the trees wasn't that good. Not like out on the prairie or even in the hardwood forests to the south where there was two or three feet of good black dirt to start with. They looked around when they occasionally went to town, and to some of them, town looked good compared to the hard, cold work of the farm. Then by ones and twos they moved themselves and their saunas to town. Some who had come so far had caught the wanderlust and left for jobs in bigger towns and cities. One could find the bones of the places in the woods they had left. You sometimes come across the remnants of whole communities who moved here, thrived for a while like some little constellation in a big dark woodsy universe, only to dissolve slowly, torn by the lure of other bigger urban constellations. Even now, north of Aitkin I drive by an old homestead, bleached and aged, old house and barn, dark against the winter white and then light against the dark green summer. Sometimes I have stopped to look at it or take a picture. The old homestead stays year after year and you know it will eventually fall, but like the people who built it, that homestead stands quietly and stubbornly, refusing to succumb.

Italian Immigrants

There are a lot of Italians in Grand Rapids and on the Iron Range. What combination of events prompted an exodus of Italians from sunny Italy to the USA, not to mention the ice-cold wilds of northern Minnesota, should be fodder for someone else's story. But the fact is a considerable number of them ended up in (oh, the horror) gloomy, cold, hard rock Hibbing. They ran the warehouses in the mines, so I'm told, and produced some of the most gorgeous women this, or any place, has to offer. And despite the climate, Italians have done very well in northern Minnesota, certainly a tribute to the adaptability of the human species. I'm not sure what the relationship is between genetics and climate, but I think the Italians, being slightly darker in complexion, suffered in the cold and dark of the Iron Range. After all, they had lived for some thousands of years in a sunny moderate climate. I knew a pretty Italian girl who worked on Fourth Street for a while. She had bouts with mild depression over the years. I explained my obviously brilliant theory about people who came from sunny areas not doing well in the dark and cold of northern Minnesota. She thought about this for a while and then left town. For California, I heard, with her boyfriend. Don't tell me I'm not convincing. Or perhaps it was my breath.

Speaking of genetics, after I was in Grand Rapids for a while, I began to notice that there were a lot of red-haired people, more than one sees in the normal population. I would mention this amazing fact to people and they were stunned at my brilliance. You could see they were impressed by the way their eyes took on a glazed look and by how they would be suddenly struck with the desire to talk about fishing or perhaps their hubcap collection. I'm hurt by this indifference, but I tell you, there are more red-headed people, adults and children, in Grand Rapids than elsewhere. So there.

July

At the beginning of July a large log that I was trying to put up on the wall slipped down a ramp and tried to squash my leg. The log weighed about eight hundred pounds. I was using a cant hook, which is a heavy wooden bar with a hook attached to it that is used to roll and otherwise maneuver logs. I had been trying to roll one end of this log up a ramp, hoping to get it leaning on the wall so that I could then tilt and maneuver it up onto the wall. This particular evil log didn't slip when I had the cant hook on it. Instead I stopped somewhere in the process, stuck a pole between the log and the wall as a brake and looked away. Incidentally, just in case you were unaware of this, stopping in the middle and looking away is almost always a bad idea if you're putting a log up on a wall.

I heard it when the log was some way down the ramp building up a nice head of steam, heading for my foot. I jumped when I heard the braking pole hit the ground (at least that's when I think I jumped) but the log still clipped my feet and flipped me between the log and the house. It didn't get me, but it was close, and it happened because I was tired and working on a hot day. Or it happened because I didn't want to wait for suitable equipment to lift the heavy log. Or because I was building a log house. It missed injuring me, except for a scraped elbow, and that is the significant point, though the vision of a crushed leg left me shaky for half an hour.

I must have really wanted that log up on the wall because I then went over to my neighbor Dale's and begged his help. I would occasionally prevail upon Dale if I didn't want to wait for mechanical assistance. He grumbled a bit, but I know he liked the break from his duties at the resort. At any rate I went over whining for help. We stood that log against the wall, secured the middle and slowly tilted it up and over until it rested on two of the walls. From there I could maneuver the behemoth to where I needed it. When we were done, Dale and I and Casey sat midst the sweet smelling balsam shavings, me sipping coffee (Dale didn't drink the stuff), talking and laughing, Casey eying the doughnut I was eating. In a little while Dale left and I went back to work.

Ten in the morning, the day is heating up. A few darkish looking clouds are hanging around off to the west over the gray-blue lake. Rain later, maybe. But the logs are dry so I climb back up on the wall to where the log is resting some seven feet up, walk along the wall balancing and carrying the cant hook, my tool belt around my waist.

I am wearing my old tennis shoes, which allow me to walk more easily along the logs. I don't have any scaf-

folding and I don't think about slipping or falling anymore. I grab the log with the cant hook, slide it a little to even out the ends. No logs are perfectly straight. The bow in the log is the crown. All of the crowns should be the same when you set them. I prefer the crown being straight up since that's the way I learned it. I roll the log back and forth, feeling its heavy, green weight and the curve of it. When I have the crown up and have centered it over the log below it, I stick a couple of log dogs (log dogs, cleats, homemade or bought; they're all wood or metal devices designed to keep the log from rolling) on each side, to hold the log in place. The crown is up and the log shouldn't move now.

A sweep of rain hangs over the lake and a freshening breeze blows the pleasant rain smell toward me off the lake. A few droplets spatter the log. The logs are as slippery as greased pigs if they're wet, so I climb down. Casey comes over and wants to be petted. We play around a little. On the ground now and it's raining a little harder. I get the step box that I stand on for low work, take the level and draw a vertical line on the middle of each end of the log, aligning the center of the top log with the lines on the others below it. The sky opens up and we head for the trailer.

The start of July found me continuing to slave away on the walls. I felt like a character in some movie with a bad plot and a doubtful ending. I was rapidly running out of materials and money, though I had enough to continue to the end of the month. After that I didn't know what I was going to do. At least I wasn't going to freeze to death. July started warm and in fact the temperature rose to about ninety degrees for a day or two. Those days were the exception, though, because that summer was a very cool and rainy one. In fact the two years that I was working on the house were marked mostly by rain and cool weather. There was a large volcano eruption in the Philippines, which I'm told caused this weather. It was so cool and wet that local people had trouble growing their gardens.

But July finally warms up to full summer. The catbirds cry in the bushes and all of the now juvenile birds follow their parents around, clumsily flying here and there, whining and begging for food. Rather a bit like I've done on several occasions. Lots of vacationers are at the resorts, and people who have cabins are here during the week. When I first came to the lake there were only a few year-round homes on Moose Lake. There are a lot more now, but mostly the lake has summer cabins. I'm only reluctant to guess how many because... I don't know. (Hey, if "I don't know" was good enough for Galileo, it's good enough for me.) There usually isn't much waterskiing on the lake until July for the simple reason that the weather and water are generally too cold for these types of activities. Vacationers are louder than locals. If I didn't know what day it was, I could tell by the noise level. At first this annoyed me, but then I realized that these people weren't harming anything. Weekend people come up to enjoy themselves and blow off steam. After a little fun and shouting they calm down and then leave, and the lake is quiet again.

The Fourth of July was like any other working day for me except that being at the lake was a minicelebration anyway since people celebrate the Fourth by shooting off fireworks. The Fourth of my youth was a big celebration in each small town, with parades and visits to the cemetery and old soldiers firing rifles over the graves, followed by ball games and other public activities. Somewhere along the line people mostly stopped that sort of celebration. When I first owned my land at Moose Lake, just a few people would ignite their fireworks around the lake on the Fourth. Since you couldn't then acquire fireworks in Minnesota of a size calculated to make anyone ooh or aah, these were paltry displays. Usually the Cities were the only ones to put on a display of high-explosive fireworks so you had to go to some specific location to see a real display. The government apparently thought too many citizens might blow themselves up if everyone got their hands on these explosives.

They are no doubt right for once, but at any rate, the Fourth of July at my lake has, of late, become a fireworks festival. Now there are enough explosives around to launch an attack on a small foreign country. For a week or so there is the constant popping of firecrackers around the neighborhood. Then for several hours on the evening of the Fourth red and white rockets sizzle up into the evening sky, exploding like flowers over the darkening forest around the shoreline of the lake, all amidst a cacophony of whistles, bangs, dogs barking, children yelling, panicked loons and confused herons flying back and forth looking for some safe haven from the racket. The air smells of sulfur and burning paper. Sometimes a great large one will go up and then the boom echoes and rolls down the lake-strewn countryside.

The rain stops. The sun is huge and hot. Humid. I am sweating already. In order to scribe the whole log, I have to get the top log so that it is resting several inches from and parallel to the one below it. I scribe around each end where it is resting on the crossing logs, changing the scribe width since one end of the log is fatter than the other end. I get the chain saw, check the fuel. It's low, so I go get the gas can to fill it; the gas can is almost empty. I set it by the Buick for tomorrow's trip to town, finish checking the chain saw, hunt around for my safety glasses and foam ear plugs, climb the ladder and gingerly check the surface of the logs. When I'm satisfied it's dry enough I remove the log dogs and roll the heavy log over toward me so I can get at the scribe marks. When I've got it tilted toward me to where I can cut it comfortably (as comfortably as one can get standing seven feet in the air balancing on a log) I reset the dogs.

The chain saw roars to life and I carefully make the first half-moon-shaped cut. It's hot, I am sweating now, the ear plugs itch my ears, pieces of wood chips fly and chain saw smoke fills the air around me. I try to be careful and finish cutting out those scribes. Finally I dance the blade end around in the cut to clean each one up and get off the wall. Down on the ground I grab the big log with the cant hook and roll it over. It settles into the scallop-shaped cuts with a nice thunk and I slide it a bit to align the marks. It is now resting roughly parallel with the log below it. I check the gap between the logs. One end is good but the butt end gap is too wide, so I grab the cant hook, roll the log back to where it was, insert the dogs again, climb back up on the wall and cut more. I'm sweating profusely. Done now, back down, roll the log again. Thunk. The gap is pretty good now and ready for the whole log to be scribed. Casey whines at me; it's time for lunch.

A hot sun now. I head for the lake, take off my shoes, walk into the cool, clear water, feeling the sandy bottom between my toes and splash and wash the sweat and sawdust off my face and head. Heaven. A loon moans somewhere in the distance. Casey dabs at the water gingerly

*with one little paw, retreats and watches me from shore,
a quizzical and dubious expression on his face.*

When I was building my house, like some traveler of old, I mostly lived under the great blue sky of the day and the wondrous vision of the starry nights. One of the nice things about living out under that huge night sky in the north is that you see the stars and the planets undiminished by city lights. Clear nights—summer or winter—the constellations twinkle in the clear air, as if they are asking to be looked at, and the milk from the breast of the wife of Zeus (the Milky Way) is a pale white swath across the heavens. Once Cecilia from Chicago, who was visiting, pronounced them the "brightest stars" she'd ever seen. They are bright, but it is an amazing thing to me that the closer we are to moving out into space on a permanent basis, the less people have a personal experience with the night skies. And it seems likely that in the future people will be less and less familiar with the starry nights, since we live in lighted warmed buildings in large brightly lit cities.

UFOs and Why Things Are the Way They Are

I kept my camera loaded most of the time in the hope that I would see an unidentified flying object, otherwise known as a UFO. Alas, I must report that I never did see a UFO, although once I did see a rather strange-looking tourist. UFOs showed up in my time, or rather the idea of UFOs became popular in my time. (No, I haven't gone totally off the deep end. Hang in here; eventually I hope to make a couple of points.)

There are several reasons for the rise of the UFO phenomenon in the United States. First there was the idea. Actually the idea of unexplained phenomena of all sorts has always been around. Where UFOs are concerned belief, not proof, seems to be important, there being a lot of the former and less of the latter. Rather like religion, most people, when inquiring about this subject will phrase it by asking whether you "believe" in UFOs. The increasing sophistication of radio, television, movies and other media during and after the middle of the twentieth century were the broth within which UFO interest developed. Radio plays like H. G. Wells's "War of the Worlds" jolted the consciousness of the rubes in the Rubvilles of the world. Media attention about UFOs began after World War II with newspaper stories about "flying saucers." Later a movie about a couple who were allegedly abducted by aliens created quite a stir. Then in the 1960s the United States and other countries began to venture rather timidly into space.

But it was the entertainment industry who quickly figured out that interest in UFOs and other mysterious phenomena was a perfect tool for extracting money from people's wallets. And presently there is a flood of popular twaddle about UFOs and aliens of every sort. Today the whole media-driven idea of aliens has sunk so deeply into the psyche of Americans that someone pointed out that the erstwhile aliens look surprisingly like the popular versions invented in the early movies.

I jokingly mentioned UFOs to a friend one morning over a delicious breakfast of burned toast and greasy eggs. A scruffy fellow with a stringy beard chimed in and said he'd seen one up toward Effie.

"You can ask my wife if you don't believe me," he said. Actually it occurred to me at that moment to speculate upon aesthetic features of any woman who'd take up with this specimen.

Repressing this thought for the moment, I went on. "Why?" says I. "Did she see it too?"

"No, but she said I was white as a ghost when I got back home," said this perfect example of the hoi polloi. He added that he had stopped his car to get a better look at the object, whereupon it disappeared over the horizon of scrub woods and swamp in the general direction of Effie. Of course scrub woods and endless swamps are exactly where your average UFO hangs out, as anyone knows. No doubt they're entomologists and biologists interested in swamp gas. Perhaps the interhuman interactions of the Effie trailer park population are of interest to them. I've got it! Maybe the bar in Effie is actually the bar at the edge of the universe and some of the aliens stop in for a bump occasionally. That would certainly account for some of the people I've seen there.

A cloudless hot sky. The sun doesn't seem to have moved. Lunch is two sandwiches, a can of soup and as much water as I can drink. A sweet, smoky smell of my balsam-peel lunch fire hangs in the air. Dessert is half a chocolate bar. I chew slowly, enjoying the sweet chocolate taste. More water. Casey finds a squirrel to annoy and I lay back, close my eyes, listening to some gulls over the lake. In the distance a truck is coming on the county road, faintly at first then whizzing by and down the hill to the west. I think about a girl I knew in college. I wonder...

I wake up in a while, slowly, like a bubble rising to the surface of a pond. Outside the balsam-peel fire is still smoldering so I puff it up and brew a large cup of very strong coffee. When it is done I sit waking, sipping the acrid coffee, feeling the caffeine jolt hit my veins.

I feel pretty good, change the blade on the chain saw and check its engine and chain oil. It is hot but less humid now. I get the scriber and slowly scribe both sides of the log, check it so I can see a continuous blue scribe line. Up on the wall I leave the chain saw balanced on a log, roll the log back over to where I can cut along the lines. Log dogs in. Some tourist women are standing on the county road above, watching. One waves, I wave back and jerk the chain saw to life.

I stand on the log, slowly backing up, tracing the scribe line with the tip of the chain saw, cutting about four inches deep. The saw vibrates and jumps with each knot. Cut a foot or two. Back up. Cut again. I'm sweating again but it's not really that hard. Just be careful. Humming some tune while I feel the vibration of the saw. From an opera, of all things. Puccini, I think. Glad it's not Pagliacci. Halfway down the log the chain saw smells a little hot. Shut it down. Take it down. Get the damned earplugs out of my ears. The blade's a little loose anyway so I get the tools, loosen it and re-tension. It was okay, a little oil spatter on the hot muffler. Up on the wall. Cutting again. In a while I'm done with the first line. Off the wall to let the saw cool down for a bit. We'll take a break.

Casey's got a chipmunk trapped in a little log pile. He'll kill it if he can. I call him over. He doesn't want to come. I yell at him. He comes reluctantly, glancing back at the pile. The chippie beats it.

The point of all of this UFO talk, aside, that is, of keeping you awake, is the connection between technological change and changes in people's lives. These things have been happening throughout our history. A good example of this in history is the Reformation. Luther wrote his ninety-five theses, thus initiating the Reformation, seventy years after the invention of the movable printing press. The press allowed relatively easy distribution of the theses among the population, some of who could actually read. Had he nailed his ninety-five theses to the church door seventy years prior to the invention of movable print, things may have turned out differently. Or maybe instead of ninety-five he might have only managed...nine. Just kidding. Sometimes these things are not so clear at the time. I don't know if, the day it was ready, anyone knew that the movable type printing press was an earth-shaking change. And anyway it didn't shake the earth; the ideas that it printed did.

Look at my world. Things are roiled up now and it isn't really surprising, considering the technological changes just in my lifetime. From the middle of the twentieth century we have confronted the impacts of the contraceptive pill, the transistor, television, computer chips, the discovery of DNA, the mapping of the human genome, cell phones, communication satellites, virtually instant worldwide communication, nuclear weapons, space travel, the bikini (for which I am extraordinarily grateful) and last, but hardly least, the Internet.

Two of these developments led to changes of historically epic proportions. The first was the contraceptive pill, which is used so universally that it is now known as *The Pill*. The pill freed women from the inevitability of having children. Its use began quietly in the 1950s, but not without strident opposition from the Catholic Church. It has never stopped affecting the world. For virtually the first time in the whole of human history, women could take charge of their lives and could plan a professional career or plan families.

The other big invention, the transistor, led to the computer chip, which led to... everything else. No really. Every gizmo of our time, from home appliances to the stuff we launch into space, runs on chips. Further, the computer chip very rapidly led to changes in communication that radically changed people's lives all over this world. In the middle of the twentieth century only a small portion of the world's population had access to such a rudimentary communication device as a telephone. By the turn of the century virtually every person in the world had a cell phone attached to his or her body. And if they couldn't afford a cell phone, they could go to a library and for virtually nothing talk to someone on the other side of the world on a computer, assuming they had a library, that is. In the middle of the century, events were filmed and mailed back home to be viewed in newsreels at the movie theater. By the turn of the century we had virtually instant communication from anywhere in the world. As I am writing this, reporters are going along on a certain military excursion we happen to be engaged in to keep the world safe for democracy. Their reports are, for all intents, instantly beamed back to the public whose need for such stimulation is exceedingly great.

The sun hangs unmoving, yellow-white, glaring hot and no wind. But I feel okay so I check the gas and oil on the chain saw, get up on the wall, grab the log with the cant hook, pull the dogs, roll the log some more so I can cut along the other line, and put the log dogs back. It doesn't want to stay. I maneuver it around and talk to it a little. Nice log, I say. Pretty log. It doesn't want to stay just at the angle I want it. Ugly misbegotten son-of-a-bitch, I say, and put dogs on all four corners. It stays. I am cutting the other line. Thinking nothing. Humming. Still with the Puccini. About halfway through now. A few sparks...sparks... Sparks! Shit! Stop. A nail. I look closer. An old nail. Damn. The chain is dull. I'm stopped.

No sharp chains so I grab three of them, fire up the truck and head around the lake to old Krantz's to get some chains sharpened if I can. Casey jumps in and leaning on me watches the road like it's the most fun thing he's ever done. Krantz totters out of his neat house in that careful way the very old walk. He is frail but clear-eyed. I explain what happened. He smiles with the bemused look one sees in babies and the very old. He sharpens one chain while we talk a little. I leave the rest.

It's four o'clock, sun is still hot. I'm back on the wall, cutting. Slowly I cut the rest of the line. Suddenly I'm tired and a little weak. My lungs don't like that chain saw smoke. Off the wall, I drink some water and heat another coffee. I sit staring stupidly, my hands tingling from the chain saw. Coffee done, I get the saw again and moving down the wall fairly quickly put perpendicular cuts in the long lateral scribed and cut piece so I can chip it out with the adze. It's knotty and obstinate and the chunks come out grudgingly. I swing the adze harder. When they do come out they fly at me. One chunk cracks me in the leg. I ignore it.

Casey stops what he is doing and stares toward the road. I can't hear anything. In a bit a car comes by. His owner's car. He looks at me and then trots off toward his home, gone for the day.

I finally finish chipping out the chunks, pull the dogs, down off the wall, position the log and roll it over with the cant hook. It settles onto the log below it and over the crossing logs with a satisfying thunk. It's five o'clock. I rock it back and forth to see how it fits. It's okay, but not great. Enough for now. Not that much left to do on this log. I can finish this thing tonight if I work at it. Suppertime now.

To paraphrase an old joke line, I've got some good news and some bad news for you. First, the good news. As a result of these inventions, many aspects of our lives were abruptly changed for the better. I'll give you a couple of small examples. The first occurred in 1978 or thereabouts. In those days I worked for a consulting firm. We produced reports containing much wisdom; the sort of wisdom generated when someone paid us. Lots of people then used Dictaphones, but we would write our reports by hand, in script. When the report was sufficiently scratched together we would give the draft to the secretary who, depending upon her (all of the secretaries I knew were female) mood, would get around to typing a draft. We would review the draft and, if we wanted to move paragraphs around, take a scissors, cut the paragraphs out of the draft and tape them in their proper places, writing any additional material around these paragraphs and then give the document back for retyping. The spell-checker was a person. If you wanted a really clean document one person would read it aloud to another person. If you made a gross error, you either had to retype the page or the whole document.

Then one day the office got the first computer, some word-processing software and voilà! You could put a document on a disk, move things around, alter it any way you wanted, check the spelling and print as many copies as you needed. And, if you could type, you could do it yourself. The world had changed.

In the 1980s I had one of the first portable cellular phones. They were huge. I mean physically huge. In addition to the phone, which was about the size of a traditional phone handset, you lugged around a large battery pack and other accoutrement. Still, when they first came out, having one was a novel and big deal. I had an acquaintance who was a rather pompous salesman who drove a huge black

Lincoln. When he went to someone's house to make a sales call, he would phone his office and tell them to call him in a few minutes. Then he'd leave the window of his car rolled down, go up to the house and knock on the door. When the person came to the door his car phone would ring. He would then make a big deal of having to go answer his mobile car phone, this to impress his client.

In most of this world, at mid-century phone service was spotty and local. By the end of the century you could call virtually anyone, from anywhere. The computer chip made communication by telephone relatively inexpensive and fairly easy. Cell phones are everywhere. I wouldn't be surprised if eventually cell phones are implanted in people's bodies, in some Cyborg future version of the eternal communicant. By the way, one problem in this for movie buffs is that the movies of twenty years ago had references to phone booths. In the near feature, few people will know what a phone booth is, so I will tell you. The phone booth is a small enclosure holding a public phone. You get in the phone booth to make a phone call (or to change into your Superman suit).

Which brings me finally to that crazed adolescent giant, that child of the military, that spawn of the zero and the one, the Internet. One day you were making a complicated (and expensive) phone call to another town, and the next day you could dial up someone on the other side of the world for diddly, using the net. Most of the population now regularly communicates across the country and the world, sending back and forth anything that can be digitized, occasionally including something important. All of these things at least arguably made our lives better.

The bad news is that a whole lot of people around the world don't like it and they don't want to talk about it.

Some of these societies have been, as one wag suggested, dragged kicking and screaming into the seventeenth century. Progress in knowledge frightens them for the simple reason they don't think it progress. A big part of this is that men identified it immediately as a threat to the power they have over women. Lots of religious fanatics yearn for the good old days when men were men and woman were their property. And they'll kill you to prove their point. A friend of mine says that it is a conflict between modernity and anti-modernity. (Or whatever the opposite of modernity is.) The inventions of modernity bypass their traditional modes of control. This angers them and they fight back. The world is still male-centered and they have had this power for a long time.

Of course some of them may have just been objecting to some of the seamier aspects of the net. Seamy, steamy, vicious and just plain crude are the grist for the net's mill, the stuff that pays the bill. Presently you can find anything on the net, residing there under the protection of the First Amendment to the U. S. Constitution. . Bomb making, slavery, child sexual exploitation, it goes on as far as the human mind can take it, in whatever direction the human mind can take it. I hardly think the Defense Department had that in mind when they pushed their little baby out into the cold cruel world.

But take smut for example. It is interesting to note that the greatest technological change in the Internet came from; you guessed it, pornography. Certain people realized immediately that one of the easiest ways of making money from the net was via porn. But to email the sort of video that was sellable as porn, there had to be improvements in data compression so that one could send the large amounts of data that make up the video. I am told that the online porn industry was largely responsible for this. Today online porn is a billion-dollar industry. Probably that will be pocket change in the future.

Of course the Forces of Darkness (I just had to use that phrase) recognized the potential uses for the Internet virtually immediately. The law of unintended consequences is never more clearly illustrated as when one examines the uses of the Internet. Terrorists latched on to the net like it was a long-lost brother and the perfect vehicle for remaining anonymous while attending to their nefarious duties. One of the curious effects of the net is that, whereas previously every little crackpot had to work in relative obscurity, or at least expend a lot of energy gathering together like souls, he now has the perfect vehicle to find every other crackpot in the world and still remain anonymous if he wants. Search engines on the net allow every individual to find other individuals of like mind, no matter where on this earth they are. This is of course good for you, but it is also great for your neighborhood nutcase. He can toil in his cubbyhole happily communing with other warpies, dreaming about making his little warped world into a large wonderful warped world.

Eventual outcomes are not clearly identified. One could argue, I suppose, that the Internet could have some therapeutic effect, that these people would live out their lives being able to foam and spout and this foaming will somehow modulate their impulses. Pardon me if I am a little cynical here, but somehow I doubt that. The jury is still out, but at best, as my daddy used to say, the results could be good, bad or indifferent. Presently good, bad and indifferent are all there on the net.

Evening. The sun is still well up in the sky but a mountain of a thunderstorm is rapidly building north of

me. Pretty on top but a little ominously dark at the bottom. It's still hot, though, so I wade out in the lake, dive in and wallow around for a while. Dinner is four or five pieces of rather greasy fried chicken, boiled potatoes, a half stick of butter, five pieces of bread, a can of pop and an ice cream bar, which I got at the resort to the west. I'm lethargic from the day and the heat and the food. I know what to do but when I try to do it I seem to stare stupidly instead of actually doing anything. My elbow aches where I landed on it. So I use the time to clean up some wood chunks and straighten up tools.

I look at the log. It seems to fit okay but it is binding in four or five places. I get a pencil and mark those spots and try to roll it over. It doesn't want to roll now that it is in place. I hang on the cant hook and curse at it. It rolls. Dogs in.

That thunderstorm is now a huge mountain, cracking lightning coming this way. The cool air blowing out from under it refreshes me. I quickly get the tools under shelter and watch as the dark, hairy cloud line of the storm marches in. Presently the storm is on me with a wild gust of cool air. I get in the little trailer. All the trees bend, the rain really starts now, lightning cracks close by with a boom of thunder and I jump a little. I don't like lightning. The storm passes and the thunder is now booming south of me. I relax and start reading a little.

When I wake it is dark and quiet with only an occasional faint rumbling of distant thunder. The air smells wonderfully fresh with just a hint of balsam in it. Crickets are cheeping and loons are hollering all down the lake. I roll over. Back to sleep.

Okay, okay, I'll get off of the techno-babble and just tell you the significant things that happened celestially at my place. Actually the first was the fact that the summer I was working on my log cabin it rained a lot. Every damned cloud that came over thought it expedient to deposit rain on my project and me. There was mildew a quarter of an inch thick. And that was on me; the house had more. Thus it was considerably surprising to me that it was dry somewhere else. So dry that large forest fires apparently were erupting everywhere in the western United States and Canada. For days a cloudy pall hung over the area. I was used to palls personally, so I didn't think much about it. The smoke was thick enough (and you thought I wouldn't get to something celestial) so that one could look directly at the sun at midday. Which I did, and in fact took some pictures. But I didn't have a good zoom on that camera and the magnificent pictures of a big red ball in the sky turned out to show a ridiculously itty-bitty red ball. I was devastated.

Two comets passed our way in those years. The first was Hale-Bopp, which showed up in late winter and was clearly visible in the northeast on late evenings or during very early mornings for some weeks, moving to the north-west after it had looped around the sun. I had not seen a comet before, and spent many minutes standing out in the cold looking at it. I also looked with a pair of binoculars and the telescopic sight on my rifle. With both it looked bigger. Speaking of how big it was, here is how you can figure that out. Hold your arm up toward the sky at full length and then hold your finger and thumb about three inches apart. That is about the amount of sky that the visible comet covered. Not that much. Or at least that is the amount I could see. The tail of the thing extended a lot farther, and one could see that faintly in the clear night sky of northern Minnesota. In the Cities this tail wasn't visible, or at least I never saw it. The arrival and eventual departure of the comet was widely reported and followed, but there was not the mystery that such a celestial object would have generated in olden days when they didn't know what such an object was. Actually we're still trying to figure out just exactly what a comet is made of. Apparently the current thinking is dirty ice ball. Very romantic.

As Hale-Bopp passed, a group of just-the-teensiest-bit-misguided cult people somehow convinced themselves to commit suicide en masse, apparently on the insane belief that when they died, they would ride on the comet up to the mother ship. I get a very tired feeling every time I think of this again. Anyway they did it, and I don't remember how many there were, but they're gone. Hopefully they were right and made it to the mother ship. For sure they're dead.

The second was Shoemaker-Levy, a comet to which the term *awesome* could rightfully be attached were it not for the fact that the word is rather commonly associated these days with such important phenomena as professional athletes. This comet broke into pieces and seven of the pieces hit the planet Jupiter. I think it was seven. I assume you can look it up if you think it necessary. For the first time, a considerable part of the whole world watched this colossal impact in a fairly close approximation of real-time. Real-time. A phrase that has wormed its way into the lexicon. Unreal-time apparently being that time spent waiting for something significant to happen. Rather a bit like reading this, isn't it? Anyway the whole world watched comet Shoemaker-Levy hit Jupiter. One impact area was bigger than the United States but basically looked like just a large blotch since the planet's surface is gaseous and not solid, and the impact was rather like punching a pillow. Still it was a great big blotch. After the blotch, we all went back to doing what we were doing before.

We also had an eclipse of the sun that summer. It was a sunny day and the eclipse caused the day to get somewhat dark. Considering the parade of rain clouds that passed over, it's a wonder I noticed.

Northern lights happen so commonly in northern Minnesota that various literary journals and such name their compendiums for these phenomena. Very many nights, particularly in winter, one sees them, mostly as a glow in the northern horizon, but sometimes very bright with wavy streamers. One night in winter I came home from the coffee house late in the evening. The northern sky was glowing white. All was silent except for an occasional muffled crack as the lake made more ice. The snow crunched underfoot and the air was bitingly cold. Suddenly a bright wall of light stood in the north, then wavy javelin banners shot overhead, all silent and wonderful. Somewhere to the north a wolf must have been watching and started a low moaning howl of appreciation.

Late afternoon, the next day. Still warm, less humid. I've fixed a tire on the Buick, peeled another log, and ran errands in town. I finish the log, trimming it, adjusting the fit, stapling insulation into the lateral groove, finally pinning it down, banging in the foot-long nails I use for drift pins with a small sledgehammer. One more log done.

At the Common Ground coffee house things were…percolating. On the positive side, we had managed to get a number of first-rate entertainers to come to our coffee house. We had been concerned that it might be difficult to get good talent to come to town. We were wrong. Shortly after the Koerner gig and by some means not completely clear, we were fairly besieged by performers who wanted to make the Common Ground one of their stops. Of course it helped that we split the gross receipts with them. Sally proved to be pretty good at tracking down talent, not that she needed to do a lot after the word went out that our coffee house was a paying gig. She was a professional in her working life, and when talking with people, she had sort of a nasally officiousness that seemed to work with the performers or their representatives. Tom had made the comment once that if we could get a certain well-known Twin Cities performer, we would have reached the top. Apparently Tom had seen him in person in the Cities, and since this fellow had appeared on TV, he was thus a figure to which we could strive. So I asked Sally to track him down if she could. This took about two days. Certainly he would come and play for money.

In one case, however, it didn't turn out well. I had heard Ramblin' Jack Elliott, liked his music, and since he was a well-known figure, we thought we would try to get him to come to Grand Rapids. (He was a big deal and later won a Grammy award.) Sally dutifully spent some days tracking him down and eventually made contact with the promotional office that managed his performing schedule.

Grand Rapids? Sounds okay, we'll get back to you.

In a few days, and after a number of phone call negotiations, including his scheduler's demand that we provide hotel accommodations, Sally announced excitedly that we had scheduled the great Ramblin' Jack Elliott for a particular date. By the way, Ramblin' Jack was not only known for his rambling, but also well known, early in his career, for the consumption of liquid refreshments and who knows what else. He and a lot of other would-be stars were then hanging around Greenwich Village. (Including, by the way, one Robert Zimmerman, aka Bob Dylan, from just down the road in that frozen rock pile known as Hibbing,

Minnesota.) Apparently Ramblin' Jack consumed rather too much on a daily basis because he began to be referred to jokingly as Stumblin' Jack. I might add that, considering the amount of mind-altering substances consumed in those days around the Village, to stand out in this regard is quite an achievement. And having done my share of stumbling myself, I can relate.

At any rate Jack was going to stumble over to our humble environs. A major figure in American music! Wow! Then one day Sally was talking with Jack's representative and mentioned Minnesota.

"What do you mean Minnesota?" says he.

"I mean Minnesota. You know, Minnesota?" says Sally. "You know, east of North Dakota?"

A momentary silence. "I am aware of where Minnesota is," Jack's guy said, an alarmed tone in his voice. "It's not Grand Rapids, Michigan?"

" No... not Grand Rapids, Michigan. Grand Rapids, Minnesota."

"Where the hell is that?" the man said coldly. "I can't even find Grand Rapids, Minnesota, on a map. We thought you meant Michigan. The east of Wisconsin Michigan," he said, with rather more sarcasm than seemed necessary.

So that was the end of that deal. But really, Ramblin' Jack should have come anyway. The people here were so starved for first-class performers in those days that they'd have jammed any place that Jack Elliott stumbled into.

On the negative side, Lon continued to act like a spoiled child and mostly sulked or gathered his little group of followers in one corner. Any pretense of civility was gone. Lon and his wife and the rest of their little group would come in and then go sit in a corner, talking and laughing and ignoring the rest of us in an adult version of a schoolyard game. If you didn't know what was going on, it would have seemed a normal situation, but it wasn't normal. It was like one of those marriages where the participants act normal, but everyone in the family knows the marriage is over, and you are just waiting for the judge's gavel to crack.

August

August passed slowly. A dream time. Exhausting long days. Boats on the lake. Faint joyous breeze drifted sounds of children screaming and playing away the hot afternoons of their innocence at the little beach along the county road to the west. A summer lake smell. The sun burning and burning, high and white in God's own steel-blue sky, settling late, hot and red, west in the evenings over the burnished, golden lake swells.

All of the machinery was working pretty well. The pumpkin-colored Buick purred straight down the hot highways, ripping off the miles with no complaint, while my sunburned arm hung out the window. I jammed the old brown truck over the gravel roads, bounced it down my rutted driveway, dragged logs here and there and generally abused it. It kept going. But I was out of logs, mostly out of money and out of energy. Every day was a long weary slog through hot, muggy, raining weather and endless work. Cut and lift, sweat, eat and sleep, daylight at five-thirty in the morning, still light at nine-thirty in the evening.

I am so worn. I'm on some sort of treadmill and the treadmill won't stop. Even a nap in the middle of the day doesn't take away the weariness. How did people do this?

How did people work from dawn to dusk? I stare stupidly at the work. Try not to look at the whole job. Just work at the task I have to do that day. Peel a log. Scribe it. Cut the ends. Start the chain saw. It's out of gas. Get the gas tank. That's out also. Forgot to get the gas. Battery's dead on the truck. Nope, battery's not dead, it's in the bulldozer, remember? Forget the chain saw. Peel more logs. You have to do them anyway. Wait until your break to get gas at the store.

I make a list of things to get done every day. An idiot's list. Two or three tasks on it. I can't seem to concentrate on more than that. Just get the first thing on the list completely done and then the next and then the next. In the afternoons sometimes I go down to a resort to the west of my place to have a pop and talk to the genial proprietors. Sometimes when it gets really warm, I wade out into the lake and swim around for a while to cool off.

Then I ran out of pine logs, but I looked around on my land and found several pine and a couple of cedar trees of sufficient size. I cut them and attached a cable to the logs. The Allis bulldozer yanks them out of the woods like nothing. Cut and lift, the sun hangs up there endlessly. Christ I'm tired.

In summer every bird in the north is screaming at the top of its lungs at the first glimmer of daylight, which seems to occur approximately ten minutes after midnight. Upon rising the first thing I would do was boil some water for coffee. When the water was hot I would make a cup of coffee, drink a little and walk to the lake with the coffee and a small towel. At the lake I would splash water on my face, towel off and then sit for a while sipping coffee, listening to the loons and quietly contemplating the still lake.

If I were out of bottled water, I would just boil lake water. In the spring I actually preferred it since it was extremely clear and tasted fine, which water from a plastic jug doesn't. However in summer, when the wind was up the lake, the lake water would be turbid. Once I tried straining the turbid water. It worked, but it was more trouble than it was worth. One of my neighbors, a great slab of a man, said he'd drunk water directly from the lake many times and "it din't bother me ta'll." Not withstanding this attestation as to the potability of our lake water, I always boiled any water that was headed down my gullet, especially from the lake.

I don't want to give the impression that I was totally bereft of conveniences. There was a small refrigerator, a propane stove, even a phone and small television (that received two channels) in the camper, all of which worked fine. But I intentionally simplified my life during this period so that my diet and other activities were simple. Thoreau, get out of town. Incidentally, I just finished a book about John Muir, he of the Sierra Club. After telling you what a great guy I am for living very lean during my period of building the house, I discovered that Muir hiked in California for many years, climbing mountains and glaciers, sleeping out in the weather. And he did it all while eating nothing more than dark bread and tea! He apparently thought nothing of this, since he made no particular emphasis upon his limited diet. I don't know whether he supplemented this diet with other foods, though one supposes he did. Further, according to him, he was also very healthy during this period.

Mostly I ate fairly well, but being in a hurry, I made a mistake that I regretted. I was in the habit of buying chicken, which was sold cheap in town. (Until the producers found they could sell it for more in Russia.) I would cook the chicken with potatoes, which were also cheap, and whatever seasonings I had, in a sort of pot-au-feu. The whole mess I would then wolf down for my evening meal.

One day I was impatient to eat my usual dinner of chicken and vegetables and bread. I must have eaten the food before the chicken was done because in the middle of the night I woke up with that oh-so-absolute feeling that what I ate was going to revisit the world. For the remainder of the evening I was either crouched over a bucket or sitting on what passed for the toilet. It was two days before thirst drove me down the road to fill up my water jug, whereupon I staggered back to bed and remained there for another day before I could sit up and then eat some soup. It was three more days before I was more or less back to normal. I had no phone then and no one showed up to visit, and it occurred to me that this little episode could have killed me and I wouldn't have been found for a week or so.

Then one day in August I suddenly realized that I had an awful craving for anything green. Remember I had no garden at this time. Once on a trip to town I bought some green beans and ate most of them raw on the way home. This I concluded was indicative. A friend had some land on the north edge of Grand Rapids where, in those days, he and his family camped on weekends. He had planted a large garden and when I told him of my greens deficit, he said I could take what I wanted from the garden. I settled on turnip greens. I would stop on my way home and pick the fresh turnip greens, trim them, wash them in the lake and then stew them in my pot with the other… stuff. These turnip tops completely satisfied my desire for greens, and I was soon back on track. I continued to get greens from his garden off and on when I felt the need.

By the way this friend had a lot of old machinery on his land and some old semitrailer boxes with large white sides. Some local teenagers had taken to hanging out there, doing whatever teens do. Apparently one felt the need to publish his views, because on the white side of one of the trailer boxes he had, in a fit of the ultimate rebelliousness, spray-painted the words, "I love satin." For some reason this alliterative misuse struck me as hilariously funny. I must not have laughed for a while and my laugh impulses had built up some, or maybe it was the fact that I had slept on mangy cotton on a very narrow bed, because I laughed until tears ran down my face. It doesn't seem that funny now, but you know, it's the truth; I too, rather like Satin.

Then one evening Tom and Will came over. We sat in the evening on chunks of wood, midst the peelings and the sawdust and with the sweet smell of a smoldering pine-bark fire, talking, drinking cups of my bad coffee and waving away the few gnats. Tom looked at my walls and asked me how many courses I was going up. Eleven, says I. "Well, then," says he, "you're just about done with the walls." And I realized right there that he was right, and for some reason the energy began to flow back into me, and we laughed and joked while the great big, huge, red summer sun slowly sank in the west, a hot red ember glowing a long while in the haze on the edge of my lake and rim of the world. That night I slept like a rock, and the next day my sister from Dallas sent me a check, so I kept going.

Housecleaning

Late in August. Since the great bear chase I hadn't seen the Big Long-Legged Bear much. Mostly he was a cautious bear and only once, just at twilight again, I thought I caught a glimpse of him moving through the brush on the side hill next to the county road. Then one day I was generally schlepping along, working at the house, I don't remember on what. I looked up from what I was doing, and there was the bear walking calmly, but with a peculiarly determined look about him, down my driveway, in the middle of the day. This was startling, since as I have mentioned, the bear usually didn't come out until nightfall. Mother Nature is a maaad scientist, and she made the black bear for the shadowy woods and they usually take advantage of darkness. But there he was, walking down my driveway in the middle of the day, headed past my house. I decided not to interfere, and anyway it would have been hard to interfere from where I was cowering in the house behind a door.

After the bear had passed, I emerged and as I considered returning to work, I heard a ripping and tearing and the sound of branches breaking. These novel and interesting sounds were emanating from the general direction of the old bear den, which hadn't been used, that I knew of, for several years. The ripping and tearing sounds and the sounds of material being thrown about continued for some minutes. I thought about going down and checking this noise out. Being fond of living, I did not, and instead confined myself to returning to work for the afternoon.

The next day, hearing nothing from the general direction of the den, I slunk down the trail, very cautiously, as you might imagine, even considering that I had heard nothing from this direction since the previous day, peering around the bushes at the old bear den. A tremendous amount of dirt, roots and other material lay on the short incline down from the den. I cautiously approached. One does not want, in that circumstance, to see two beady bear eyes staring out of the den. It was empty. The bear had totally cleaned it out, biting off roots and tossing the material and loose dirt out for a distance of ten to eighteen feet. Some of the roots that the bear had bitten off were more than an inch in diameter.

Apparently black bears do this to their dens in late summer and in fact may dig or clean out several. I think I'm one of the few people who've been there while it was happening. It was nice to have the bear considering the reuse of the den. I went back to work, but then thought better of it, got out the shop vac and cleaned up a bit.

And then one day in August I finished the walls. This milestone would have passed with little celebration or notice. But the friend who had come down with his backhoe the previous summer stopped in about then, looked at the eight-foot-high walls and then at me and wryly said, "I didn't think you'd do it when I came down last summer to dig those footings." It was true, the walls were done. Eleven courses were done and that was all I did, and that fact led to one of the mistakes that I made.

Most of the mistakes in my life have been due to not thinking and planning. You don't have to plan every single thing that you do. In fact it's stupid and stifling to do so, but when you undertake something, have a plan, for God's sake. Believe it or not, I've always been pretty good in that regard. This particular mistake became obvious much later when I started cutting the rough openings for the windows. I realized that I couldn't locate them high enough for my height. You can't cut the top log, and because I am a very tall person, that meant the windows ended up a little low for me. I was staring at the top of the window when I looked out while standing up. And by then I'd already started framing the roof timbers. I couldn't, rather I wouldn't, stop and add courses to the wall. Furthermore the front door and the sliding glass door had to be reengineered to make them fit properly. All because I didn't have enough log courses. Yeesh! The windows are perfect for a person of normal height. My house would have worked a lot better with twelve log courses. Everything came out fine in the end, but it would have been better with a little proper wall planning.

By the way, when you plan the windows, you put in "drift pins," foot-long nails in each course of logs next to the window locations. And of course over time you lose the marks that show where those drift pins are. When I was cutting the rough openings for windows, I hit several of these steel spikes with my chain saw. Not a pretty sight. Sparks and pieces of metal.

At the Common Ground we had lost our common ground. There was no longer any pretense of civility between Lon and his group and the rest of us. Oddly the tension of pretending to be civil had seemed to depress him, and now that he didn't need to pretend anymore, he seemed happier. The gallery put on one of their art shows at which Lon was asked to play his guitar for an hour. He had done this on a fairly regular basis and was very good at the jazzy guitar noodling that these events warrant. Strangely, he and I talked during a break as if nothing were going on.

This state of affairs affected Glen, who was one of Lon's cadre and who reacted to these events by steadily retreating from the rest of us. Not that he didn't try in his own way. He had a good heart. At least I think he had a good heart. I was never quite sure what was in there. Sometimes the calm place that you see in a person is merely empty space. Maybe there was more to him and less to us. But at any rate Glen came up with the idea of trying to have a sort of a circle discussion with a "talking stick" in which each person is given a chance to speak his or her piece. He said this was how the Native Americans did it. We were having this discussion about how to have a discussion and bring peace, when Bonnie the drunken lady staggered in again and wandered around breathing various fumes on the participants.

Some guys from the local alcohol treatment center came in on a Saturday night with their minders. Our island of rum-free virtue was apparently their award for being good during the week. Minnesota is of course the land of ten thousand treatment centers, and Grand Rapids, being interested in commerce, has taken to this new market with an enthusiasm born of a thin economic base. Alcoholism and drug-related treatment programs are huge markets for the state. The treatment center at Hazelden was one of the first in the country, and people drag their abused bodies and minds to that place and others for help. This is a phenomenon of fairly recent vintage. When I was young there were your town drunks or just people who hid a bottle. It was well known that this illness was around, but the approach to it was a morality tale. Alcoholics Anonymous is a fairly recent phenomenon founded in the twentieth century.

On that evening we did our usual thing, talked and played a few tunes. A version of Bob Dylan's "I Shall Be Released" seemed to strike a chord. One of the inmates, if that is what one is supposed to call them, was a black guy who we encouraged to sing along. He did but couldn't carry a tune. He yodeled on painfully somewhere between registers. Amazing, a black guy who sang off-key. Well I never.

In the summer we see more juveniles at the coffee house. It is the perfect place for them, since adults run it and the teenagers can come in and act like adults. Some of them read their poetry, and though most of it is bad, it is generally very intense, being generated by various teenage hormones. The teens seemed to respond well to the coffee house, spending their time talking quietly or sometimes playing music.

On one occasion two teenagers came in and sat down, listening to the music and generally minding their own business. After a while two guys with crew cuts who looked like something out of a bad movie for young Republicans came into the coffee house and stood next to the juveniles, making some rather strange comments. Sort of pleasant threats. After a bit I asked them what they were doing. They implied they were the law of some sort. I told them that they weren't in uniform, in that case, and that if law was what was needed, to either call some real cops or do whatever they were legally able to do. Otherwise, they could sit down and have some coffee or get out. They apparently were some sort of security service for the shopping center that the art gallery was in. Tom then strolled up alongside me, and the two Republican minders left, not having felt the need to either apply the law or have coffee. Shortly thereafter the two juveniles left, and we never saw them or the security guys again. Ah yes, the raw underbelly of life and crime in the north.

September

The preacher who lived around the lake a mile or so north had, of all things, a couple of apple trees. I didn't think apple trees would survive the winters this far north, but there they were, big as leafy life. And damned if they didn't produce apples, which of course in September are green and just getting a little size if not a good flavor. The Big Long-Legged Bear didn't care. He must have tired of fish heads and his diet needed a little variety, so he stopped in at the preacher's little orchard and ate a bunch of the apples that had dropped off the trees after a windstorm and were lying around on the ground ready to be eaten. Still hungry for apples, he then decided to go to the source, so he reached up six or seven feet, broke off a few limbs and got some nice green apples that way.

Done with the apples, he went for a little desert of birdseed on the preacher's back porch. While he was there, lapping up birdseed, the apples must have acted as something of a laxative since he spewed greenish bear poop all over the porch. The preacher, hearing noise, came to investigate, whereupon the bear left greenish tracks off of the porch, back to the woods. The preacher was of course mad about the apples, not to mention the greenish tracks on his porch. And rightfully so, I might add. I feel obligated to agree that it shows a healthy portion of ingratitude to crap on a preacher's porch after you've eaten his apples and had dessert. I wouldn't recommend it, even if he is a fundamentalist.

Which, I don't know if that's all true, and it doesn't have much to do with my place anyway, except that Dale came over one day to help and mentioned this tale in passing and said that the preacher was interested in buying his resort.

As for me, I was finally working on my roof. When I was thinking about building my house originally, it had been my intention to get the walls done, then plop prebuilt roof trusses onto the walls, put on the plywood and roofing and presto! I would have a sturdy, good-looking roof and the house would be enclosed. But in August I virtually ran out of money. Not willing to stop, I changed the plan and decided to build five large log trusses and link them together with horizontal logs called perlins. These trusses and perlins would substitute for the prebuilt trusses and would be the structural base for the roof. There are good illustrations of this process in Milne's log home-building book.

So I spent an interminable period of time peeling logs for trusses and poles for rafters. I built the trusses in place on top of log beams placed across the top of the house. For aesthetic purpose I left two of the beams in their original round shape but two of the beams I kerf-cut and then chipped the sides flat with the adze. When I finished making the beams, I dragged them down to the house with the truck. Then on a weekend morning, a goodly number of friends came over to help me place them. We stuck the beams through a window hole and into the house and then,

226

using a pulley, hoisted the beams into place. The roof rafters, which I got from a friend's land, were long, slender maple poles, thin and very strong when dry. This seemed like a good solution. It wasn't in the long run, but I didn't have the time, inclination or money to argue.

The whole job of building trusses, cutting the angles for the supports, cleaning and preparing the logs, drilling and nailing or bolting the trusses together is better done on the ground. You then lift the massive truss into place with a crane. I couldn't do that since I had already put up the beams under each truss and anyway didn't have the large equipment necessary to do that. So I borrowed some scaffolding and cut, peeled and shaped each truss component. Remember me talking about the T bevel? That tool is very important here. When each truss was cut, I carried each (heavy, they are logs) component up onto the scaffold and drilled and nailed it into place. I was in good shape then, though not any smarter, and I recall putting one eight-foot-long green log that was about eight inches thick on my shoulder, and I carried it up a metal ladder, hoping to high heaven the ladder wouldn't collapse. The basic problem with this approach, aside from the distinct possibility of bodily injury, was that it took longer. Placing trusses, sheathing and roofing can be done easily in two weeks. When I was forced to build my own trusses, I was committing myself to a month and a half's work. And though I didn't think much about it at the time, I was rapidly running out of time.

Speaking of placing the logs as I have mentioned, I hired a neighbor periodically to come over with his cherry picker to set logs. He was another sturdy northerner, logger, farmer, excavator, etc. Toward the end of my job, just as I was running out of energy and money, he became more and more reluctant to come down. It's true, I hadn't paid him much money, and he was doubtful that I'd ever do so. I was beginning to wonder myself. (By a year after I'd finished, I'd paid him everything I owed him, which really wasn't that much, plus some extra.) Still, I don't blame him (the cheap SOB) for being reluctant to come down. You don't survive in the north by doing charity jobs.

The maple poles that I used for rafters were very strong. I thought about using them unpeeled, but I couldn't stand the thought of unpeeled rafters being under my roof and continued until they were done. The poles were nailed at the top and butt end with appropriately sized pole-barn nails and bolted to the Perlin in the middle, so that the whole truss, Perlin and rafter assembly became one extremely strong, well-connected unit. The plywood sheathing for the roof was installed over this framework. Lucky for me, attaching plywood sheathing on the house and roofing it with asphalt shingles was relatively easy. By the end of September I was finished and my house was roofed. I about fell over, as they say.

By the way, in the interest of accurate reporting, the roof that I installed then is no longer on the house. When it was done it was strong as hell. Maple is a very strong and flexible wood, and those poles dried hard and tough. But the roof was uneven. This was because the maple poles weren't as straight as pine poles would have been, and I didn't do a good job of leveling the nailing surfaces under the sheathing. So the roof was, shall we say, quaint? It rolled around here and there, like the shallow waves on the surface of a lake. No one really noticed unless I called their attention to it, or they were too polite to mention it. But then my brother came up to fish, and said my roof looked "rustic."

That did it. I knew I would rebuild it, and several years later when I wanted to put on a new metal roof, I stripped the entire roof off the house in sections, and during this process, replaced the poles with standard rafters. Incidentally, I left the trusses and Perlins in place although I didn't really need them. So if you're reading this in the future, wondering why there's all that wood under there, including all of those truss elements, it's because I got aggravated by that remark that my brother made. I couldn't stand an uneven roof, and ripped it off at the first opportunity. I did reuse the maple poles for various purposes and they were around for some years.

Let me say a few words here about steel roofs, which have been growing in popularity in our area. Essentially they are a variation of the old corrugated Quonset hut roofs that the military used. At first they were used in sheathing and roofing for pole barns on farms. Then some marketing genius got the idea to paint them nice colors and to promote them for residential uses. They can be bought in any length and many colors, and they have gradually been used more and more in areas of the county where there are a lot of forest fires and snow. People also like metal roofs because they are easy to put on. They cover a lot of roof quickly, especially if you order them cut to fit from the ridgeline to the lower edge of the roof. One of the attractive aspects of metal roofs in our area is that snow slides right off the roof. They come in three-foot-wide sheets and generally you need two people to put them on, mostly one person to hold the sheet and one to screw it down. The roof also comes with the same screws of the same color with rubber grommet sealing rings.

Actually anything slides off of them fairly easily, including myself once. When they are dry and you have rubber-bottomed shoes, you can stick to them like

Spiderman, like a fly on the ceiling, like… (enough, Mike). You get the point. But don't go up there when it is wet. Or even moist. Once I was installing panels on a very hot day. I was sweating profusely and it was dripping on the roof. I apparently stepped on some of the sweat, because the subsequent panic dance I did would have done justice to Nureyev. When the windmilling was done, I had managed to catch hold of one screw on the corner of a window. Actually, had I slid off of the roof it wasn't that much of a drop to the lawn. For a split second, however, in my mind you'd have thought I was falling off a cliff in the Tetons. I subsequently crawled along the ridge and off the roof, quivering more than a little and went and had a drink of my Gatorade and water mix.

A couple more things and I promise, on my mother's sacred honor, that I'll drop this. You can cut the metal sheet roofing with a skill saw. You just use any old skill saw blade. I used one with carbide-tipped teeth. Then you place a board under the sheet of metal to keep it off of whatever surface you're cutting on, and a board on top of the sheet to slide the skill saw along. I did my cutting on the lawn. Remember trying to keep yourself from getting injured? Stick hearing protection in your ears, your protective glasses on, gloves on your hands and cut slowly, not fast. The skill saw cuts through the sheet metal like butter.

Chipmunks

Approximately the same time as the house was well roofed, the chipmunks moved in. Apparently they'd been watching from the woods. They didn't mind that I was there. To them the house was nothing but another pile of logs. And what was nice was that this particular pile came with food. Gee, isn't that cute, I thought, as a chipmunk used my living room, or rather what would become my living room, as a racetrack. Gee, this has to stop, I thought very shortly thereafter, as a couple of them used my kitchen counter for an obstacle course, while another rummaged through my garbage looking for something to eat, or perhaps read.

One day after waking from a nap in my newly roofed place, I looked down and there was a chipmunk ogling me, no doubt wondering if I was, by some chance, edible. Being at that moment of an irritable mien, I considered getting the shotgun and making chipmunk mincemeat of this impertinent critter, thought better of that idea and settled for tossing a tennis shoe at him, which he easily dodged. More chipmunks began to forage for food inside my house. Then it occurred to me one day that perhaps the chipmunks were merely hungry. Why, I asked, hadn't I thought of this before! I would feed them elsewhere… outside, for example. This would allow me, a gentle but firm human, to develop a rational plan to deal with these lovable but misguided creatures. True, they are cute but…

Did I tell you they're rodents? How much can it take to outthink a rodent? And not really a very smart rodent, after all. Many other rodents are smarter than a chipmunk. No doubt about it. Your New York City rat, for example, is a veritable genius in comparison. Let us suppose you throw some food to a rat. The rat goes to the food and eats it, right? Throw some toward a chipmunk and what does the chipmunk do? It runs the other direction. I rest my case. Chipmunks, cute but stupid.

Thus I would devise a sensible plan with myself as (forgive my bombast here, but I only say it because it's true) the leader; we would coexist while respecting each other's intrinsic rights as sentient beings. I fairly beam with pride. To each according to his need, or something like that. Karl Marx, you've got nothing on me. I would feed them outside. There are but two or three chipmunks. Mixed birdseed is cheap. They can't eat much, can they? I would provide a little sustenance and they would gather up the seeds. Thus provided for, my friends the chipmunks would sleep away the cold winter, and I would go about my life unhindered by chipmunks pole-vaulting over my dishes.

Thus does the ladder to hell have rungs labeled "good intentions."

I bought a bag of seeds. One could almost see the smile on their little faces as I generously distributed a little seed here and there. The chipmunks scurried around picking up the seeds, stuffing their little cheeks full and then off to who knows where. My, my, but they can stuff a lot into those cheeks. In the meantime, I did my part and firmly chased any chipmunk that entered my house. One day, however, I noticed that several of the chipmunks apparently commute via a route that crosses my living room. Oh, isn't that interesting, they think it's more direct and safe to be inside my house instead of outside. Well I guess that's okay. They are merely passing through. I understand that perfectly. Let them. In fact, one gets a little warm spot in one's breast thinking about my house being a safe place for them.

What's that? There seem to be four chipmunks. Probably a mistake, a miscount. They all look the same, you know. The seed bag is empty and the chipmunks are still here. There really are four chipmunks. A fattish-looking one with half a tail and an evil temper has showed up. Whenever he is around, he chases the others rather vigorously and grabs the seeds, or rather as much of the seed as he can stuff into his pig-like cheeks. Which I repeat is an amazing amount. Exactly how much, I ask, does he need to safely pass the winter? Good gracious, this isn't a bird-seed retirement fund for chipmunks. The only reason the others get any seeds at all is that he has to go back to his den.

Anthropomorphism aside and all apologies to Jane Goodall, I have named him Stubby. I think there is another one. Where did that one come from? Oh, and another thing. I have noticed from throwing out the seed that the chipmunk does an odd thing. Remember me mentioning the fact that if you throw some food at a chipmunk, they invariably scurry the other direction? Well they scurry every direction. They scurry randomly until they find something to eat. It doesn't matter to them where you throw the food. Now that is slightly irritating. They don't know, and don't even seem to care, where their food—which I might add is purchased with my hard earned money—comes from.

Chipmunks don't like each other. This is easily discovered from observation. Since I have begun to feed them and more of them seem to be around, the opportunity for observation has no bar. In fact they seem to hate each other. They chase, attack and bite the other one's tail. How they produce little chipmunks is beyond me. Each chipmunk seems to have a den in the woods. In my case they seem to live in a wooded embankment along the county road. They defend their dens and the surrounding territory rather vigorously. And, you won't believe this, but they steal from each other's dens. Since they really don't like each other, how then, one asks, do they show up together at my place?

It is a week later, and I think I have figured it out. Apparently, instead of making a deal with me, they've made a deal with each other, a truce, so to speak, the better to gather Mike's seeds. Did I say they all look the same?

This isn't strictly true—there are differences. This one is smaller, that one has a bump on its shoulder that looks like some sort of growth but doesn't impair his seed-hoarding activities. Stubby is fairly obvious, and another two are smaller—they are juveniles.

The juveniles are really the most interesting. They are just like children, hopping around without a care in the world, sniffing this and tasting that. The juveniles don't play with each other much that I can see, but they do sort of play investigate the world. They are true innocents, and it's good that they have this period of their lives, because the chipmunk world, I have discovered, is a very rough one. The father's contribution to their lives consists of approximately five seconds (if that) of lust behind the log. The mother chipmunks have no concern for their offspring once the little ones are juveniles. The period between being born and being juvenile is very short. They are then thrust into the world and either ignored or attacked by everyone else, including their mothers. Juvenile chipmunks don't seem to realize what the real world is like. To them it seems a wondrous place. They hop around here and there, nibbling this and sniffing at that, sitting in the sun and, in their small way, trying to figure things out. They are the most charming of chipmunk society and remind me of my little nephews and nieces. Most juvenile chipmunks are food for hawks.

But chipmunks, even the juveniles, have evolved defenses. They have extremely good vision and hearing, and the one thing on which they cooperate is the spotting of danger. They have a danger call, a steady chirp, chirp, chirp, which penetrates through the woods and which the others can hear. And when all fails and the predator gets close, they are amazingly quick.

Chipmunks have opted as a species to store food for the winter, instead of storing it on their bodies in the form of fat à la the bear. The red squirrels apparently do both, fattening up and burying acorns, rousing themselves from their winter sleep during the warm spells to hunt for the acorns and seeds. Chipmunks assumedly sleep away portions of the winter, only getting up to eat some of their stores to rebuild their body fat. Two different strategies, both risky, but they seem to work. The equation is pretty simple. If they don't have enough body fat, and they don't get enough seeds and they can't forage a little, they die. It's as simple as that. I have seen some of them scurrying around in the woods in March, looking for food. At the time I thought nothing of it. Isn't that cute, a chipmunk out in March. Probably that chipmunk is starving. As a matter of fact, chipmunks sleep away large portions of the year, even in the middle of summer. They do it because sleeping is energy efficient. And except for gathering food and sex, there isn't a reason for them to be out.

There are now six chipmunks and one red squirrel. The red squirrel is practically hysterical when I'm around, or perhaps he's hysterical at finding this much food. He chatters at me constantly, hoping I'll leave. I'm not leaving. The chipmunks, of course, don't mind me a bit. My presence in this equation constitutes a bonanza for them. The perfect chipmunk welfare society has been created, and I am now going through one five-pound bag a week. There is no need for desperation in the hunting of this or that seed, since one merely hauls as much as one can stuff into one's cheeks back to the hole. And the chipmunks weren't satisfied with just a small amount of seeds every day. They would gather that, hustle it off to their dens and be back, waiting for more. No amount satisfied them.

No problem. Flexibility is the signature of human intelligence. I would lock up the seeds, feeding only once every few days. Did I tell you that some birds showed up when the birdseed was thrown out? Well they did, and what fun! The chickadees traipse and flit back and forth. I dug out an old bird feeder someone had given me somewhere in the past, hung that on a branch and filled it with birdseed. It is plastic and has glass walls. The little birds came and I enjoyed them. I gave no thought to chipmunks. How could your nice, but obviously limited, little chipmunk get to the seeds in this thing? They couldn't. I chuckled.

The bird feeder's inviolability lasted approximately twenty-seven seconds. And there are seven chipmunks. At least I think there are seven. They are coming and going all day, and they are never there at the same time. Several of them still use the route through my living room. Newcomers have to be swept out of the kitchen. They go grudgingly.

Remember the feeder? I happened to be resting and looking out a window when the chipmunks ran out of seeds on the ground—or rather disdained the little work involved in casting about for seeds on the ground—and decided to examine the contents of that thing hanging from the branch. Up the tree, out the branch, down the wire, onto the roof, pause to consider what to do, sniff over the edge. (Here I laugh, watch the miserable little rodent fall ignominiously to the ground. My, my, but your attitude toward chipmunk society has changed.) Then zip!! over the edge and there the little thief sat, pigging out on a bonanza of seed! I went outside. The chipmunk saw me coming and shifted uneasily, a guilty look on his face. I approached. He leaped for the tree and ran off in the general direction of his den. So what. A smart one. They all can't be like him. And anyway, how much can they get out of the feeder?

They were all like him, only smarter. The first one was more aggressive than the others, not smarter. Most took to scampering up the tree, examining the situation for a moment, and merely jumped from the tree to the ledge of the feeder, thus skipping the somewhat problematic, over-the-edge maneuver of the aggressive chipmunk.

The good news is that the number of them has seemingly leveled off at six. Or seven, I can't really be sure. I'm sure there's only one red squirrel. Who, by the way, has gotten over his nervousness and who apparently does not store seeds and so once he eats himself full, he flops out on a branch in the sun, his feet hanging over the sides, like some fat American on a winter cruise.

They aren't cute little chipmunks. They are thieves. It has been going like this. I fill the bird feeder. The birds come and demurely pick their seeds. This lasts until the chipmunks get there. The chipmunks then rummage around on the edge of the feeder until all of the seeds are gone. I go out and chase them off. They wait until my back is turned, then back onto the feeder. It doesn't matter if there are seeds on the ground. Apparently they have figured out that the seeds on the ground will mostly stay there until later. They can't be that clever, can they?

They have now figured out I'm not inclined to hurt them and they refuse to leave the feeder. I take to rushing out, yelling at them, sweeping them off with a broom or poking them off with a stick. They look at me with the leaden, porcine expression of a fat person in one of those fast food restaurants. They go grudgingly, when they go at all. Once in a fit of outrage at an especially fat chipmunk, I took a swing at him with the broom. The chipmunk jumped the wrong direction and I conked him on the head with the corner of the hard part of the broom. He fell onto the ground, laying inert with his little feet sticking straight up toward the blue sky.

I was awash in guilt. He was merely doing what I had induced him to do. I was a brute. I picked him up and carried him to the porch. He lay inert on my porch. One is at a loss for what to do about a conked-out chipmunk. Mouth to mouth is out, at least for me. Long minutes passed. His large eyes were glassy. Suddenly he blinked and certain awareness flowed back into the inky black depths of those eyes. Then he flipped over and scurried away, no doubt back to his den, where several others who had heard of his demise were sniffing around already.

I bought a new feeder. The chipmunks can get some seeds from it, but only after spending a considerable amount of energy, since I modified it so that they don't have anything to hold onto on its plastic sides. It's quite amusing watching them examine the new feeder like little rodent safecrackers.

And there we shall leave it. I resigned as the supreme leader of the chipmunk society, though the welfare state went on. Cecilia from Chicago who had come to visit exclaimed, "Oh, those are the fattest chipmunks I've ever seen!" She was puzzled at my grumbled response.

Squirrels

A few words about squirrels. Red squirrels are fairly commonly carnivorous. Food in the form of seeds can be hard to come by occasionally, and the red squirrel will kill to get its food. Bird nests are its the first choice. I've also heard of red squirrels killing chipmunks, but I've never seen that. Once I heard a racket on my new porch and went to investigate. There was a large female red squirrel, obviously pregnant, being attacked by two enraged robins. The red squirrel, upon my entrance to the situation, ran up onto a post and calmly sat there, looking down at me. The robins retreated to the environs of their nest, still screaming their outrage. The red squirrel had killed one of the baby robins. Mama squirrel's mouth was bright blood-red from the robin she had been eating. She retreated from the scene but came back later that day. The robins abandoned their nest, knowing that their babies were doomed.

I have no black squirrels at my place that I have seen, but black squirrels are fairly common in the deciduous woods toward Grand Rapids. They are very pretty, about the size of a gray squirrel with glossy coal-black fur. They are a distinct subspecies, separate from the red and gray squirrels or, just as rare now, fox squirrels. I believe the black squirrels are a remnant from the old forests wherein the woods were much darker with less open spaces. There is a town in southern Minnesota that has a large population of black squirrels. Probably they inhabited a larger area of forest in that area and retreated to the town as the woods were cut for farmland.

At the Common Ground coffee house things were about the same. Glen the California hippie had tried his best to bridge the gap between Lon and the rest of us. It hadn't worked, but to his credit he persisted. He would look at people with his big soulful nonjudging eyes, talking quietly and trying out various ways of getting people to get along. But nobody was having much of it. Lon was working behind the scenes, playing politics with the art board members. And the rest of us were being stupid about it and ignoring him.

Speaking of coals to Newcastle, the Veteran came in one night, sat around for a while and made ready to sing several of his lugubrious missives. Then, halfway through one of them I realized I liked it! Slap me upside the head if I didn't! Actually two of his latest were pretty good. Hundreds of songs and years of effort and damned if he hadn't written something pretty good. Then I thought for a moment that it might have just been the comparison with his previous songs. Nope, the new ones were pretty good.

I hadn't talked with the mystery writer lady since the caramel corn incident. No it wasn't poison. Probably. At any rate one night she showed up at the coffee house and announced happily that one of her manuscripts had been accepted for publication. I was happy for her and somewhat amazed. Then she told me the name of the publisher. It was one of those self-publishing companies who get paid to turn your manuscript into a book.

She talked on happily about this and I made no comment. Lots of people have done this and sold their product directly. Who knows? Several months later I met her again. This time she was very discouraged. Her counselor at the county had been telling her she had to quit writing and do something else with her life. It wasn't working, he said. No one wanted her work. He was concerned about her mental health. I asked her what it was she liked to do, and she told me she liked to write. My opinion was that she should do what she was happy doing. She had no children to take care of, nor any other obligations. She seemed happy about this. As far as I know she's still writing, probably surrounded floor to ceiling with manuscripts, and will die in the middle of a huge pile of paper. Could be worse.

Another writer was a rather bushy-haired individual who lived with his mother. He looked like a reject from a bad fifties bebop movie. He was a genius, someone (possibly himself) said, and a good musician. Still another writer was working on some psychological novel or lengthy book related to psychology. He and his wife lived in the woods and worked on their home. I'm not sure what else they did. He worked on his book all during the time I was working on the house and eventually finished it, I hear. I never could figure out exactly what the book was about and never read it. Perhaps it was just about doing it. That I understand.

Later in the evening Russell the smart kid came in again, smiling and waving to everyone. I hadn't seen him for a few weeks. Lon's group was sitting at one table, ignoring the rest of the people. He visited with everyone and, sensing the tension between the groups, tried to elevate the atmosphere. Russell's effort wasn't working and in a while he sat quietly talking with someone, his expansive expression and intelligent eyes taking it all in and for once growing concerned and sad at not being able to find a solution to a problem that wasn't his to begin with.

Building Your Log Home, Part Three

Finishing a log home has five components, actually six, if you include dying of boredom. They are curing the logs, sanding and cleaning them, treating, chinking and finally staining. Then once you're done with all of that, you throw down your tools and swear you'll never do it again.

Curing Logs

Most log houses are, as previously mentioned, laid green. This is done for good reasons, several of which I can think of, but now that I do think of them, they don't seem that important. It is said that this allows the logs to bend and to settle into each other. And that is somewhat true, since the joints become tighter as time goes on. Still, I'm not certain of the earth-shaking importance of that. Instead, cutting, fitting and laying green logs is probably done because green logs are what the log homebuilder has got to lay. At any rate they are put up green and have considerable water content. As much as 30 to 40 percent of their weight, I'm told. As a result of this, the logs spend a couple of years reducing their moisture content. This process is called curing. Log houses, including mine, seem to work better after the logs are cured. It is best to let the logs thoroughly cure before staining them.

Sanding and Cleaning Logs

Logs can be cleaned and dressed up by sanding. Remember me blathering about how wonderful the orbital sander is? Mine is a DeWalt, but there are other brands, of course. You remove the hard head on the thing and replace it with a rubber head, which you can buy at the sander store. I used heavy grit sandpaper. (Wear protective paraphernalia when you do this. I know I don't really have to say this again. But for God's sake, wear eye protection, breathing protection and any other protection, since things are flying everywhere when you do this.) The reason I'm so enamored with my sander is that this little tool can make a crummy log job look good. It removes all of the dirt and detritus of the building process and about anything else for that matter. You could sand the log down to a toothpick if you wanted.

Another popular method of cleaning logs is power washing. With a power washer, which you can either buy or rent, you can thoroughly clean the logs quickly. There are of course other methods of cleaning your logs. I investigated sandblasting and corn blasting when I was finishing my place. I know these methods work, but they seem expensive. At any rate I haven't done these and don't know enough about them, so I am just mentioning that they are available. As for corn, I don't know how one could clean anything with rural humor.

Treating Logs

Logs should lose most of their moisture prior to you staining. But it is best to spray or paint the peeled logs with fungicide as soon as they are peeled. This is because if you don't your logs will gradually turn from a wonderful creamy yellow to an ugly gray. Your basic fungi apparently love sap, it being sugary water. Further, you won't notice that the logs are turning ugly gray, because you're working every day at your project and the diabolical little fungi are there, right under your nose, having a party on the sap you so generously provided, drinking it up like Kool-Aid and turning your house gray—ever so slowly. This was easily apparent to me when I finally looked at the first pictures of my house and then at the later ones. There was fungus amongus. So use a good fungicide. Use a lot, if a little fungicide gets on you, maybe it'll subdue your athlete's foot. I treated the logs with Penatreat, which is a product, I'm told, "highly toxic to wood-destroying insects and fungi." After reading this somewhat alarming verbiage, I enthusiastically sprayed my logs with Penatreat. I also sprayed a considerable portion on myself in the process and was concerned about that for some time.

Speaking of fungussy walls, my neighbor Dale looked at a picture of one of my walls after it had turned gray. "Look, a cross," said Dale. And it was true. There on the wall was the shadow of a cross. After that he thought my house was a blessed event. I'm sorry to say I got a good bit of work out of him on the strength of that one picture.

Chinking

Chinking is the process of filling the joints between the logs to impede airflow, heat flow and bug flow. Historically log homes have been chinked with almost anything, including mud mixed with grass or straw and oakum (also known as jute) and used in ships to seal seams. Actually oakum is, I understand, mostly used as a backing for synthetic chinking. Chinking is one aspect of log home building, which has, without a doubt, benefited from advancements in science. Modern synthetic chinking is reasonably easy to use, expands and contracts with the house, comes in several colors and can be stained over. It is really two products: the backing, which is a polyethylene ropelike product that you stuff into the crack, and the chinking itself. Your supplier is happy to talk about chinking, since it is a pricey product.

In modern log homes chinking is part of the final aesthetic effect in addition to its beneficial effect of keeping heat in your home and cold out. It is part of finishing and should be done in its proper place, next to last, before staining.

Staining

A little knowledge is certainly a dangerous thing. When I was first considering how to finish my log house I began to ask questions about stains. Most of the answers I got differed from the other guy's answers. Now I'm not overwhelmed with the impulse to know everything about everything. In fact I have absolutely no interest in knowing anything about stains. Just sell me something and I'll put it on. But no one said the same thing about stains and this bothered me.

Oh, that's not completely true. They did repeat one thing, which basically boils down to "you get what you pay for," meaning they want to charge a lot for their products. I understand this. You can't stay in business without charging money. And it is invariably true the best quality things cost more. The problem with this is that it didn't seem that the best quality stains lasted any longer than any other product. Further, it seemed that even the best oil-based stains had linseed oil as a base ingredient. This, I had been told, was not the case. So the following is what I know, or think I know, about stains. And then remember "taking advice" way back at the beginning of this? Do your own thing.

Most stains are mostly some form of oil and have linseed oil (look in the small print) with a colorant and other chemicals thrown in. So is paint. Stain is usually just thin paint. The companies loudly proclaim the UV-resistant characteristics of their formulas. Actually it appears that the best UV-protected stain is paint, the thicker the better.

In the end I made my own stain. I did not want to do this, but neither did I want to spend forty or fifty dollars a gallon for stain for my house. It seems that the various businesses that want you to buy their stain dwell at length on how their product is better than anything you could make up. Further, they argue, do you want to risk your effort and investment on something you made yourself? God, what are you thinking?

I'm going to tell you exactly what I used to stain my house. No doubt I'll burn in hell for doing so, but here it is. Get a five-gallon bucket and mix one gallon of boiled linseed oil with one gallon of mineral spirits. To this, add a quart of golden oak stain and half a quart of number 705 russet-colored Pittsburgh Paint stain to achieve a more ruddy hue. This last addition is one that you want to add and then test the result on a section of your logs. At first I used more of the russet-colored stain and it was too orangey, so I reduced the amount. It looks great now. I further added a fungicide, which is easily purchased and comes in plastic squeeze tubes. Finally I added an insecticide to the mix, though I thought the better of that last one.

By the way, some years later I was going to stain something and bought a gallon of off-the-shelf stain. It worked fine, looked good and cost much less than the stuff I made and far less than the expensive stuff. Also I might add that I was going to apply my stain using the sprayer, but I found that the stain goes on very well with a large soft-bristled brush. It is true that you need to brush in the stain anyway, so since you're using a brush in the first place, why not just use it for everything? The lady at the store said using a good quality brush would make the job easier because good brushes hold a lot of stain. She was right, and the actual staining was easy. I still think spraying might be okay, though.

Old Norwegians and My Sand Point Well

Most people, including my friend Cecilia, when invited up to visit would think for a moment and then ask whether there was "plumbing." By which they meant is there a toilet and a shower? Now, I am sympathetic to such notions. For the first year or so of my house, I didn't have running water. I built an outhouse and carried my water most of the time.

In summer I would often collect rainwater and heat it for washing my hair. Nothing is better for washing your hair than rainwater. I know that water softeners produce water that is supposed to be as soft. Believe me, it isn't. So if you read this somewhere in the future, try this when it rains. Go out and collect a basin of rainwater, heat it and wash your hair or stick your head under a downspout, soap up and rinse your hair with that. This of course assumes rainwater isn't toxic and that there are still such things as downspouts. At any rate if you do wash with rainwater, you will see what I'm talking about.

By the way, I had a friend who lived in the Cities with his girlfriend who was rather well endowed, but not apparently with modesty. She liked rainwater shampoos so much that every time it rained she would throw off all of her clothing and stand au naturel under the downspout on their back porch. She liked the soft water for her hair and said the chilly water... stimulated her. Several old geezers across the way who sat on their porch got an eyeful every time it rained. Ah, the pleasures of old age.

At the beginning of the twentieth century until surprisingly late ('50s and '60s) people would collect rainwater in barrels and cisterns, but in general the advent of modern plumbing and subsequent "soft water" systems doomed the collecting of rainwater. People give up the old too quickly in some cases and collecting rainwater may be one of them. Other changes are more understandable. Fuel oil lights are wonderful to reminisce about and to have as antiques or at the cabin, but average people took to electric lights without looking back. Prior to the twentieth century, most Americans probably didn't take a bath more than once a week. If that. During the twentieth century people began to work more and more off of farms. When you've got to get up every day and haul yourself off to some factory you don't have a lot of time for a long bath. It was the advent of running water powered by electric pumps that led to frequent bathing. Showers came later.

At any rate, after several friends remarked about the plumbing, it finally occurred to me that I too had better begin to make provision for running water. I might add here that for all the castigating of myself regarding planning, I had installed the plumbing pipes when I built the interior walls, so all I needed now was a source of water outside of my house. I could then pipe it into the house. I resolved to get water by driving a sand point. A sand point, which I could do myself, seemed to be an elementary way of providing for my needs.

Not knowing much about how to do a sand point well, I asked an old Norwegian by the name of John whom I had met in Grand Rapids how it was done. He was seventy-five years old or so, polite, pleasant, grizzled and hobbled, but still spry, working every day on the farm and as a small contractor for various people. He had grown up on a hard-scrabble farm hacked out of the woods up there, had always worked, was frugal and still driving an old truck. His only luxury, it seemed to me, was coming to town for coffee every day to visit with his friends. At any rate, he gave me a lot of advice and loaned me his tripod, pulley, rope and pounding device, which consists of a heavy pipe with weights welded onto one end and a loop to attach the rope. Then he went along to the hardware store to make sure I got the right pipe, connectors and pipe dope. Thus equipped I headed for my place, my future well to make.

So how is it done? A sand point consists of a steel "point" which is about two feet long with screened holes in the sides. This point is screwed to a fitting that then attaches in turn to lengths of pipe. The fittings are hardened, that is they have the strength to withstand the pressures of being pounded into the ground. You augur a hole as deep as you can and then set up the tripod. Next you put pipe dope on the threads of the point and screw on several lengths of the hardened pipe. You can tighten them but you really don't need to do it, because as you're pounding the pipe into the ground, you are supposed to turn the pipe every so often (in the direction that tightens the joints) using pipe wrenches.

On the pounding end of the pipe you screw on one of the joint fittings and use this for a pounding head to be discarded when it is too beat up, or the job is finished, or you are too beat up to finish, whichever comes first. Mine lasted until the end of the job. The pounding device, which pounds the point and pipe into the ground, consists of a section of steel pipe about three feet long that has one end welded shut and a loop welded onto that same end for the pulley rope. This contraption is pulled up using the pulley and let down over the pipe. You are now ready to pound.

And here's where paths vary. Remember me talking about the quick versus the slow, steady way of doing things? Well, with this job it is good to have help. A friend that I know called up several friends and, by tempting them with beer, got them to come over and help, whereupon they pounded through two cases of beer and into water. Lacking beer or friends who are inclined to hard physical labor, one does it oneself. In these matters advice from friends is easier to come by than actual physical help. Bribes and lying help here. Still, one takes what one gets, and good advice is appreciated. By the way, the type of soil that one is pounding through is very important. Rocks are bad for pounding a sand point. If there are a lot of rocks, you're probably screwed. Go get a well driller. You can't pound a sand point through a rock. Sometimes you can get by the rock, but often you have to pull out the pipe if you can, and start over. Part of the reason for auguring the pilot hole is to get through the overburden soil and avoid rocks.

Once I had augured down four or five feet I had to pound through blue clay. The good thing about the clay was that there were no rocks. The bad thing about pounding this pipe through clay was that it was sticky and dense and progress was slow. About three-quarters of an inch for

250

every fifty times the pounding head was lifted and dropped. Or less. Pound, pound, pound. While sweating buckets during this process, I found that by drinking a mixture of half water and half Gatorade I could work longer. The other trick that refreshed me was to take a drink of pickle water out of a pickle jar and then take a drink of regular water.

In this fashion I went down ten, then twenty feet. The pipe got too hard to turn in the sticky heavy clay. Twenty-five feet, and I couldn't turn the pipe at all. Another local guy who had pounded a number of sand points said I would know when I hit a sand vein with water when the rate at which the pipe went into the ground abruptly increased. Then you pound the pipe down about a foot and a half farther and stop. The way you tested whether you were in a water vein was to pour water into the pipe. If the water just sat there you weren't in a water vein. If the water went away in the pipe, you were in a sand vein with water. Possibly.

Thus enlightened, one day suddenly I noticed the pipe going into the ground four or five inches for every fifty blows of the weight. I followed instructions, pounded a little more and stopped. I poured the pipe full of water. It disappeared immediately! John the Norwegian had given me a hand pump for this situation. I screwed the pump onto the end of the pipe, hooked it up and voilà, water! I was flabbergasted. I pumped for quite a while. Water. My own water! I danced around!

I pumped for several days, using the hand pump, to make sure of the volume of water. There seemed to be plenty. Later my friend Doug came over, and we hooked an electric pump onto the pipe and tested the capacity. There was plenty of good clean water in my sand vein below twenty-seven feet of clay. I then disconnected the pipe four feet down into the ground after we dug a trench from the well to the house, installed an elbow and ran plastic line into the house where I hooked it up to the main pump in the house.

Actually the water was under enough pressure that it trickled out the top of the pipe when we disconnected it four feet down. I have used the water from this well for quite a while. It is very good and gets better with use. I do filter the water since it is relatively cheap to do so, removes most of the impurities and makes the water taste great.

I am relating this because it is probable that this sort of self-help activity will be gone fairly soon, so I wanted to tell you how I did mine. People who make their living by drilling wells are agitating to make this sort of well a thing of the past. They have managed to convince the counties and others of the extreme health dangers of the sand point well. Of course they have no problem with drilling innumerable "pump-and-dump" systems to run air conditioning, which depletes the pure water veins. After all, the deeper you have to drill the more money you make. So if by chance you read this in the future, sand points will probably be a thing of the long, lost past. Of course the principal danger is to the well driller's pocketbook if people get the idea that with a little effort they can get water cheaper.

In Grand Rapids at Cole's Hardware, and I suppose other places, you could buy the makings of a sand point. And the guys who worked there, after selling you the pipe and other paraphernalia, would include considerable advice as to how to go about pounding a point to boot. Undoubtedly several of them had done it themselves. Which reminds me of how things are rapidly changing.

For the years that I was building the house, Cole's Hardware was housed in an old wood-framed building, circa 1900. I don't know how long they had been there, but over the years more and more hardware and other useful things accumulated in the building, until the place was crammed with paraphernalia for every conceivable use. The basement was a low-ceilinged dark warren of narrow aisles. The place was undoubtedly a hazard, but an interesting hazard what with every corner filled with stuff.

Further and most interesting, the guys (and women) who worked there generally knew where everything was; could thread a pipe on the spot; sell you an old, used, but still good, electric motor or as in my case, sell you the stuff for a sand point and get you on your way with good advice regarding that endeavor. At that time people didn't automatically throw things away when they were done with them. Products were purchased with the idea that, if they broke, they would be fixed, not thrown away. Part of the value of those local stores was that in addition to the products, they sold knowledge, though they weren't formally educated very much. They mostly worked with their hands and learned from experience.

They were products of an agrarian society. The farm. In the middle of the twentieth century when they were young men, blacksmiths were common in small towns. A large percentage of the population had been born on farms. People still got together in the fall to thresh oats and wheat. When these men were young everyone could fix a car or truck and did so commonly.

You can't fix a car or truck anymore. Well, not many people can, and soon it will be virtually impossible without the electronic and computer tools. Oh, there are still farms and people who can fix things, but the numbers are dwindling. Since those days Cole's has moved to new, larger quarters and still is a good place with good people who actually know hardware. But it is likely that this is a passing phenomenon.

These guys will likely give way to people who smile brightly, try to act as if they actually know something and when asked about the availability of a particular widget exclaim, "Just what's there, sir, just what's there!" And then these just-what's-there birds wander off chirping to anyone else who comes in, "Just what's there."

These gargantuan modern box stores are chock-full of stuff and empty of people. And most of the people who do work there, to use a descriptive phrase, couldn't pour piss out of a boot if they were given instructions on how to do it. That is, of course, my opinion. In the interest of fair reporting, a friend of mine suggests there are good aspects to these stores. They are open all of the time. Those old stores were generally open eight to five during he week, and ten o'clock to five on Saturdays. They were closed on Sundays, which, it could be argued, was a good thing. But if you needed something and the store was closed, you were out of luck until the start of the workweek. Now you can go to a store virtually any time and buy products cheaper. There is value to this.

Thus endeth my compendium of suggestions regarding log home building. If you're a professional home-builder, no doubt reading this has provided a few laughs, and if you're an amateur, you might get the idea you can do it better. You are right.

October

December may be the end of the calendar year, but October is the end of the natural year in the north. All of the green growing things bow their heads, die back and settle down to wait out the winter. For a while there is that wonderful organic, leafy smell of full fall. It is a time of urgent movement in nature. All of the ducks and geese and loons now wheel and bank crisply in the cold air. Fishes move with the changing water and the lakes begin to steam in the chill mornings. There are days when the Witch rides a hard cold wind down from the north, triumphantly screaming all of the way of the death of the year. But then, in a while, she sullenly retreats and some days are calm and sunny, the air still and clear as a bell. The lake reflects the blue sky and it is very quiet.

Once I was far out on my lake in a boat, and it was so quiet that I could hear a conversation between two neighbors talking two hundred yards away on shore. I'm sorry to say there was nothing interesting to report. The tourists and most of the bugs are gone except for the blood-sucking gnats, which apparently wear little fur coats and latch onto your ears anytime the sun comes out and the temperature gets over forty degrees. October is a great time for fishing. The fish are feeding up for the winter. The big northern pike and muskies chase the bait fish, and the walleyes are on the move. One can find a little solitude on the lake.

October is a perfect time for everything related to work. People clean up and get ready for winter, stacking things where they can get to them when the snow is deep. People all over the north suddenly pay attention to their woodpile, and either look with smug satisfaction at a well-stacked large pile or frantically look around for dry wood to cut up. By fall you can't really split green wood for burning, even if you dry it until late in the winter, although my neighbor used to stuff his outdoor furnace full of mostly dry wood, and then put in a few green chunks. Said it kept the furnace going longer. But spring is the time to cut and split green wood. Get out there in late March or April, cut and split it and leave it to dry in the summer.

I was working hard to finish my place by the end of the month. I had finished the roof and by the second week in October I was framing and insulating the ceiling inside my house. The weather was changing too. In the mornings there was ice on the driveway puddles. I worked steadily, trying to reach my goal of enclosing the house and getting it to the point that it would hold heat. Some friends came up, but I could only visit as I worked. They headed off to sightsee and visit the Lost Forty forest, and I kept on. My friend Don was helping me make a front door and frame. We made it from leftover pine floor joists that were two inches thick. The door was not easy to frame because it has a round top. But Don is a professional woodworker and so the door came out fine, the proof being that it is still on the house and it is the thing that everyone comments on.

Then I cracked the blade on the bulldozer, and followed it up by breaking the fan belt so that it overheated. Since I had only a few minutes of work left, I then tied a belt around the fan rails, cinched it up and duct-taped the connection. This didn't really work and the bulldozer overheated again. It hissed ominously, so I parked the dozer and it didn't move again.

The only other significant thing that happened early in October was that, while I was working, I slipped with the portable electric drill that I was using and stabbed my left hand with a Phillips head screwdriver. Naturally it hit a hole in the glove. I left a bloody trail as I went to get my hand into some cold water. I let it bleed a little more, washed it with soap and water, wrapped it tight, put the glove back on and went back to work. It stopped aching in a while, but the Phillips head had damaged some muscles and it took some weeks to heal thoroughly. I still had the scar a year later.

Newt the Weasel

Newt the Weasel showed up in late fall of the year that I moved into my house. Mostly, up till then, the chipmunks had happily grown fat from feeding on my seeds. My place was still fairly crude, but the chipmunks and the mice didn't mind. I was standing by the front of the house on a brilliantly blue day with a chilly northwest wind, but warm in the places where the sun shone. Some chipmunks were plundering my bird feeder as per usual, when a little brown blurry form shot past, hard on the tail of one of the chipmunks. The chippy beat it for the top of a tree with the blurry thing in hot pursuit. The chipmunk then shot down the tree and off into the brush and weeds. There was then a loud squeak but I don't know what happened after that. I learned later that chipmunks aren't really prey for the weasel. Not that a weasel wouldn't kill a chipmunk if it could. Actually if a weasel weighed twenty pounds it would have taken a run at me.

It's just that chipmunks aren't that easy to catch since they are amazingly quick and have teeth, though they mostly use their teeth on seeds and nuts and each other. But still, they have them. Mice are the real prey for your weasel. Nonetheless a stoat (a weasel) can kill a chipmunk or at least threaten one seriously, and so chipmunks get very quiet when the weasel is in the neighborhood. Suddenly those freeloading chipmunks had a new factor in their little birdseed welfare-scheming lives. When the word was out that the weasel was around, they approached the feeder very carefully. I named the weasel Newt in honor of a certain Republican politician rampant on the field of Washington politics at the time who, when occasion necessitated it, railed about welfare cheaters.

Newt kept me company that first winter, coming and going through the various holes in the walls. Once I saw him trotting across the floor with his brown back and cream underbelly, his neck arched proudly, holding a mouse, heading back to his lair. Another time I found part of a grouse under the stairs. I don't know how he would have killed it. The snow was very deep that year, and the grouse often sleep under the snow. Perhaps he hunted one down there. Maybe he found it on the road. As the winter deepened, Newt turned pure white with just a black tip remaining on his tail.

Normally he hunted at night. If he showed his whiskers during the day, I learned that meant he was very hungry. So I would leave him some deer fat that I kept frozen in a box on my porch, or on occasion, even some lunchmeat. Once in late winter there must have been a dearth of mice. I had no meat for him that day. He kept fooling around my garbage, and I finally realized he was interested in a can of Dinty Moore beef stew. So I set it out and he licked out the whole can.

Life is hard and short for a weasel. I've had a succession of Newts in the house over the years. I purposely didn't chink up the little hole in the northwest corner of the house so each Newt could get in and out. I liked having Newt around for the simple reason that when he was there, the mice, which can get as bad as chipmunks and are a worse health hazard, were kept in check. And at least the chipmunks lived elsewhere most of the time. Once when I was between weasels, or the weasel was occupied elsewhere, the mice practically overran the place. They had a chorus line going in my kitchen at night, and they weren't singing the theme to Cats. This went on for some time, until just about the point that I was going to break down and get some traps, when, just in time, the weasel appeared. In a week or two Newt ate his way through the mousy dance troop, and the world was all right again.

Cutting Boughs

Periodically during the time that I was working on the house I would run out of money. Mostly this was more of a nuisance than anything, since I lived small and didn't really need much. And I'd had some money from the selling of my land, which I carefully parceled out over the year. Still I would work for money when I could. Once in early spring I worked for the Department of Natural Resources (DNR), stripping walleye eggs from the fish in the fish trap they operate over at Leech Lake.

The other thing I did once for money was to cut boughs. Bough cutting is currently a local industry that springs up each fall in late September and October and continues into the early Christmas season. In the fall buyers all over the north put up rudely painted signs advertising "Boughs Bought Here" or "Bough Buyer" or just "Boughs" along the highways. Upon the springing up of these signs, a considerable number of locals head into the woods, or into their neighbor's yard, and gather the balsam and other conifer branches.

One day as I was rattling along in the truck, it occurred to me that I didn't know a lot about cutting boughs (actually I knew nothing except that you got the raw material off of a pine tree). It also occurred to me that since, as per usual, I had spent all of my money on construction materials and my stomach was sending me letters threatening divorce if I didn't feed it more regularly, I needed a few bucks.

So I stopped into a bough "factory" to see for myself exactly what they were up to. Inside the pole building there were about thirty ladies and high school students all lined up snipping apart the rough boughs. The bough factories are the next level in this production system. They are the local places, ranging from someone's garage to heated industrial buildings, where the boughs are assembled into door-hanging wreaths and other decorations. The wreaths are then shipped by the ton to cities in Minnesota and across the United States.

The smell of this place was wonderful! It was like the best Christmas you've ever seen and smelled. A pungent, balsamy, steamy air with music playing (not Christmas music) and the workers chattering. One of the ladies said she had been assembling wreaths for several years. Her fingers flew here and there and presto! the boughs became a wreath. I commented on the wonderful smell of this place. She shrugged and said she couldn't smell it anymore, but that when she got home her husband said she smelled like a balsam wreath even after she'd showered. He liked it.

The finished product was worth about fifty bucks on the retail market. Actually from one end to the other bough cutting and wreath making is governed by the harsh laws of capitalism. Too many wreaths? The price goes down. Too few boughs available? The buyers raise their prices and the bough gatherers are encouraged to go out and get more. A buyer showed me which boughs he wanted and how to bundle them. They're tied with twine into approximately fifty-pound bundles. The good thing about this is that you need very little except some means of transportation, a clipper of some sort, and a place to cut the boughs. When you have gathered as much as you can get into your car or truck, the bough buyer then weighs them and pays you in cash on the spot. It's not hard. It's quick money, and one can work in the woods without having to think too much about anything.

Of course there's a dark belly to every white thing. The bad aspect to the local bough industry is that, left unchecked, the forest might end up looking like a green lady with her skirts cropped off. The Department of Natural Resources has had to develop rules for the cutting so that the lady will keep some of her clothing. Because of this it may well be that this industry won't be around in the future. So I wanted to tell you just how wonderful that factory and the ladies smelled. I cut boughs only that once, but I liked it. It made me a couple of hundred bucks, I felt good doing it, and like the ladies in that factory, I smelled good, like Christmas.

Hunting Grouse with Casey

Then on a windy, gray, late October day I got back to the house from town. I was supposed to be installing my pine slab front door, but it wasn't ready, so I decided not to work and instead to shoulder my old shotgun and head out hunting. Something about the day was made for being in the woods. You know what it's like if you live in the north when most all of the leaves are down, blown off of the trees in the weeks after that first hard freeze. Then it rains, and in the cool mornings the lakes are steaming and there is that pungent, organic smell of decay and wet leaves in the air. In the sky the geese and ducks are all blown downwind and everything is moving with one wild voice. Woodcock come south during the nights and some days, if you hunt them, they're everywhere in the thickets. I don't hunt woodcock anymore—they're too pretty and unusual—but it's the perfect time for hunting grouse.

When I got to my house that day, Casey wasn't there. He wouldn't have stayed if I wasn't at the house, so I put on a hunting jacket, tossed a box of shotgun shells on the seat, stuck the old shotgun in the truck and went looking for him. He came rushing out of his garage home, barking like mad, until he realized who it was, and then he wiggled himself into a frenzy in greeting. We jumped in the old Chevy truck with Casey sniffing the shotgun and box of shells and sitting on the seat watching the woods, shivering and whining in anticipation.

There is a place around the other side of my lake and then up into the Suomi Hills, not more than five or six miles, where there are trails that go a long way back into the woods. It is an area of deciduous trees, mostly maple, but some oak also, and it is here that I stopped the truck and let Casey out. He bolted from the truck and scampered around wildly. I let him go for a while so he could burn off energy.

There was no one around except the trucks of a couple of bough cutters. The hunters of early in the season, they of the expensive new trucks and all-terrain vehicles, were gone. A solid mat of leaves covered the ground. Here and there a mushroom, one left from the wild explosion of mushrooms of earlier and warmer September and October, still poked up among the leaves.

Casey calmed down and I got organized and we started down a trail. I tried to hunt slowly, but Casey was impatient. He is a little demon, everywhere ranging back and forth and wanting to run ahead. I picked up my pace, talked to him to get him slowed a little. In a while we get into a certain rhythm, with him working in a good ranging arc back and forth about ten to twenty yards in front of me. The day is iron-gray now. Most of the woods we are working are mature second or third growth. The mature trees have prevented the brush and berry shrubs from growing. It's too open to offer good cover for grouse, and we see no grouse. But the grouse like to, so we keep working into the woods.

The grouse grow leery of trails, which are used by so-called hunters in all-terrain vehicles. But the trails are the best food sources, so the grouse come out to eat clover and other leaves and learn to spend as little time as possible on the trails. Late in the year the grouse prefer to run rather than fly, and they scuttle back into the woods at the slightest provocation. They can run like hell, and when they do fly, they tend to fly at least several hundred yards. About a half mile into the walk we moved off of the trail a little ways and then parallel to the trail around a small lake.

We cross a little marshy area, working through some cover that looked more promising. Here and there high-bush cranberries grew, their bright red bells hanging over some broken brushy cover. No grouse. We kept on. The sky lightened and it was a little warmer, or maybe I was just warmer from the walking. In the distance the sun came out a little and turned the other end of the lake from dark to blue, illuminating some bright white birch on the steep hillside of the little lake. We kept on, the shotgun felt good, easy on the arm, smooth and dark brown. When I paused, I could smell the pleasant odor of gun oil and burned powder.

We left the lake behind. The cover is much better here, some young aspen, a few yellow aspen leaves now dry and rattling loosely on the trees. Grouse eat aspen buds. A tangle of brush and shrubbery ahead. Good cover. I'm working slowly now, walk ten paces. Pause. Casey, who has been working steadily here and there, starts working a little faster. "Easy, easy," I talk softly to Casey. I move ahead again. I tell myself to concentrate. Don't be startled by the explosion of wings. Focus on the head. I'm a little warm now and my back aches a little. Move ahead. Stop. Find another lane and move to it.

On the far side of a hill, Casey suddenly started working excitedly. He shot forward, turned, whirled and stopped, stock-still. I moved up slowly. Three grouse exploded from a brambly tangle. Two of them beat it to the west toward that lightening sky, but Casey had confused them by ranging ahead and flanking them from the far right. One flew down and across in front of me, streaking low and to the left, then snapping downhill toward some thickening woods.

Per usual, the sudden explosion of whirring wings had completely startled me, and besides I was halfway through stepping over a dead tree, so I wasn't ready when the grouse got up. But I got off a desperation shot, and, amazingly, one of the grouse went down. Casey was on him then, holding the struggling bird down. I killed it while Casey watched impassively, his job having been done. He sat watching, shaking a feather out of his mouth and eyeing the grouse intently to make sure he wouldn't come alive and fly off.

The sun came out a little and we sat on a hillside in a place where there was a little grass. I lay the grouse on the grass and Casey snuffled it for a moment, but it was no more his business. I took out a lunchmeat and cheese sandwich, split it in two. This was of great interest to Casey who gulped his half, cheese and all. I chewed mine slowly and drank deeply from a bottle of water that I had brought. Casey showed interest in the water, but I had no container for him, so I poured some water into the palm of my hand and Casey lapped it all up. I poured more into my palm and he lapped more. When he had had enough, he settled down into the grass and began to groom his paws and his fur, finally cleaning a place in his fur where I'd pulled a burr out for him. Then he lay down beside me and watched the woods in case any grouse were out there.

Then something about the killing of the grouse, or the day, or whatever, made me terribly sad and I could think of no reason for it then. I just sat there, pinned to the world full of every good thing and every bad thing I'd made myself into. It was Casey, finally, who shook me out of it, sitting upright abruptly, shaking himself and then with a preemptory nudge at the grouse, looked at me and stood up whining and looking off down the trail as if to say, "Enough of that crap, let's get back to business."

We got back to business and hunted our way back for an hour. But we saw no more grouse. It turned colder, sleet fell and a familiar low moaning wind rose in the bare tree-tops. At the end of the hunt Casey figured out that there weren't any more grouse and walked in front of me on the trail sniffing the air occasionally.

At the truck I decided to take the long way home and stopped by Don's cabinet shop where I picked up the pine slab door and its frame, talked for a while, then drove slowly home. Casey curled up on a blanket and slept all the way. At his driveway he hopped out, turned, looked back at me and then trotted off toward his home in that alert confident way of his.

In fading sun I worked on the door over the next couple of hours and finished hanging it. There was a sudden brightening when the waning sun cleared a cloud, then gray and chill again. In the background the lake had a hard blue glint to it. The wind rose, gusting, and some leaves finally came loose from the top of a stand of popple and fluttered to the ground. Sleet began rattling again in the alder and a little snow whirled around. I hadn't done it for a while so I stuffed some dry balsam peels under the grate, lit a fire and heated some icy, clear lake water for coffee. When the water boiled, I stood a while sipping the acrid, piney-smelling coffee, admiring my handiwork. The inside of the house was framed and the ceiling insulated. I had a wood stove that supplied a little heat. My brother would be up to hunt in a few days. I had reached the goal I'd set out toward the year before. My house was done.

Epilogue

That winter I came to the Twin Cities to work. I hadn't given a lot of thought to what I was going to do. But it was clear that, although the house was livable, it was very roughly livable, principally good enough for me, the chipmunks and the weasel, but not for much more than that. The rest of the construction was going to require more money. I could either stay north and eek out a living working at some low paying job, or I could go back to work at a job at which I would make a living and work on my house in my spare time. I've told you that, while I tolerated being poor, I didn't like it. If I had to occupy my time working daily I'd rather make a lot of money.

And then there was that old business with Dale my neighbor. It had bothered me that I had not done as much as I could to help. He's done fine, but I really felt I could have helped in a more constructive manner, and this stuck under my collar like a burr. I decided that eventually I'd get back to what I knew something about, namely land. At first I worked part-time in the Cities at whatever job I could get. I once took a job for a week as one of those guys retrieving carts in a shopping mall. Later that year an acquaintance needed help, and so finally I started working full time at my present occupation.

There is sort of a tally in my mind that I use to score my time up north. I grew mentally stronger there in ways that are hard to explain. I suppose that is a natural thing, but it occurs to me that it might have been different and one could have been beaten down by the experience. Perhaps the strangest thing about the whole time period was that despite the strain occasioned by the precarious state of my finances, I don't remember being depressed, or even feeling down for more than a day or so. On the contrary, once I got going I quickly gained strength no matter what my place, my cars or I looked like.

I was in good health all of the time I was up there, except for that time I poisoned myself with poorly cooked chicken. This despite the fact that I didn't always eat as well as I could have, and that I physically exhausted myself rather frequently.

I built my house myself, mostly with my own hands, and best of all, I borrowed no money building it. Speaking of money, my time up in the big woods turned out not to have cost me and actually made me a lot of money. Not that I would have changed it anyway, but in effect, I saved a lot of money since the house is worth a considerable amount. And amazingly, I have become well off financially. Since I came down, I've been around the world, to China and Europe, and I spend part of each winter in Central America.

In any case, I dove into the roil of working life again, but in fact, I have never completely left the north. In the years that followed I gradually improved my log home by driving north virtually every weekend to work on it. By the next year I'd installed new hardwood floors and had sanded and finished the interior walls. I just kept working at various components of the house. Truth be told, I never really stopped working on it. I think of myself as having my home in the north and sort of living on the road in the Twin Cities.

I made good friends there and they are still my friends. There is nothing more important than this.

There is a saying that once you get out of town it's hard to get back in town, meaning the contacts and general familiarity are lost. But that didn't happen with me. Being out of the Cities didn't really make any difference. In the years that I was preoccupied up north, things hadn't really changed that much. I am a land broker with clients in land development, and when I picked up my professional life, people that I had known were still there (several acted as if I'd been on vacation), and I developed new clients.

What a great gift is time spent alone. I am so grateful and more than a little astonished at the result. But let's not make a mountain out of a molehill. I wrote this to tell you how it was, not to tell you what to do. And this certainly isn't a suggestion to go out and build a log house. There aren't enough trees in the woods. Live your own life. There are as many ways to live a life as there are lives to live. I just wanted to make a record of that time, so that I might leave some sign of my passing to tell you how it was that I lived for one brightening season of my life. Think of this as a message in a bottle, thrown into the sea, by a child of the twentieth century. If it washes up on your shore and you enjoy it, good enough.

My House

I continued to work on and improve my house. As I've mentioned, I replaced the roof, installed hardwood floors and improved the heating system. Basically for years I worked four days a week in the Twin Cities and three days up north. They say it looks quite good and is worth a lot of money. That wasn't the point, but I found I liked to do several things at once, and one of them was working with my hands, so I just kept on working. Like they used to say back in the sixties, it's all good.

Dave the Old Gentleman Who Got Me Started

I didn't hear from Dave again. A couple of years later I talked to Jim, the guy who'd cut and delivered the semi-railer load of logs for the house. He said that Dave had died at the nursing home the winter after I finished my house. Jim and his family had watched out for Dave, and when it was obvious that Dave was sick, saw to it that he got in a nursing home.

Dave lived his life for building log homes, gunning and hunting dogs. He got along fine. Life isn't fair, I know, but lots of people don't get to live their lives on their own terms, and Dave mostly did that. It could have been a lot worse.

The Big Long-Legged Bear

Didn't make it, I'm sorry to say, though he did make it through two more years. This time it wasn't his fondness for Le Tourist Garbage Restaurant that got him in trouble. But it was still just a matter of time, I'm afraid. The bear and I got along and he never bothered me, but maybe that was because I was mostly starving and didn't throw out anything edible. At any rate the bear hung around for the next year. It's not like you would see him much, but I would fairly often see his tracks in the mud on my driveway, and several times I saw him ambling down my driveway in the twilight.

Then one day the bear was somewhere near the lake poking around some tourist cabins and decided that he just had to see what actually went on inside a cabin. So he stuck his head in through an open bedroom window to have a gander. And, as I said previously, he had a very, very large head. You and I both know he didn't mean any harm. Probably just curious, or he smelled the bacon cooking or maybe he was interested in ladies' underwear. You can't really blame him. Whatever his motive, the tourist lady who was alone in the cabin was apparently looking the other direction when the bear stuck his head into the window. When she turned around, she was nose to nose with the bear.

I wasn't there, but my neighbor said you could hear the scream for a long ways, even given that she was indoors. Scared the hell out of the bear. So naturally, when the furor died down, they came and trapped him again and this time took him a long way, and I haven't seen him since. I hope he lived out his life and that they didn't kill him, though I don't have a good feeling about that.

The Truck, the Buick and the Bulldozer

A year after the house was mostly done I had shifted my car affections to a red sedan, a Japanese model, that didn't work as well as the truck, but looked better in the Twin Cities. How fickle thy human. Then later I got a new truck. The old brown truck sat dispiritedly over in one corner of the yard, drooping a little from low, rather balding tires. It had a hole in its gas tank, a lot of rust and the muffler was held on with wire. But even after a couple of years it would still start readily, so long as you filled it with the various fluids that it ran on. Anyone could see that the thread of its life was thin and frayed. Finally I told a neighbor he could have it.

He didn't want it, but he said he thought he knew someone who needed it. Presently a rather scruffy, stringy, unshaven fellow who looked as if he originated from some Ozark famine showed up. The truck, which hadn't been started in months, seemed surprised at our attentions and balked a little, but then roared to life. At this the fellow seemed anxious that I would change my mind and keep the truck. My scruffy friend fixed the gas tank leak, filled it with fluids and pumped up the tires. Then roaring and smoking, the truck happily bounced down my driveway onto the county road, off to hold some other reject's life together for a while. I did not see it again.

With almost the last thing I needed to do on the house with the bulldozer, I managed to overheat it and fry the cylinder head on its engine. This occurred because, as I have related previously, I used a jury-rigged belt in place of the fan belt, hoping it would last long enough to finish some dirt work I was doing. After that, the bulldozer sat in back of the house, like some great immovable yellow objet d'art. Someone suggested, rather cruelly I might add, that it looked like the world's heaviest planter, since there was a flower and some grass growing on one of the treads.

Then one day some guys who happened to be driving by saw it and came down to ask about it. They claimed they collected antique tractors and bulldozers. What, they asked, was I going to do with the bulldozer? I told them that if they could start it and get it out of there, they could have it. Then I left for a week and when I got back it was gone. There were bulldozer tracks where it went up the driveway. I don't know where it went. Maybe it got scared and went and hid in the woods.

I drove the pumpkin-colored Buick until I got the red Japanese thing. It had gotten me around for a year and made it to south Texas and back. And for all of that time it had gotten nineteen miles to the gallon of gas. Except for the muffler I had fixed in Oklahoma, it had cost me no other repairs, although at the end the rear bumper began to sag and had to be wired up. With the new acquisition I decided to let the Buick retire gracefully to the junkyard. The day I was to retire the Buick, I mentioned it to a local guy who asked if he could drive it. The upshot was that he bought it from me for a hundred bucks and he drove it off. I saw it rolling down the county road six months later, as ugly as ever, but still rolling.

The Bear Den

The bear den is still there. Its walls have crumbled a little and the popple and brush have grown up around it some. I walk the path to it every so often to have a look. It's still a pretty good location, and I keep expecting some enterprising bear to clean it out again and snore away the winter. So far none have.

The Chipmunks

Of course they're still there. Stuffing their little piggish faces full of my seeds. They also still use my living room as their personal highway between their dens and the food supply. We've more or less reached equilibrium. I feed them, and they take as much as they can get. In this way it is an equitable situation. Stubby is long gone and not really missed. But the other day I saw another fattish chipmunk with a familiar, chunky rear end rush out and rudely chase a couple of other chipmunks away. And then it occurred to me; Stubby must have gotten more than just his share of food.

Newt the Weasel

Newt is still around. Or at least a weasel is still in residence and that's okay with me. When the weasel is around the chipmunks are less inclined to run roughshod over the place. And there are few mice. Just last weekend I was at the house working as usual and so hadn't bothered to cook. I had some store-bought roasted chicken in one of those plastic containers. I left a piece for the weasel, and it was shortly gone so I knew something was around. In the evening I heard a noise, and there was Newt or one of his descendents on top of the plastic container, trying to figure out how to get the lid off. She was pure white with that black tip on her tail, as pretty and deadly as you can imagine.

My Neighbor Dale

Is doing fine. Last I heard from him he was working at a sawmill, hauling firewood to the Twin Cities and living in a house he'd bought. He lives on air with a little salt on it, so I don't worry about him.

Doug

Doug is still going strong. Full of bull, but ready for action when the chips are down.

John the Old Norwegian

I was eating breakfast at my favorite greasy spoon restaurant when I last saw John. He greeted me in his cheerful and earnest fashion, walking quickly in the door in his peculiar bowlegged hobble, which, if I get to be seventy-five years old, I'll be happy to hobble like. Earlier in the spring I'd mentioned that I needed more manure for the garden, and that if he found some, to just deliver it and pile it on one end of the garden. I then promptly forgot about that conversation and some weeks later got a load of rotted cow manure from a farmer about forty miles south. The next week, there alongside of my garden was another pile of manure. Naturally John hadn't forgotten about it and had delivered. That last time I spoke to John he was making outhouses for people in the area. Mostly they were summer cabin outhouses, which people still use out of nostalgia or disdain for environmental regulations. He says he builds and delivers ten to twelve a year for people at five hundred bucks a pop. By the way, as I was writing this some time later, the State Board of Health or some such organization came in and closed the greasy spoon. Too bad.

Tom

Tom continues to do his art and is still his cheerful and energetic self. Lately he's taken to traveling in the winters since the northern cold gets into his bones. More and more he's reluctant to come off of the road.

Russell the Smart Kid

Russell the very smart kid went on being a bright light in this ordinary world. I heard he had a very bad accident several years later. The last I heard he had moved to Florida and was living there.

The Common Ground Coffee House

The coffee house lasted a good while. The split between the faction who wanted just a small group and the rest of us couldn't be worked out. So we just muddled along until the next winter.

Then one Saturday night we had a good crowd, including some rather attractive young ladies. One of the young ladies, a high school student with huge, brown, innocent eyes, was going to read some of her poetry and asked me if I minded whether it had some swear words in it. I asked her which words. She mentioned (a bad word) and one or two others. I replied that, while this language didn't bother me at all, I couldn't speak for the others. She went on stage and her poetry was pretty good except that some of the language would have scalded the hair off of a dead boar. I am not bothered by swearing, but hearing some of this language come out of that innocent looking mouth was, I admit, a shock. Some people practically went into cardiac arrest.

"Make her stop!" said one of the board member ladies somewhat plaintively, in the middle of one of the girl's poem.

The young lady finished (to stunned silence) except for a smattering of applause from several of her friends.

I thought it no big deal. Apparently, however, several rather influential patrons of the Common Ground thought differently. They were shocked, simply shocked, at this affront to their sensibilities. One wanted to get back at me for that remark I had made about their bad art way back in the previous winter or whenever it was. Several of them, backed by Lon's group, convinced the board to cancel our rights to use the place, which they did the following day.

And that, rather too abruptly, was the end of the Common Ground coffee house. It had lasted for some years and was a very good idea of my friend Tom. Most of the friends that I acquired in the north were found at the Common Ground. I'm sorry it ended, but I'm not sorry the young lady used those words in her poem.

The Weather Witch

I haven't heard from her for a while. And, to answer your question, no, I haven't gone completely balmy; she was always just a nice part of my imagination. The weather seemed so personal when I was building my house, when I was living closer to her. I think this is a natural thing. Humans have lived close to nature for most of our evolution. For many millennia we lived out under the stars, bracing ourselves against the wild cold winds of winter, standing in awe at her lightning storms and reveling in her green life. To think of nature in personal terms is human.

But it is hard to conjure up the Witch when you live in a climate-controlled house and drive a comfortable car stored in a comfortable parking garage. Still, I know she's there, up along the prairies and the woods of the borderline. They say she lives in the screaming storms along the coasts of the ocean, too. Once I was fishing some bonefish flat in the land of the Southern Cross, and about the time I was getting comfortable, she showed me two huge spinning waterspouts leering down out of a black cloud face. But she was just playing a little joke, and afterward there was a bright rainbow as a smiling reminder. I miss her. She has no pity and she will kill you if she can, but she will also find what is left at the bottom of your heart. What you do then is your business.

Casey the Dog

A year after I want down to the Twin Cities, I was still coming back to my house on weekends and working. The habit of working with my hands had gotten into me and I couldn't leave it alone. Plus, the fact was, the house wasn't totally finished, so I kept on. In the intervening year Casey had come over to visit fairly often when I was at the log house. He had figured out quickly that I was mostly there on weekends, and I would hear him scratching at my door. A couple of times in the next fall we went hunting grouse, and it was just the same as before. But over the next months I was gone more, and Casey came over less and less when I was there. Then I was gone for the middle of that winter.

I finally got up there in late March, to continue some interior work that I hadn't finished. Also late March is a good time to cut brush. In the early mornings the snow that has melted in the bright March sun is frozen hard enough to walk on. This is the time I cut the brush in the wet areas between the house and the lake. In the predawn darkness I was surprised to hear Casey on my porch and went to the door to let him in. He wiggled and whined his greetings and sniffed the place out, to make sure I wasn't harboring some strange competitor. I was happy to see him, of course, and in the habit of getting up early anyway. So I put on a pot of coffee.

With the coffee perking, I went out on the porch to see the sky. Hard frozen snow still covered the ground. The temperature was about twenty degrees, though there was no wind. In the east the planet Venus was very bright just above the horizon, and to the northeast the comet of those years stood on its end, fairly bright, its tail fanning back toward the northwest. I watched for a while until I was chilled and then the smell of coffee drew me back in to the fire and a good, big, hot cup. Casey stayed around for a couple of hours, but you could see that he had other things on his mind. Finally he went to the door to be let out. He trotted off in his purposeful way. It was, after all, a weekend and he had his people at home and they'd be getting up about that time. Or he had other places and people to visit.

I never saw Casey again. I hope his life was all right and that he was well taken care of. Or if he didn't make it, I hope for him what I hope for myself: that when the end comes it happens fast and he doesn't suffer too much.

When I saw the comet that morning, it had already swung around the sun and was heading back out into the great enormous dark. It was gone a month later. For a while, me and the Big Long-Legged Bear and Dale and Tom and the coffee house and Casey were part of the same orbit. I felt it at the time and I feel it still, and though times have changed like they always do, things were very good for that little while when they took me in and made me part of their ellipse.

So that's it. That's my story. It's mostly true, as I said at the beginning. You can see for yourself. Stop in if you want. Afternoons are best, but anytime is okay. I'll show you the Big Long-Legged Bear's den if it hasn't crumbled all in by then. You can even look at the canoe paddle with the chunk bit out of it that Bob used to ride the great fish. We'll sit on the porch, have a pop or some coffee, tell some stories and laugh and spin out the day.

—The End

About the Author

Michael N. Felix was born in Shakopee and grew up in Prior Lake Minnesota. Educated at the University of Minnesota and Mankato State University, he holds a BA in Economics and an MA in Urban Planning. He presently works professionally in and around the Twin Cities, but considers his log home on Moose Lake to be his residence.

For additional information about the author;
www.theweatherwitch.net